NEW INFORMATION TECHNOLOGY
IN EDUCATION

New Information Technology in Education

David Hawkridge

CROOM HELM
London & Canberra

© 1983 David Hawkridge
Croom Helm Ltd, Provident House, Burrell Row,
Beckenham, Kent BR3 1AT
Croom Helm Australia, PO Box 391,
Manuka, ACT 2603, Australia

British Library Cataloguing in Publication Data

Hawkridge, David G.
    New information technology in education.
    1. Computer-assisted instruction
    I. Title
    371.3'9445   LB1028.5

    ISBN 0-7099-1286-2

Printed and bound in Great Britain by
Biddles Ltd, Guildford and King's Lynn

CONTENTS

PREFACE

With Gallic vigour and hyperbole, the French call it 'Le mariage du siècle', the marriage of the century, the marrying of information technology to education. Is this wedding as propitious as M. Christian Beullac, Minister of Education, made out when he coined the phrase in Paris in November 1980 (Ministère de l'Education, 1981)? Is it to take place this year, next year or on some more distant date? Should we expect a long partnership or will there be a quick divorce?

This book offers my own answers to these and related questions. Like many others, I have been aware of the potential impact of technology on education for many years, but since 1979 I have been studying in particular the potential impact, for good or ill, of new information technology on education. I am fortunate to have been able to do so in the course of my work at the Institute of Educational Technology of the Open University and also while writing an earlier volume, *Organizing Educational Broadcasting* (1982), with my friend John Robinson, formerly Education Secretary of the British Broadcasting Corporation. I decided to plan and write a book that might convey to others what I had myself learned from many sources. In 1981 I heard that the British Government was going to name 1982 Information Technology Year, making such a book particularly timely. Now, too, the United Nations General Assembly has declared 1983 as World Communications Year.

I hope that those who read this volume will find in it the sense of excitement that gripped me as I explored. For me, new information technology offers challenges, new frontiers in education. It can also be very dangerous in the wrong hands.

Plan of the Book

To me, it is important to think about how education can take advantage of technology, rather than the other way round — how technology can take advantage of education. We may all be tempted simply to gape at amazing inventions that can do much more than their predecessors and to declare, 'These *must* be used in education!'

In reading this book, some people may feel I am encouraging them to gape, but that is not my purpose. I decided that first I ought to provide something of an introduction to the new information technology and establish a working vocabulary. It seemed to me that those who knew all about it could skip on to Part Two, where I wanted to report examples of how new information technology is already being used in education. These experiments have raised many issues, revealing problems and constraints. I decided to devote Part Three to discussing such matters, but to avoid being merely retrospective in a period of such rapid change, I chose to look forward to the year 2000 in Part Four, in an attempt to show, first, how opinions may become polarised and, secondly, how education may in time take greater advantage of new information technology or fall victim to it. Therefore the plan of the book is as follows: Part One surveys new information technology, setting out to provide readers with an introduction written as far as possible in non-technical language.

Part Two describes, with many examples, applications of the technology in education at all levels, ranging from young children at home to secondary school students and to adults learning at work, thus including formal and informal education.

Part Three considers the problems and constraints in using new information technology in education. It spans educational, social, political, economic and technical issues.

Part Four consists of three forecasts for information technology in education in the year 2000: optimistic, pessimistic and my own forecast.

Throughout the four parts I refer to many recent sources for further reading, including some that trace the history of development in this field, which I have not attempted to do because I considered it more important to be up-to-date.

Acknowledgements

I thank first the Open University, which uses new information technology itself in many ways, not least to help its 80,000 students to learn at home and at work. The University granted me funds to visit the East Coast of the United States in 1980 and the West Coast in 1981 to gather material for this book. In that country many friends and former colleagues, too many to mention individually, spared time to talk to me at universities, research institutes, government bureaus, schools, factories and libraries. I am grateful to them, as I am to those in British institutions who did the same, to my colleagues in the Institute of Educational Technology, to co-members and staff of the Council for Educational Technology, to staff of the International Institute for Communication, to John Robinson, who helped me to sort out my early ideas and to Juletta Broomfield of Link Resources Corporation, who kindly provided me with technical material.

Finally, I owe much to several people whose enthusiasm for taking advantage of new information technology in their own education has impressed me greatly and persistently. It would embarrass them to be named, but one at least lives in the house where I live.

Milton Keynes

PART ONE: A SURVEY OF NEW INFORMATION TECHNOLOGY

Part One is an introduction, written as far as possible in non-technical language and aimed at clearing the ground for Parts Two, Three and Four. I have tried to define, describe and explain the new technology in Part One. Chapter 1 begins the task of pinning down the concept of 'new information technology'. Chapter 2 is about the technology's functions, or what it can do. Chapter 3 discusses the symbols, codes and languages needed to operate the technology, and the principal modes of human communication. Chapter 4 is a full, if long, catalogue of the devices and systems belonging to the new technology, ranging from videotex, satellites and fibre optic cable to pocket calculators, videodiscs and microcomputers. Chapter 5 says a little about who makes and sells these devices and systems. Finally, Chapter 6 discusses briefly who is buying and using them. The rest of the book is about new information technology being used in education.

1 WHAT IS NEW INFORMATION TECHNOLOGY?

The Dawn of New Information Technology

The two words, information technology, used together, have acquired special meaning in the last few years. If we had heard them used separately, or even together, as recently as 1976, we probably would not have attached to them this special meaning. At that time, perhaps technology signified materials, tools, systems and techniques, although modern definitions of technology vary (see Bugliarello and Doner, 1979) and to the Greeks technology was 'a discourse upon the arts, pure and applied', because *techne* meant art or craft (Nuttgens, 1981). In popular parlance, information was facts, knowledge, data and news. Libraries, the printing industry, telephone exchanges, television studios, billboards, computers and sky-writing all encompassed some aspect of information technology, but scarcely anyone used these two words in everyday conversation. In fact, as recently as 1981, a British opinion poll (reported in *The Times*, 14 January 1982) showed that 80 per cent of those interviewed then had not yet heard of information technology.

In the Western industrialised world (that is to say, Western Europe, North America and Japan in particular) people are suddenly becoming much more aware of this, the new information technology. In a number of countries, governments have started to tell their constituents that information technology is an important factor in maintaining and perhaps enhancing economic well-being. The British Conservative Prime Minister, Mrs Margaret Thatcher, said in Parliament, 'The Government fully recognises the importance of information technology for the future industrial and commercial success of the United Kingdom and the central role that the Government must play in promoting its development and application' (Hansard, 2 July 1981). Her remarks were backed up by the newly-appointed Minister for Information Technology, the first in British history. In France, under Giscard d'Estaing, the Direction Générale des Telecommunications began a few years ago to promote 'la télématique', the French term for information technology, coined by Nora and Minc (1978). Both the British and the French

3

Governments are placing special emphasis on introducing computer methods and skills into schools. In Sweden, a Commission on New Information Technology (1981) recently reported its findings. Other European governments have taken a similar line, if not with as much publicity. Canada and the United States have placed high priority on developing information technology. We can now see in Canada what is probably the widest range of working examples of the technology. In the United States, many companies are seeking to sell new information technology products and services. Commercial competition between them has increased dramatically as laws and regulations controlling communications have been amended or even rescinded in the name of adding to national economic well-being. Borrell (1981) reports that during the 1979-80 Congress, 857 bills concerning information were introduced, of which no less than 113 became law. Japan shows signs of leading the world in many sectors of the new field: the Japanese Government has fostered awareness of the technology's potential in industry and commerce, and has actively encouraged investment and collaboration, so that major companies now share research and development costs in an effort to outstrip their American and European competitors.

Governments are saying to us that new information technology is the key to economic growth. They are also saying that it is likely to bring about substantial changes in our society. Their awareness-raising campaigns are to some extent aimed at reducing what Toffler (1970) calls 'future shock'. Information technology, in its new guises, may change our lives, for better or worse, within a very short time. Preparing us for change may be one way of helping us to reap advantages rather than collapsing under the strain. As Bowes (1980) suggests, however, 'information utilities' (i.e., organisations dealing in information) are attractive to governments not only as profitable new industry but also because they can be presented as an improvement in the quality of life for many people. Proponents claim that information will be more accessible and that more information at low cost will increase opportunities for all, with the greatest gain being to those at present at a disadvantage education-ally and 'informationally'. On the other hand, Stonier's (1981) aphorism strikes home: 'An educated workforce learns how to exploit new technology, an ignorant one becomes its victim.'

To a remarkable extent, information is a source of power in Western society. Information technology is becoming a means of wielding power. Robertson (1981) provides estimates of the size of the information explosion in the United States: 30 billion original documents are created each year, with 630 billion pages of print going through the postal system and 100 billion pages coming off photocopiers. For each employed person, this is enough paper to fill four filing cabinets, containing twelve miles of paper. These figures will probably double in five years, he says, before the new technology takes effect. The new information technology is overtaking the old, providing more and more powerful ways to create, store, select, process, deliver and display information.

It is vital for us to arrive at some understanding of new information technology and of what benefits it can bring to many fields, including education. We must bear in mind, of course, Scriven's (1981) dictum that information is not education. Nor is information necessarily knowledge, although knowledge is based on information (see Rich, 1980, for a discussion of knowledge in society). Bell (1980) suggests that knowledge is 'an organised set of statements of facts or ideas, presenting a reasoned judgement or an experimental result', and distinguishes knowledge from news or entertainment, though all contain information.

Institutions that produce or distribute information in some form are, however, classed by Machlup (1980) as belonging to the 'knowledge industry' sector. Knowledge industries, producing and distributing knowledge *and* other information, rather than goods and services, are increasing steadily their share of the national product in Western countries (Drucker, 1969; Bell, 1980). Knowledge is arguably the most important single input into modern productive systems (Stonier, 1981). It is a fact that information (including knowledge) is accumulating in many fields at rates far exceeding a worker's capacity to absorb it. A researcher specialising in one-thousandth of the field of science and technology, amounting to 10,000,000 characters printed in, say English, needs twelve years of reading 13 hours a day, every day of the year, at 3,000 characters a minute, just to cover his part of the field once. During those twelve years, as many new characters would have been published (Licklider, 1966). Kilgour (1981) tells us that during the year to June 1980, 1.5 million titles were added to the principal North American computerised catalogue for libraries. Can new information technology help?

But what is new information technology? It would be useful to have a one-line definition to throw into dinner table conversation. 'New information technology is new technology applied to the creation, storage, selection, transformation and distribution of information of many kinds.' That is more than one line and does not say very much. We need a more comprehensive approach, which takes up more space and is, unfortunately, less suitable for casual use. The definition adopted by Unesco is 'the scientific, technological and engineering disciplines and the management techniques used in information handling and processing; their applications; computers and their interaction with men and machines; and associated social, economic and cultural matters' (quoted by Raitt, 1982). Perhaps that says too much and certainly it explains very little. What is needed is a layman's introduction to new information technology, what it is and how it works. Part One of this book is aimed at giving just such an introduction.

One way of defining a new technology is to say what it can be used for, what functions it can perform, and to describe the symbols, codes and languages that support these functions. Another way is to survey the devices and systems that have so far grown out of the technology. But let us first look at how this new technology differs from the old.

Old *v.* New Information Technology

It would be a mistake to think that the boundary between old and new information technology is perfectly sharp, but we can certainly notice very distinct differences. If change has been gradual in some branches of the technology, it has been abrupt in others. Stonier (1979) suggests that the industrial revolution brought us devices to extend our musculature, but the electronic revolution is bringing us devices, such as television and the computer, that extend our nervous system. Similarly, Hubbard (1981) points out that our old information technology depends largely upon mechanical means of carrying out its functions. The postal service, the press, the book publishing industry, the film industry, the sound recording industry, even the telephone system, could not operate without depending upon machines that have a large number of moving parts. All, including the best, of these machines are subject to wear and tear, the more so as designers find ways to speed them up. Why should machines be speeded up? To many of us, they seem fast enough already, especially those which handle information. But to others, it is very important to obtain faster means of dealing with information, with less chance of breakdown. Higher speeds mean that much more information can be handled within a given time, and information is often a source of power. People who can get vital information first, and who can select it quickly to suit their needs, are in a very powerful position indeed in Western society. This utilitarian view applies in education as well as in industry and commerce, in politics and the military.

The new information technology depends far less on mechanical means. Instead, its machines are electronic. That is to say, the moving parts have almost entirely disappeared, being replaced by 'flows' of electrons. We have an example in desk calculators. Twenty years ago, whether manual or powered by electric motors, they contained intricate systems of levers and gears which carried out the calculations. They were essentially mechanical devices. Today, desk calculators have no levers, no gears, but contain much more intricate systems of switches. If we press the buttons, this sets the switches in particular patterns, guiding the flow of electrons to accomplish the calculations as commanded. 'Flow' is perhaps not quite the right term to use: it is more accurate to think of the electrons packed into the circuits from end to end, and when the current is turned on at one end, the 'push' is almost instantly felt at the other end. Thus our calculation can be done almost instantaneously once the switches have been set. We set the switches in two ways: we press keys for the numbers and we press others for the functions (add, multiply, subtract or divide, for example). We use the function keys to tell the calculator what to do with the numbers.

Electronic calculators are a rather simple example of the change from old to new. New information technology depends on three complex technologies that have recently converged: computing, microelectronics and telecommunications. In each of these technologies new materials, systems, tools and techniques are being invented at an astounding rate. The three in combination offer opportunities for use or abuse that few of us ever imagined, and these opportunities are now beginning to be apparent in many fields, not least education. Can education take advantage of technology?

Computers

Jarrett (1980) offers us a popular definition of the computer as a 'fast rule-following idiot machine'. It is fast because it is electronic, although the first ones were mechanical. It is rule-following because the patterns of its switches and the logic of its circuits are designed so that, when it processes information it will indeed follow rules that have been worked out beforehand, and it is an idiot machine because it has to follow these rules, incredibly complex though they may be.

Computers are surrounded by their own jargon, much of which is not essential to the level of understanding this chapter provides, but a few terms ought to be introduced here. The machine itself, with its various accessories, makes up the hardware ('everything you can touch', as somebody said). The rules or commands for the computer to follow are the software, written in one of a large number of programming languages. A set of commands is called a program (a universal spelling in English-speaking countries) and kept in electronic or other forms either in the computer itself or elsewhere. Programs can be printed out on paper, but untrained people cannot understand them, because first they must learn the appropriate language. If we want to use one of the programs to process information, we make sure that the program is in the computer or at least accessible to it electronically. We then put in ('input'), one way or another, the information to be processed. Processing takes place very quickly, and our processed information can then be stored or displayed, or both. The display is the computer's output and can take a variety of forms, not all of them visual displays, as we shall see.

It is quite incorrect, by the way, to think that computers can handle only numbers, because they can actually deal with words, pictures, charts, music and much else too. Consider an example: the typescript of this book was written on a 'word processor'. Part of the word processor was a computer already programmed to undertake a number of functions. In addition, a special 'editing' program went into the computer before the first word of this chapter was typed in. Typing was the process of input. Editing by the author was done easily, something most writers would appreciate. The computer simply manipulated the information, that is, the words, in accordance with commands given as the text was typed or edited. Even the more complex commands, such as to move a paragraph to another page, or to another chapter, were executed very quickly indeed, with no retyping. The computer's display of the text was on a television-like screen at first, but it stored the text in coded form on a magnetic disc. When the final version was ready, the computer controlled a printer which produced a typescript automatically at a speed of about a page a minute.

Later chapters in this book will give details of many types of devices that are used for inputting and outputting information. For the moment we should note what happens inside the computer during processing. Like the desk calculator, the computer has intricate systems of switches and circuits inside its central processing unit. These switches and circuits differ from those of the calculator in being far more intricate and more commandable. Each switch, as in the calculator, can be set in one of two electronic states: on or off. It is the pattern of ons and offs, so to speak, that provides the basic code for all information processed by the computer, including the commands or programs that it needs. This code is termed binary because it employs only two symbols: 0 for off and 1 for on. Yet combinations of 0s and 1s can be used to represent numbers, letters and other symbols. In fact, the binary code is extraordinarily versatile.

The 0s and 1s that make up the binary code are called bits, the term being derived from '*bi*nary dig*its*' (Bell, 1980). Four 0s and 1s make a 4-bit word (e.g., 1010), and since there are 16 combinations possible using not more than four 0s and 1s, a 4-bit word, using only four switches, can represent in code any one of 16 symbols. Words of eight bits (e.g., 00100110) offer 256 combinations, enough to represent all the numbers and letters on a typewriter keyboard, while 16-bit words give over 65,000 combinations. From these figures, we can gain at least an inkling of the potential of computers for dealing extremely efficiently with large amounts of information.

What does the computer actually do with all this coded information during processing? The programs, converted into binary code (switch settings of 0s and 1s) and stored in one part of the computer, act upon the information to be processed, which is coded and held in another part of the computer ready for processing. We cannot see what is happening in the circuits, but we can imagine switches changing from off to on and from on to off. These changes represent complex changes in the patterns of states among all the switches in the set of circuits being used. The patterns of states, in turn, represent changes in the information coded into them. Thus, to take an example that does not even need the power of a computer, we can calculate 256 times 347: 256 and 347 are both coded into 0s and 1s (offs and ons), and the command 'multiply' (which is really 'add so many times') is put into the computer too. The answer is computed, in 0s and 1s and then converted back into the figures we understand, giving 88,832 in the twinkling of an eye.

The same broad principles apply in much more complex processing tasks, such as arranging in strict alphabetical order all the entries under A for a new dictionary in preparation. Entries are typed into the computer's memory, where they are stored in coded form, automatically, as 0s and 1s represented by states of switches. To put them in alphabetical order, they are acted upon by the commands contained in the computer's programs. These commands rearrange the patterns of states, so that when the computer displays, on its screen or via its printer, the new patterns in the form of (decoded) typescript, all the entries are in the right order. Even extremely complex processing tasks, requiring vast amounts of information, employ similar principles. Most of us have heard the often-quoted examples: how telemetry (measuring distance and position) data from spacecraft could not be processed by mathematicians with pencil and paper alone because it would take many lifetimes, or how every day international financial corporations process hundreds of millions of pieces of information regarding banking and other transactions.

Thus at the heart of the computer, in its central processing unit, is the means to use information to create new information by changing the old, whether through adding up money totals, by compiling a dictionary or by computing the new signals to be sent to spacecraft that are slightly off course. The computer is immensely powerful as an information-processing machine, better even than our brains in some respects. It remembers everything it is told and works very quickly indeed: the most advanced models carry out as many as a hundred million instructions per second (Ince, 1982), although those described in this book work more slowly. Such machines, available now at reasonably low cost and requiring little energy, are fundamental to the new information technology.

Microelectronics

We have seen the real cost of computers fall fast in the last few years, together with the amount of energy and physical space they require. By contrast, we have seen a steep increase in their processing power and reliability, a burgeoning of uses for them and a real improvement in their 'user-friendliness', the jargon for saying that they are easier for relatively untrained people to use.

To a large extent these changes can be attributed to the development of microelectronics (Evans, 1981). Microelectronics is the result of miniaturisation, of making incredibly small the switches and circuits of processors and their accessories. Miniaturisation has been made possible by the invention of new manufacturing processes and by using new materials. Electronic elements used in today's computers serve more or less the same functions as mechanical and electrical elements in much larger machines of twenty years ago, but in those days each element was made separately and then wired to other elements. Now they are produced in microscopic form, already connected by extremely thin 'wires', on chips a quarter of an inch square. These chips, called microprocessors, can be manufactured by mass-production methods in tens of thousands, so that a single such chip may cost very little, much less than a school textbook, yet contain most of the switches and circuits needed by a particular electronic device, perhaps a computer.

Miniaturisation has progressed so far that it is not easy to grasp what can now be put on a chip. Micrographs (photographs taken through a microscope) of chips reveal the complexity, but inadequately. By the time this book appears in print, a single chip may contain as many as a million elements and their circuits. Many chips, of varying degrees of complexity, may be used in combination or a few well-designed ones may suffice. For example, Sinclair, the British microcomputer manufacturer, reduced the 21 chips in his ZX80 model to only four in the ZX81.

The process of manufacturing chips begins with a slice of material, usually pure silicon, about four inches in diameter and 15 thousandths of an inch thick. The circuits and electronic elements needed for the particular kind of chip being produced are 'printed' onto the base in a succession of layers, with insulating layers provided wherever needed. The printing is done by a series of photographic and chemical processes, leaving extremely thin lines of conducting material rather than wires as such and at the same time depositing other material that makes up the elements for that particular chip. The slice can be cut into quarter-inch squares afterwards, each one being an identical chip ready for testing. By such methods, Texas Instruments, one of the major American manufacturers, makes over 20 million chips a year of one type alone (the

TMS1000), for use in digital watches, microwave ovens and other consumer items.

The circuits and elements to be printed onto each chip must of course be planned and drawn beforehand. Designing them is a difficult task now carried out with the assistance of computers. The artwork is produced on a large screen and is about 250 times the size of what goes onto the chip. With computerised controls, the circuit designer can try out very quickly a variety of layouts. In fact, the computer often selects the optimum routes for the circuits, given a set of conditions. Up to eleven layers may be needed on one chip and each has to be designed completely, down to the last detail, before photo reduction.

Where do chips fit into computers? A small computer, nowadays known as a microcomputer, needs a microprocessor for its central processing unit, designed to process or change information. It also needs electronic input and output units, often linked to keyboards and display devices respectively. And it needs two kinds of memory. The first of these is fixed: the information in it cannot be changed and it is called a ROM, short for read-only memory. The second, called a RAM (for random access memory), stores information that can be altered (see Chapter 4). It is quite feasible for one chip to contain a microprocessor, input and output units and both kinds of memory. By itself, that chip does not constitute a microcomputer, however, because it must be linked to a power supply, to various input and output devices and perhaps to other pieces of equipment, depending on its designed functions. Miniaturisation has influenced these additional items, too, therefore the whole system is likely to be small enough to fit on top of a desk, as in the case of microcomputers now being used in schools and other educational institutions.

The next size up in computers has been affected by miniaturisation, too. Minicomputers are too large to fit on a desk but only require a small room. They have become as powerful as the older very big computers. The largest computers, usually called mainframe (although this term is also applied to some minicomputers), require a large room but are very powerful indeed. They can process extremely large amounts of information at very high speed. Miniaturisation has also led to the development of networks of micro-, mini- and mainframe computers that help each other, so to speak. For example, together, a number of microcomputers can provide as much information processing power as a mainframe computer. What is more, the microcomputers can be scattered widely in different locations, thus providing a fair amount of local power as well as the greater power of the whole network.

It is easy, but wrong, to think of microelectronics only in the context of computers of various sizes, particularly the micro-computers that are widely advertised for use in education. It is wrong because the coming of the chip has revolutionised many control devices that are not strictly computers but have a place in helping students to learn. For instance, in workshops micrometers that use a chip give precise measurements in a digital readout. Blind students can now search Braille texts rapidly by using a device that stores some 200,000 Braille characters on a single C60 audiotape cassette; it can play back voice-recordings while providing a Braille output of eleven characters at a time.

Telecommunications

Both computers and microelectronics are having great impact on telecommunications, and developments in telecommunications have considerable   significance   for   future   use   of   computers. Telecommunications provide the means to deliver information over distances great and small, accurately and speedily. Each year the pace of development accelerates, meaning that more information can be sent faster and more faithfully. There is also potential for lowering the cost of telecommunications. The real cost has dropped noticeably over long distances, as in the case of Transatlantic telephone calls.

Computers are taking their place as controllers of telecommunica-tion systems, as well as being generators and transformers of information to be delivered via these systems. There are many well-known examples. If we are credit card users, our credit is checked in seconds via telecommunication channels that span oceans and continents to a computer that is asked whether our credit limit has been exceeded or the card stolen. A microcomputer owner in New Mexico can use a special telephone network (Tymnet) to gain access to information of many kinds held on The Source's computer in Virginia. Using a terminal in an office in one city, a clerk can call up any of hundreds of thousands of insurance records on his or her screen, linked by telephone line to a computer, in another city, that searches optical videodiscs (see Chapter 4), each one containing 40,000 pages of information.

The most significant changes in telecommunications in recent years have been in new transmission channels and new ways of sending information through these channels and the older ones. The 'old' channels, still extremely valuable, are those used over the past 50 years by radio and television broadcasting, and by telephone and telex. Telecommunications are being influenced by microelectronics as miniaturised components make possible more powerful satellites, including those that can broadcast direct to homes and institutions such as schools. Similar components are going into switching devices and equipment to step up the strength of signals during long-distance cable transmissions. Take the telephone network, for example. In most countries at present, messages pass through it in analogue form: that is, variations in the current in the wire are analogous to variations in the sounds spoken into the mouthpiece. New information technology will convert such networks so that messages are coded in digital form, that is, in binary code, as 0s and 1s, making the signals compatible with computers and at the same time increasing the quality and efficiency of transmission. Converted networks will be able to handle numerical, textual and visual information, all coded digitally (see Chapter 3), and their capacity to inform will be increased greatly. Copper cables, used everywhere for decades, will be gradually replaced by glass optical fibre cables (Chapter 4) that can carry signals as pulses of light instead of in the form of electrical impulses. Again, systems' capacity to inform will be increased because such cables convey many more messages than copper ones, and, a minor point, they are also much more difficult to tap.

These are a few examples of the confluence of computers, micro-electronics and telecommunications, but lest the sheer technology enrapture us, we need to be fully aware of its potential functions and, later, its limitations.

2 FUNCTIONS

Information and Communication

What can we do with new information technology? What functions does it serve, and does it serve them better than the old? To answer these questions we must first define one or two terms. The fundamental function served by the technology is that it enhances our ability to communicate information. But what is 'information' and what does it mean to communicate? We say that human communication is based on interchange of information, but we need to be more precise.

Paisley (1980) suggests two ways of defining information, structurally and functionally. Structurally speaking, information is 'an encoding of symbols (for example, letters, numbers, pictures) into a message . . . communicated through any channel'. That is what information looks like, if only we could always see it. Needless to say, these encoded symbols take many forms, as Chapter 3 shows. Functionally speaking, in terms of what it does, Paisley suggests that information denotes 'any stimulus that alters cognitive structure in the receiver . . . something that the receiver already knows is not information'. Or, in the words of Stafford Beer, information is what changes us (quoted by Knott and Wildavsky, 1981).

Information, says Paisley (1980), varies in quality, depending on its relevance, timeliness, comprehensiveness and authoritativeness. Its value depends on not only its quality but also its specifiability (distinctness of representation), locatability (distinctness of location), acquirability (ease of acquisition, including cost) and usability (suitability of form and content for intended use). In other words, much information is of no or low value to particular individuals at any one time. In education, above all, we are obliged to develop selectivity.

Information has been defined even more technically. It is widely accepted among communication scholars that information is 'a difference in matter-energy which affects uncertainty . . . where a choice exists among a set of alternatives' (Rogers and Kincaid, 1981). What is a difference in matter-energy? Such differences appear in the physical world as differences that humans can sense.

15

Thus we imperfectly sense, by sight and touch, differences in form. We attach meanings to what we sense and construct a psychological reality for ourselves from these perceptions. We perceive printed words, and each of us interprets what they mean. Or we hear music and interpret it each in his or her own way. We use the differences in matter-energy to alter the uncertainty we possess, in whatever degree, concerning what we already know. We learn nothing from messages that contribute nothing to the resolution of uncertainty (Pierce, 1961). We want information to increase our understanding.

Clearly, it is possible for us to create differences in matter-energy for others to perceive, as well as perceiving such differences, in varying ways, for ourselves. Human communication consists of exchanges of information, of differences in matter-energy. Education must surely entail such communication. New information technology is surely at our service here, to store, collect, select, transform, send or display information. Education can take advantage of this technology.

Models of Communication

We must therefore look carefully at these functions of storing, collecting and so on, but first we should consider one or two models of how humans communicate. The best-known one is Shannon and Weaver's (1949), depicted in Figure 2.1. In this model, a message emanates from an information source. It is converted into a signal or series of signals by a transmitter. En route, this signal is mixed with or contaminated by 'noise', that is to say, various kinds of unwanted interference coming from noise sources. The received signal is decoded by a receiver, being converted back into the original message, more or less, which is what the receiver (or destination) receives.

Shannon and Weaver's model seems straightforward. It recognises that encoding and decoding occur. It takes into account the problem of interference: 'noise' is a term from electrical engineering, denoting electro-magnetic interference. Noise arriving with the signal makes it more difficult to decode accurately, as we all know from everyday experience.

This model has been criticised, however, because it is linear. That is to say, it accounts only for the act of sending and receiving. It is a one-way model, based on engineering. In fact, this was the dominant

Figure 2.1: Shannon and Weaver's Linear Model of Communication

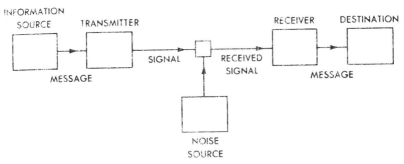

Source: Reproduced by permission from Shannon and Weaver (1949).

model for a quarter of a century (Rogers and Kincaid, 1981). The thinking behind it was probably reflected in the thinking of many top managers in organisations in the field of communications. Broadcasters, for example, thought of themselves as primarily responsible for sending out messages, and perhaps for reducing noise to a minimum, but not for receiving them back. Broadcasting organisations put most of their resources into production and transmission of programmes, and much less into listening to audience opinion.

To convert Shannon and Weaver's model into a two-way model of communication, we must add a feedback channel, complete with transmitter, encoding, noise, decoding and receiver, all to deal with messages returning from the receiver to the sender. It could be said that we are simply working Shannon and Weaver's model in reverse, but in fact we are working it almost simultaneously in both directions. In this two-way model, the feedback channel can be vitally important to the original receiver as a means of seeking clarification of the original message. Feedback channels, verbal and non-verbal, continually serve this purpose in human communication. And, as we shall see, in some situations new information technology enables us to engage in far more two-way communication than did the old.

Shannon and Weaver's model, important as it was when it was first published, has also been criticised because it did not provide for the complex nature of relationships among humans, and other scholars (for example, Schramm, 1977 and Kincaid, 1979) advanced models intended to fill this need. This is not the place for a lengthy discussion of these models, none of which has yet gained wide acceptance, but they do remind us that it is easy to over-simplify explanations of our own communication processes.

What are the characteristics of a model that helps to explain the functions of new information technology? First, it must be a two-way model: the channels within it must allow for two-way traffic. Secondly, it must include all the functions and, thirdly, it must show how these functions are integrated. Ideally, it should also exhibit the complexities of both human-human and human-machine interaction.

Figure 2.2: A Model of Functions of New Information Technology

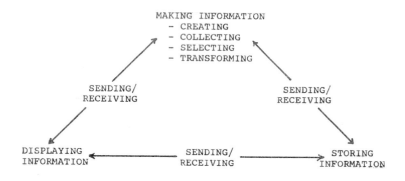

Figure 2.2 establishes four principal functions: making, sending/receiving, storing and displaying. Making is sub-divided into creating, collecting, selecting and transforming. Sending is of course complemented by receiving. We can look at each of these functions in turn and examine their interrelationships.

Making Information

Do humans make information? Or do they simply discover it? These are interesting philosophical questions, but if we are in the business of *creating* 'differences in matter-energy' for others to perceive as information, we can afford to take an empirical view and say that the answer does not really matter. We may read a book as an original 'creation', yet freely acknowledge that it and every other book include amalgams of information *collected, selected and transformed.* Some books are more original than others: Shakespeare's plays, for example, owe less to others than does the *Encyclopedia Britannica.*

Collecting information may call for channels to bring it from stores or sources of many kinds, from many places and in many forms. The rate at which information is available to us will depend on the capacity of these channels. The variety of information they can bring in depends on their flexibility. The quality of information they provide, including the amount of noise present in it, is determined in part by the efficiency of the channels, with noisy channels yielding noise-ridden information. New information technology enables us to increase the capacity, flexibility and efficiency of channels for collecting information.

We can find examples of new information technology being used to collect information in industry, agriculture, medicine and many other fields. The head of a manufacturing company collects sales information from retail outlets through data networks that transmit the figures at high speed over telephone lines. In the same company, the production manager collects information continuously from the automated assembly line, using remote sensors linked to computers. Even the nightwatchman, one of the last of the unskilled workers, has at his service a closed-circuit television system that collects information unflaggingly and in all weathers. In agriculture, new information technology, in the shape of a satellite carrying infra-red cameras, collects information about weather and the state of crops over a very large area at frequent intervals. In medicine, new information technology monitors the condition of patients.

Selecting information precedes and follows collecting. Totally indiscriminate collecting leads to information overload, therefore we need to be able to select information. We set up criteria of many kinds, sometimes to include information in our collection, sometimes to exclude it, and more often to sort it into categories. In other words, we switch information through complex paths and into various stores. We merge information, too, after selecting it from different sources. As the sum of information circulating in our society has increased, however, so has our need to select information efficiently. We have used technology to assist us for many decades, in the form of indexes and mechanical sorting systems. Now we can use new information technology for this purpose and it offers us the power to search and select quickly from very large stores indeed.

An example from the entertainment world: a pop group makes a recording of its music. The recording is a process of collecting information from each performer, from each instrument or vocalist, on a separate track. Afterwards, the producer uses new information technology to select what he or she wants from each track. A particular track may be enhanced electronically. On another, more sounds may be added. On another, the volume may be changed or sounds may even be eliminated. The end-result is an edited version of the original. In the television industry, producers follow similar procedures in the 'post-production' videotape editing room, again using new information technology to select information that finally makes up the broadcast. Even during live broadcasts, producers are busy selecting information by switching from one camera to another and by instructing the cameramen to take particular shots of the action.

The police force, dependent upon information to solve crimes, uses new information technology to search criminal records, including fingerprint records, notoriously difficult to search by any other means. Of course, the technology may also be used to select information by people intent on committing crimes, who can search more easily for sources of wealth they want to expropriate, and 'computer crimes', in which crooks break into electronic systems to select information they want, or to corrupt it, are becoming more common.

The new technology excels at selecting information when the stores are massive and the criteria for selection are complex. It can handle with ease the task of searching among a few million items for those which belong to certain sets. For example, if we wish to select from a store of research studies all those published in the last ten years concerning the use of television for teaching foreign languages to adults, we simply specify these sets: (1) the dates, (2) television, (3) teaching foreign languages, and (4) adults. The computer counts how many there are in store within each of these sets, and how many there are in the intersection of the four sets, that is, where they overlap each other. If we wish to be even more specific, it will count those for the particular foreign languages in which we have an interest. In any case, we can request a listing of all the studies it finds for us. Impressive as this may sound, it is an even more remarkable use of the new technology when we bear in mind the fact that the search can be done on a terminal in a European library, linked by telephone line to an earth station that sends the signals via a satellite stationary at 22,000 miles above the equator to an earth station in America, and then by telephone line to the computerised databank.

The information selected comes back, by the same route, barely seconds later.

Transforming information that has been collected and selected entails rearranging it, reordering it, preparing it for presentation in various modes (see Chapter 3). The transforming function requires the ability to manipulate information, to analyse and synthesise it at high speed and with great flexibility. It also requires a facility for trying out transformations, so that we can see whether they fit our purposes, before we finally choose one out of a number of alternatives. Here again the new information technology is at our service: we can use it to create 'mock-ups', based on trial transformations, and to compare these and refine them until we have the one we want. For example, computer programs enable us to rotate, in several axes, three-dimensional engineering drawings of working mechanisms so that we can check whether clearances are adequate between adjacent parts.

Sending and Receiving

Sending and receiving information are further functions performed excellently by new information technology, which enhances transmission. Chapter 4 provides details of devices and systems serving these two functions, and they can be divided into three broad classes depending on the means of transmission. One class includes those which depend on electrical waves or pulses transmitted through wires or similar conductors. A second class includes all that depend on electromagnetic waves or pulses broadcast through the atmosphere, and a third class includes devices and systems that depend on transmission of light pulses, produced by lasers. Information is delivered, on its outward journey from the 'making' source, to a device or system that serves either the *displaying* or the *storing* function, but may also be returned to the source for reselection or transformation, hence on Figure 2.2 the arrows point in both directions. There can also be interchange of information between devices and systems that display or store it.

Storing and Displaying

Information is stored in many forms, and new information technology makes conversion into the most economical form very much more feasible. Thus thousands of pages of words can be stored as very dense magnetic patterns recorded on tape or disc, for display on a screen or in print. Millions of 'bits' of information can be stored in microscopic indentations in a videodisc, for display as colour television pictures and sound. Chapter 4 contains many examples.

Integration

Integration of these functions is made possible by new information technology, which combines in single systems, large or small, components for input and display, for storage and delivery, for selection and transformation of information. Technical reliability improves with greater integration and costs tend to fall. Integration is increasing as more system components use digital codes and as they become compatible with computing equipment that can process information at high speed and with great reliability. In Chapter 3 we look at symbols, codes and languages used in carrying out all these functions.

3 SYMBOLS, CODES, LANGUAGES AND MODES

Human Communication

Education, by any definition, depends on human communication. Many forms of human communication are enhanced by new information technology, which can increase the fidelity with which messages can be transmitted and the variety and amount of information in these messages. Fidelity improves as 'noise' is reduced. Variety increases as ways are found to transmit more of the full range of messages sent by humans, including complex messages made up of many 'bits' of information.

Humans (and machines) communicate by means of signals. A set of signals makes up a message. Messages are transmitted through one or more channels or media. As we saw in Chapter 2, messages are encoded by the transmitter and decoded by the receiver. All messages are 'shaped' by the codes used. These codes are usually chosen by the transmitter, affected by noise and the media used, and decoded by the receiver. If the receiver is human, decoding always occurs against a context; this may even occur when the receiver is a machine.

Without technology we communicate through, for example, auditory, visual and tactile channels. In the auditory channel, we send and receive sets of sounds that make up messages; these sounds may be verbal, musical, shouts of laughter, cries of pain, and so on. Technology extends our senses and breaks the bounds of time and space for us. Some signals we can receive only with technology to help us, as when we listen to the radio. All this is elementary and much has been written on this subject (see, for example, Innis, 1951; McLuhan, 1964; Gumpert and Cathcart, 1979; Salomon, 1979; for a complex theory of 'conversation', see Pask, 1975).

Symbols, Codes and Languages

We need to distinguish, however, between symbols, codes and languages, all of which are vital to transformations of information.

Without transformations, we would not have civilisation as we know it, with recorded knowledge and near-universal communication. To achieve transformations, humans arbitrarily assign meanings to symbols or groups of symbols. In countries of Western Europe and North America, symbols called alphanumeric characters are used to represent numerals and letters. Groups of letters in certain combinations make up words corresponding to spoken words. Groups of numerals have certain meanings. Groups of characters by themselves cannot convey much meaning, but when combined according to a syntax they become languages, capable of expressing abstract ideas. Languages are principal tools of transformation of knowledge.

Alphanumeric characters can also be used to devise codes, in which the original 'plain language' messages are hidden, compressed or otherwise transformed. One code can be translated into another, according to a given set of rules. Codes are essential to new information technology, not to hide information but to deal with it efficiently, to carry out the functions discussed in Chapter 2.

Binary code (in 0s and 1s, see Chapter 1) is the basis for machine language, the most primitive form of language used in the computer (Jarrett, 1980), but there are languages at higher levels. Next up the scale is assembly language, a relatively simple form used by programmers to avoid working in binary code direct. The computer translates assembly code into binary code, for the programmer, before carrying out the instructions contained in it. Almost every make of computer has to have its own assembly language, not transferable to others, therefore assembly languages are termed low-level. High-level programming languages are less exclusively linked to particular makes, although few are freely transferable. They need more translation (by the computer, not the programmer) before they are in binary code. Examples are COBOL (Common Business Oriented Language), FORTRAN (Formula Translator), BASIC (Beginners' All-purpose Symbolic Instruction Code), COMAL-80 (Common Algorithmic Language), which was developed from BASIC in Denmark (Atherton, 1981, 1982 and Bramer, 1982), and PASCAL (named after the French mathematician, Pascal), the last three being more commonly used in education. LOGO, developed by Papert (1977, 1980), and Smalltalk, developed at Xerox's Palo Alto Research Center, are examples of languages originally developed with children in mind, although the latter is now being used for other purposes in addition to education. All these programming languages include a large number of plain language (English, for instance) words combined with abbreviations and special terms and symbols. BASIC, in various 'dialects', is the programming language most widely used for microcomputers, although it has a number of disadvantages for educators. For example, it is not very suitable for presenting text on the screen and lacks the kind of structure needed for educators' information processing. It tends to lead to the development of programmes that are extremely hard to read, modify or debug (repair), according to Bramer (1982). On the other hand, it is relatively easy to learn and is readily available (for a good primer, see Dwyer and Critchfield, 1978).

Digital and Analogue Signals

We also need to distinguish between two forms of electronic signal in new information technology: digital and analogue. Martin (1977) points out that information of most types (aural, visual, tactile) can be converted into one of these forms. Analogue signals can be changed into digital signals and vice versa. In old telephones (which most of us still have), the strength of current in the wires directly varies with the frequency of the voices. By contrast, new digitised telephones encode voice frequencies as a stream of electrical pulses. Each group of pulses represents the binary code for a particular voice frequency. This may seem to require immensely long strings of pulses to reflect faithfully the original voice, but sampling and compression techniques reduce the actual number of pulses to be transmitted, without significant loss of fidelity.

Digital signals have the advantage of being compatible with digital computers, which now far outnumber analogue computers. They can be easily amplified for long distance transmission and are not susceptible to electrical noise in the same way that analogue signals are. Electrical noise corrupts analogue signals, but digital signals are coded as pulses therefore interference has to be very strong to overwhelm the pattern. Moreover, streams of digitised signals interfere with each other less than streams of analogue signals. The capacity of lines carrying digital signals is very much greater than those carrying analogue signals, resulting in cheaper transmission.

Digital and Analogue Information Storage

Digitised storage forms are displacing analogue forms, too. Here we should look at 'analogue' in a wider context. On film, we record an analogue of what we see through the viewfinder of the camera. But in using an electronic videocamera, say in a television studio, do we also record on tape an analogue of the scene? Do videocassettes contain an electronic analogue? The answer to both questions is at the moment usually 'Yes', although it soon may be 'No'. Magnetic tape in videocassettes does not carry digitised information, although it can and soon will for most new cameras. The cameras on spacecraft that take pictures of Saturn, for example, convert into digital code the colour and light intensity for each of a large number of 'spots on the retina', so to speak. These digital signals are transmitted by radio to Earth, where the pictures are reconstituted.

All magnetic tapes and discs used in computers carry digitised information, however, and the 'move to digital' is almost accomplished in other parts of the electronics industry. We can now buy digital recordings of music. When these were made, the original sounds were transformed into digital signals, then recorded on a master tape. Most of us do not yet have digital players, for audiodiscs or tapes, therefore the master tape must be used to create old-style analogue pressings or tapes, suitable for our equipment. Digitising the original recording is worthwhile, however, because it eliminates one major source of noise and retains high fidelity during editing. Digital audiodiscs are esteemed by connoisseurs even though the needle still has to move along the groove, which is shaped as an analogue of the sounds it helps to produce. We shall look at other digitised information technology, such as videodiscs, in Chapter 4.

Analogic, Digital and Iconic Modes of Communication

Finally, we need to return to human communication, to distinguish between its analogic, digital and iconic modes. In the digital mode we employ characters and digits, letters and figures. Each character has little meaning in itself, but strung together in particular ways and placed in context, characters convey deep meaning, as in a book. If we read the book aloud however, we shift into the analogic mode, since the spoken word is an analogue of the written. The distinction is clear when we compare a digital watch's changing numerals with the sweeping hands of an 'analogue' watch. Print without illustrations is in the digital mode. Print with illustrations is in both the digital and the iconic (pictured) mode. Radio broadcasts are in the analogic mode, but the scripts from which they may originate are in the digital mode. Television (sound and pictures) is certainly in the analogic and iconic modes, but can also be in the digital mode when titling appears. Printed tonic sol-fa music is in the digital mode, but performed music in the analogic.

In each of these modes, information is structured and conveyed differently, that is clear. Moreover, as humans we have become accustomed to the patterns, called symbol systems by Salomon (1979), in which information is structured in each mode. Salomon takes the view that we overlook the potential of particular media, operating in one or more modes, to cultivate our skills of pattern recognition. Thus in film we become accustomed to the symbol systems used by film makers and expressed in analogic, iconic and sometimes digital modes. Some symbol systems require more 'mental translation' than others, some contain more ambiguity, as in the case of Japanese characters (see below).

Much primary schooling is taken up with learning how to communicate in the digital mode ('reading, writing and arithmetic'), which is the dominant mode of education generally in our industrialised society. We value a 'bookish' education that teaches students how to excel in the digital mode. Less attention is given to learning how to communicate in analogic or iconic modes, despite the fact that many concepts are difficult to explain in the digital mode. The analogic mode is vital, for example, to drama and performed music; the iconic mode to design, fine art, engineering, town planning, architecture and cartography. It is possible that we shall soon see more learning in analogic and iconic modes, and perhaps less emphasis on learning in the digital mode, which has actually proved difficult for large sections of the population. It is already clear that some digital modes of communication, such as writing and (silent) reading are being made less essential in our society.

One reason why these shifts are likely to accelerate is that new information technology is capable of handling human communication in all three of these modes, despite the challenges of the most demanding mode, the iconic. To be able to generate, select, transmit and receive information in the digital mode over vast distances, as a telex system does, is impressive. To do the same with voice or music, as radio does, is more impressive. But most impressive is the capacity to generate, select, manipulate, store, transmit and receive in iconic mode, with great speed and fidelity. New information technology can do this with ease. It can also achieve already certain transformations from one mode to another: for instance, within limits, it can change what was originally in digital mode (say, the printed word) into analogic, as in voice synthesis, and soon it will accomplish the reverse transformation.

The Special Case of Japan

It is interesting to note some of the special problems being overcome by the new information technology in Japan. In Japanese writing and printing many thousands of traditional Kanji characters are used to represent ideas and they bear no direct relationship to spoken words. The Japanese thus face unusually complex tasks in information processing, as examples of new information technology applications indicate. In CAPTAIN, a pilot Japanese videotex system (see Chapter 4 for details of these systems), the need to display Kanji characters has resulted in the development of different techniques from those used in systems that display alphanumeric characters (Ito and Harashima, 1981). The latter are small in number, whereas there are 3,000 Kanji characters in common usage. Kanji characters are also very complex, containing many 'strokes' compared with our characters. In videotex systems based on alphanumerics, information is stored, selected and transmitted in binary coded form, then transformed within each terminal into the dot patterns that make up the characters within each terminal, for display on its screen. In CAPTAIN, the character generator must be much more elaborate and is too expensive to put into each terminal, therefore it is located centrally, alongside the large computer that stores the information and selects it. Then dot patterns needed to make up each character are transmitted to the terminals, which do very little decoding. This means that transmission time for the information is longer and costs more, but the technology does provide a solution to a difficult communication problem.

In another application, computerised databases for scientific information (again see Chapter 4), Japan has similar problems, as Komatsu, Hara and Taoka (1981) point out. There are few large databases in Japan such as *Chemical Abstracts* in the United States or *Excerpta Medica* in the Netherlands. Although there is a Science and Engineering File in romanised Japanese, containing about two million entries, only 15 per cent of these are for articles originally written in Japanese, the rest being translations into Japanese (subject to extra time-lag because of the need for accurate translation). The language structures of Japanese and Western languages differ fundamentally. What is more, ways of conceptualising ideas also differ widely, say Komatsu, Hara and Taoka. Translation of Japanese characters into alphanumerics (Roman characters) occurs in Japan through three rather different methods, two of them in wide use, and a reader who does not know which method has been used can misinterpret the romanised Japanese text. Takano (1982) provides details of other problems, such as using Japanese together with alphanumeric characters in new information technology systems in Japan. Clearly, these systems are helping the Japanese to solve difficult communication problems.

Conclusion

Knowing about symbols, codes, languages and modes helps us to understand how new information technology can be used in education, and to appreciate how information can be transformed. The power to transform information increases the capacity of our society to store information and to select it, in one mode or another, for use in multi-media systems. In education, the Open University is a prototype of such systems. Learners may benefit from opportunities to learn in more than one mode, often in more than one medium. Each medium employs a different combination of symbols to convey information (see Lindenmayer, 1981), therefore learners who find difficulty with learning in one medium may have less difficulty in another. New information technology increases our capacity to provide opportunities to learn through several media.

4 DEVICES AND SYSTEMS

Classifying Devices and Systems

Which are the devices and systems that belong to new information technology? What can we do with each? These questions are quite difficult to answer in the face of a great variety of inventions, with new ones being added every month. In general, the new technology is marked off from the old because it is electronic rather than mechanical or electro-mechanical, and the new technology often uses microelectronics: most of its devices and systems take advantage of miniaturisation, the chip and its integrated circuits. But it would be a mistake to draw too sharp a line between old and new, because devices and systems belonging to the old can be modified for use alongside the new. For example, existing electro-mechanical telephone exchanges can accommodate data transmissions between computers, and paper remains an important storage medium in many settings where new information technology is bringing substantial changes. This merging of old and new is only to be expected. To replace the old is very expensive, particularly when huge sums have been invested in, say, copper cable under the streets.

One way to classify the devices and systems of information technology is in terms of its function or functions. We saw in Chapter 2, however, that the functions of new information technology overlap and it is also true that many devices combine two or more functions. Systems, made up of different devices, always combine functions, sometimes all the functions, displayed in the model of Figure 2.2 (page 18). This chapter looks first at devices used mainly for putting information into information technology systems, then at storage media, before going on to consider transmission devices and systems. Finally, it looks at output devices and at systems that integrate by serving most or all functions.

Input Devices

The first, and best-known, input device is the keyboard. The

30

standard QWERTY keyboard has been fitted to typewriters and tele-type machines for decades in all English-speaking countries using the Roman alphabet, with minor variations to suit different cultures. By placing much-used keys some distance apart, separated by less-used keys, the original designers enabled typists to work faster without jamming the key bars. In Europe other arrangements of the letters (e.g., AZERTY) are in use, but the QWERTY keyboard is close to being the world-wide standard for typewriters and computers using the Roman alphabet, and Gates (1980) assumes that it will not be displaced easily, despite its inefficiency. In the United States, QWERTY keyboards are standard, although for its Sesame Place educational playground Children's Television Workshop installed teaching computers with ABCDE keyboards (*Time*, 21 September 1981), and Texas Instruments' educational game, Speak & Spell, also uses an ABCDE keyboard. Computer keyboards usually have additional control keys for various functions. Often computers have a separate numeric keyboard for use when large quantities of numbers must be keyed in. Computers used for word-processing, like the one on which this book was first written, have special keys for moving around the text, deleting characters, words or para-graphs, and so on. Many computers have specialised keys for use in programming. Sometimes a keyboard will have dual uses for the same keys, with the second use being written on the front of the key rather than its top. The second use is actuated by first pressing a control key.

Keypads are small keyboards with only a few keys. Pocket cal-culators, remote control devices for television sets or videocassette recorders, push-button telephones and check-out tills in stores all have keypads. Keypads are usually intended for use with one hand only. A keypad recently appeared on which the user presses various combinations of keys ('chords') to produce letters of the alphabet, numerals 0 to 9 and punctuation marks. This is enough for most writing tasks. A 14-character line of what is being written appears in a small window above the keys. The number of keys? Only five, one for each finger.

Keyboards and keypads used to be entirely mechanical, with levers moving in response to each keystroke. New ones are electronic, requiring much less energy from the user. Some keys are spring-loaded switches, which make contact when pressed quite gently. The most advanced are touch-sensitive, requiring only that the user makes contact with them.

Touch-sensitive boards, made in several sizes, consist of a set of squares which can be coded. Input is simply by touch, therefore a young child can learn to use such a board even before learning to use a keyboard (see Chapter 7).

Similarly, touch-sensitive screens are available. They look like television screens but are linked to computers which are able to record the coordinates (the 'cross-references') of any spot on the screen when that spot is touched. Therefore even an illiterate can make an input when asked to touch a particular part of a picture shown on the screen.

Another device, the graphics tablet, combines the capabilities of touch-sensitive boards and screens. The author or artist writes or draws on it with a special stylus connected to the computer. Whatever is drawn appears on the computer's screen and can be stored in the computer's memory. The tablet works in much the same way as the screen, but is easier to draw and write on because it can be held at any suitable angle and does not have a slippery glass surface. Some tablets have additional facilities: for instance, Apple makes one accompanied by programs that enable the user to select with the stylus from a menu of functions specified by the user in advance.

In a somewhat different version, marketed by Rediffusion, a British company, anyone can write the numbers 0-9, the letters of the alphabet and 22 other symbols on the paper surface of the tablet in ball-point pen or pencil and the device identifies the characters and their position on the tablet, signalling this information to a computer, which not only records it appropriately but also flashes it back to the tablet for display in a small window. Thus the writer can check for errors.

Some microcomputers have 'paddles', usually a pair, and these are levers that can be used, for example, to draw on the screen by steering the point of light that draws lines.

Computer-assisted design devices go further than the graphics tablet, which they can easily incorporate. The computer's keyboard is used to instruct the computer to draw lines between different spots on the screen. Sometimes, as in designing the layout of a chip, the computer will solve intricate logic problems before 'deciding' where to draw the line. In architecture, sets of rules and lists of standard components can be programmed into the computer. In engineering, strain factors and the like can be taken into account, quite apart from the fact that the screen offers an almost limitless range of scales. If the database contains data for three dimensions, objects can be constructed and viewed from any angle on the screen. Moving parts can be 'moved' through their complete cycles to check clearances, and so on (see *Computers and Education*, vol. 5, no. 4, 1981, or *Microvision*, no. 18, Autumn 1981). But the means of input remain the keyboard and the tablet, often used in conjunction with a cursor, or pointer, on the screen.

Xerox Corporation has produced a versatile input terminal, with a larger than usual screen, plus the normal keyboard and a mouse. The mouse is a device for easily controlling input, rather than for making inputs itself. It fits under the user's hand and runs on the desk surface next to the terminal, being connected to it by a thin wire. In its back are two switches. The user moves it around the desk and each movement of the mouse is paralleled by a movement of a cursor on the screen, except that the cursor moves faster, therefore further, than the mouse. The user points the cursor at, say, an item in a list of commands on the screen and then presses one of the two switches to execute that command. Alternatively, the cursor can be used to define the corners of a figure to be drawn on the screen. Since the terminal is backed up by a large and sophisticated computer, experienced operators acquire great versatility in using the mouse.

Lightpens look like pens without nibs or points. They too are attached to computer terminals by a short length of wire, and each contains a photoelectric device responsive to light displayed on a terminal's screen. A user simply brings the pen close to the screen or even 'writes' on it. As with touch-sensitive screens, the computer is able to register the coordinates of the points touched by the pen. It is quite possible to use a lightpen to draw on one screen, in various colours and shadings if desired, in a way which is visible both to the author or artist and to those watching a number of screens elsewhere, linked by telephone line (see Chapter 12 for the Cyclops project at the Open University).

Optical character recognition devices are an important new group of input devices. They are used to scan written or printed characters, to recognise them, and, usually, to convert them into digitised code for storage, transmission and further processing. Among the simpler kinds, they are devices that read the numbers on cheques or the marks made by respondents on questionnaires and multiple-choice tests. The optical wands in stores, and recently in libraries too, to read black stripes of varying widths printed on part of the packaging of goods or on a label placed inside each book, are optical recognition devices. The stripes represent coded letters and numbers, and the data from them are used for stock control. More advanced devices will read several typefaces or fonts, including typescript. The most sophisticated read almost all fonts now in use, with remarkable accuracy and at very high speeds. Thus it is possible to insert into one of these machines a mixed set of magazine clippings, typescript from several typewriters, plus material from existing books or journals, and from it will come, if we desire it, an edition set in whatever typeface we specify. As Gates (1980) says, such devices have the advantage of being able to transform text into digital codes for processing, at high speed.

Voice recognition devices are still being developed. Their potential value is obvious and by the time this book is in print some of the technical problems may have been solved. We are of course familiar with microphones as input devices, connected to other equipment, and with optical cameras. These are scarcely new technology. Video or electronic cameras are new, however, combining as they do optics with electronics to turn the images entering the camera into analogue and, more recently, digital signals to be stored on tape. The size, weight, power requirements and price of these cameras have dropped sharply, while their efficiency has greatly improved (Hawker, 1981). A slowscan television camera can send pictures along ordinary telephone lines, a frame at a time, ideal for applications such as surveillance or calling up drawings from a distant archive.

Once one of these input devices has been used, how is information stored, or, to use the jargon, what are the storage media and devices?

Storage Media and Devices

Paper remains, for the time being, an important storage medium. Printed paper, product of the Gutenberg revolution, is far from being excluded by new information technology (Williams, 1982). True, the 'paperless office' has come to a few large companies and will come before long to many more, large and small. But we do not yet know how paperless they will remain. The advent of optical character recognition actually favours retention of printed paper as a storage medium, since recognition devices form a technological bridge between our immense stores (in libraries, offices and law courts, for example) of printed paper and new forms of electronic storage. We must recognise, however, that printed paper stores information at a relatively low density, and for many applications is likely to be overtaken by storage media that provide much higher densities. The differences are emphasised by Evans (1981) who compares the 'data units' of print (the letter or number, two to five millimetres long) with those of computers (switches only thousandths of a millimetre in size).

Punched paper tape used to be vital to computer technology and to telecommunications by teletype. The 'ticker tape' of New York welcomes is still in use for teletype machines, but it is a fading part of computer technology, even if some schools are still obliged to use it. Information is stored on the tape in code represented by the punched holes, which can be read back later. Punching it is a slow process and reading is not much faster. Paper tape suffers from being not very durable and comparatively bulky to store.

Similarly, punched cards used to be much more important in computer technology than they are today; they do not belong with microcomputers at all, for instance. Each card is punched with a series of holes which represent coded information, and the cards can be read by a card reader attached to a computer. This form of input is still in use for some purposes: for example, the responses to a questionnaire from one individual may be punched onto one or more cards which can thereafter be held for processing in various ways. Punched cards are again rather bulky to store although they are more durable than paper tape.

Magnetic tape is a standard storage medium in new information technology. As the tape, coated with oxide, passes over a series of drums it is magnetised by one or more 'heads' in extremely dense patterns that can later be read back by the same heads. The magnetic patterns, which can be recorded at very high speed, may represent coded information from a computer, or frequencies or pulses from a microphone or videocamera. We can speak of audiotape, videotape and computer tape, but there is some interchangeability. An audiotape can be used to record a computer program, for example, and is indeed used in this way with several makes of microcomputer that employ an ordinary tape recorder as a storage device. Magnetic tape suffers from one or two disadvantages: the magnetic patterns can be damaged by mishandling or heat or a magnetic source, and it is quite difficult and slow to find information on a magnetic tape unless a high-speed tape drive is being used, as in mini- and mainframe computers. The reliability of this tape is signified by the numbers of magnetic tape videorecorders (about 800,000 in the United Kingdom, 1 million in the Federal Republic of Germany, 3.3 million in the US and 3 million in Japan at the end of 1981).

Magnetic discs are divided into two categories based on the flexibility of the material from which they are made: floppy and hard (sometimes called rigid). In both cases, information is stored on them in much the same way as on magnetic tape. A 'head' passes over the disc as the latter rotates at high speed, and the disc is magnetised in extremely dense patterns that can later be read by the same head. As the head's movement across the face of the disc can be controlled with microscopic accuracy, it can 'address' any part of the disc to store information there or retrieve it, very quickly indeed. Hard discs, commonly known as Winchester discs, offer greater density and therefore greater storage capacity than floppy discs (floppies), although the latter can now store more than 300,000 characters on a single side, or over 600,000 characters on a double-density, double-sided eight-inch floppy. As a general rule, microcomputers and specialised computers such as word processors use floppies, although there is a trend towards hard discs. Both kinds can be damaged in the same ways that magnetic tape can be.

How do the different forms of storage compare in terms of capacity? Morgan (1980) suggests that we take the Concise Oxford Dictionary as our standard: a 5-inch floppy will hold 40 pages, a C60 audiocassette (magnetic tape) will hold 80 pages, a 15-inch hard disc two dictionaries, a 2400-foot magnetic tape four dictionaries. But optical and capacitance videodisc technology offers the most capacity, therefore it must be explained in some detail.

Optical discs, one kind of videodisc, store information as patterns that can be read by an optical device. Since such discs are attracting considerable attention, we should look at the principal types. Philips, the Dutch electronics company, are making a 12-inch disc which will store about 25,000 pages, coded into a spiral groove with 45,000 usable tracks (Klimbie, 1982). A very thin layer of a tellurium alloy is deposited on both sides of a metal base, and the groove is pressed into this layer. Every track is separated into segments, each segment having its own 'address'. To record on the disc, a laser beam melts holes at appropriate points in each segment, the holes corresponding to digital code. Each hole is less than one micron (about 35 millionths of an inch) in diameter, giving an information density much higher than magnetic discs (Schubin, 1980). Recording can be done only once. To read the disc, the same laser beam is bounced off the track. When it hits a hole it bounces back at a different angle. Since the laser can be directed to any track and any segment, immediate access to data is easy. A set of these discs held in a sort of jukebox provides a very large information store that can be consulted electronically from terminals in many places. One American system, manufactured by Teknekron Controls, is designed to store 22,000,000,000,000 bits of information.

The first optical videodisc system in public use was the MCA laser-read disc, very similar to Philips' disc, with very small pits in an aluminised surface sandwiched between protective layers of transparent plastic. A laser beam is reflected differentially by the pits, which again represent signals encoded in binary, and the beam's position is determined by other encoded signals alongside the pits. One side of an MCA disc can carry all the signals required to record half an hour of colour television, including two sound tracks, or, if we prefer it, for no less than 54,000 frames or over 40,000 pages of print holding about a million words.

An optical disc is durable, since the laser beam reads pits that are below its surface and ignores scratches or dust on the disc surface. There is no contact with this surface, therefore the laser 'head' lasts a very long time. Specialised equipment is needed to make the discs and it is much more expensive than, say, videocassette recording equipment. A videodisc player is rather more expensive than a videocassette recorder/player, although the prices may soon be very similar. The discs themselves are comparable in cost to videocassettes, but only when reproduced in large numbers. On the other hand, these discs are more compatible with computers and other digital information processing devices and transmissions systems than are videocassettes (Otten, 1980).

Another optical system in public use is made by Thomson-CSF. It has many of the features of the Philips/MCA discs, but instead of bouncing the laser beam off a pitted surface, it shines the beam through the disc to a detector on the other side. The beam is modified by pits pressed into the surface of the disc. By changing the focus of the beam, it can be made to read either one side of the disc or the other.

Capacitance discs, another kind of videodisc, store information in grooves, rather like audiodiscs. The two principal types were developed by the Radio Corporation of America (RCA) and the Victor Company of Japan (JVC). In the RCA system the grooves guide the player's stylus across the face of the disc. JVC's system depends on signals in the grooves to guide the stylus, more like an optical disc. Capacitance discs are made of vinyl impregnated with carbon to make it electrically conductive. The stylus is diamond-tipped (JVC's is said to last ten times as long as RCA's) and it registers differences in electrical capacitance as it passes over pits in the floor of the groove. The discs contain one hour of videorecording per side, twice what is available on optical discs. Both systems provide for some random access, although JVC's is more flexible. At present, capacitance discs carry only one sound track, although this may rise to two quite soon. The discs have a very high information density, like optical discs (Schubin, 1980), but suffer the disadvantage of being subject to wear by the stylus, especially where freeze frames are used. This problem may be serious enough to prevent much use of capacitance discs in education (Schneider and Bennion, 1981).

We should not forget that the chip itself can be a storage device. Indeed, most chips contain some storage. Within their miniaturised circuits information can be stored as electrical charges or as voltage or current levels: their switches can be set in particular ways which represent coded information. This form of electronic storage is particularly useful when relatively small amounts of information, say for control purposes, must be stored in a very small space.

One further type of storage: microform. Images (digital or iconic) can be reduced photographically to microscopic proportions and recorded on film. For several decades information has been stored on microfilm, but as optics and film manufacture have improved it has become possible to reduce the images drastically. Microfiche are pieces of film the size of an index card, each piece containing reduced images of up to 98 pages (Teague, 1980). Hyperfiche or ultrafiche are similar, but contain up to 3,000 pages. Although microform storage is not electronic, it is worth mentioning here because systems exist that combine microform storage of, say, the documents of an insurance company, with new information technology. In one major system being marketed, all incoming documents are put onto microform in random order, each document being given an identifying number or address. Any document can then be called up very quickly, if not as quickly as in electronic storage, and its image transmitted elsewhere in the system as required. Moreover, 'micropublication' is possible (Otten, 1980) at the original size either on a screen or on paper. The Open University uses laser equipment which puts into microfiche computerised data, such as student records.

Terms employed for different kinds of storage or memory are, unfortunately, somewhat confusing. Let us start with serial and random access memories. Serial memories store information in sequence. They are relatively cheap per item of information stored, but finding a particular item takes comparatively long. Random access memories, by contrast, store information in rows and columns or in some other form that is instantly addressable, resulting in retrieval of an item of information with practically no delay (and are sometimes called direct access memories for this reason). Magnetic tapes and capacitance discs are examples of serial memories. Magnetic and optical discs, under the control of 'players', are random access memories. Chips are produced that have both kinds of memories. Then there are volatile and non-volatile memories. Volatile memories forget everything if the power is cut off, but non-volatile ones do not. Most of those we have been examining in this chapter are non-volatile, but some kinds of chips are volatile, so that, for example, many pocket calculators do not, after being switched off, remember the last answer. Finally, there are read-only and read-or-write memories. Read-only memories, known as ROMs, store data when they are first made and the data cannot be changed thereafter. Some chips are ROMs, and we could consider the optical disc as a further example of a ROM. Certainly the audiodisc or record is a ROM. Read-or-write memories contain information that can be retrieved and changed. Again, some chips are of this type, being confusingly labelled RAMs. RAM stands for random access memory, hence the confusion, although Morgan (1980) suggests that it might more appropriately stand for read and modify. We may note in passing that ROMs in microcomputers are now of four sub-types: those on which programmes are stored during manufacture (mask-programmed ROMs), those that are programmable later, but only once (PROMs), those that can be programmed many times, called eraseable programmable read-only memories (EPROMs), and, lastly, those that are electrically alterable read-only memories (EAROMs). The most important point to note here is that the distinction between ROMs and RAMs is being eroded.

Processors

Next, we should consider processors, that is, devices and systems that are used to select and transform information. At the simplest level these are electronic calculators that can do no more than add, subtract, multiply and divide. Pocket-sized devices that go by the same name now carry out many more mathematical functions. Some are specialised to meet the needs of engineers, architects, navigators, businessmen or scientists. Almost all of them are designed to work with numbers, but it would be a mistake to think that this will always be so. Soon similar pocket-sized devices will be widely available to process words too; the first models are in the marketplace. In the meantime, we need something larger, a desktop microcomputer, to provide sufficient power and the peripheral equipment required for word processing. If we want very large storage and immense processing power, we may need a mini- or mainframe computer. To analyse a large amount of statistical data, for example, may well be beyond even a minicomputer if the statistical manipulations required are complex. To store many pages of text may not require a minicomputer, but to manipulate those pages may.

So far we have looked only at the processing of numbers and text, both sets of digital symbols (see Chapter 3). New information technology can also process information in analogic and iconic modes. Computers help to edit audiotape and videotape. Sounds and images can be altered, enhanced or diminished electronically. Computer graphics is a fast-developing field, in which computers are extending the creative powers of designers and artists through giving them precise control over a graphic medium (see below).

Transmission Devices and Systems

Within the electromagnetic spectrum are frequencies used for radio and television, for conventional broadcasting. We should start by considering devices and systems that use these frequencies, which lie between about 300 kHz and 300 MHz (Hz stands for Hertz, the unit of measurement, named after Heinrich Hertz, a German scientist, and equalling one cycle per second). Radio and television signals are broadcast by transmitters, normally through tall antennae, and picked up by much smaller antennae, which feed the signals to receivers. All this is well known. The range of transmitters varies considerably for radio, depending on the wavelength being used, while television transmitters have a maximum useful range of about 65 miles. To provide national networks for television, countries build repeater stations, which pass signals to each other, usually at microwave frequencies, above 300 MHz, and along line-of-sight paths.

Satellites, which also use microwave frequencies, are bringing sweeping changes to broadcasting. Until very recently, satellites used for broadcasting were of relatively low power; indeed many of these are still operating. It is necessary to set up costly ground stations to receive signals from these satellites, in addition to the cost of building transmitters to beam signals up to them. Broadcasting companies take advantage of the services offered by satellite companies to bridge great distances, and round-the-world television broadcasts are commonplace. The most recent development in this field, however, is the direct broadcast satellite, which is very much more powerful and can broadcast signals direct to small dish antennae suitable for purchase by individual householders. These antennae require a converter, which pushes up the total cost a little, but no expensive earth receiving station is necessary. As satellites can broadcast to very large areas indeed, this is a significant development. A direct broadcast satellite is already in use in Canada, enabling television signals of high quality to be received in the remote communities of the northern parts of that country as well as in the more heavily populated south. Direct broadcast satellites are planned for several other countries, and are being adopted even in such a small and heavily-populated country as the United Kingdom, where the case for such a satellite was widely considered (Home Office, 1981) before the final decision was taken in 1982.

Other telecommunication tasks, as well as broadcasting, can be carried out by satellites. Voice and data transmissions are increasing greatly every year, and satellites are part of national and international telecommunication systems. American businesses that want immediate access to specialised market data can tune into a satellite which broadcasts market reports at regular intervals, in code, to those who have paid for the service. Similarly, specialised satellite broadcasts can supply continuous weather information over a wide area to farmers who have the equipment to pick up the signals, or to navigators at sea or in the air. Inexpensive narrowband channels on satellites can carry signals for slow-scan television, suitable for teaching, tutoring, testing and teleconferences (Nettles, 1981).

Satellites have already proved so successful in telecommunications that the cost of sending and receiving signals is becoming less and less dependent on the distance they have to travel. Other terrestrial transmission systems being installed are also helping to make distance and cost less closely related so that, for instance, telephone subscribers are seeing international tariffs fall while local ones rise.

Some 20 years ago, each scattered community in countries like Canada had a tall television mast to capture signals from the nearest station or repeater, which might be 60 miles away, close to the line-of-sight limit for transmission. The signals were fed into a cable connected, for a monthly rent, to most dwellings in the community. Those on the cable were able to see very clear pictures on their domestic receivers, while their less fortunate neighbours could often see nothing but 'snow' on their screens. Often the mast captured signals from more than one station, bringing variety of programming, perhaps for the first time. The cable was of a special type, termed coaxial, and provided a one-way channel into the home for signals which occupied a fairly large amount of the Hertzian spectrum and were therefore called broadband, as opposed to the narrowband transmissions of radio or along telephone lines.

Within the past five years or so, a major change has occurred in cable systems (Smith, 1981). Businessmen and others have realised that the cable systems already installed in thousands of communities in Canada, the United States, Japan and several Western European countries, offer profitable opportunities to exploit the potential of new information technology in general, not simply television (see Large, 1982a, for comment on British proposals). At the numerous 'ends' of a cable system, users may have at their disposal, within a few years, many of the devices and systems described in this chapter, plus those still on the drawing board. Most cable systems at the moment are one-way only, reminding us, perhaps, of Shannon and Weaver's model of communication, and the experimental two-way systems such as QUBE in Columbus, Ohio (described more fully in Chapter 13), are not without their problems (Kaiser, Marko and Witte, 1977). Clearly it is cheaper merely to deliver signals into homes and institutions, but two-way systems may be the norm for all new installations, at least in urban and suburban areas, within ten years. Much will depend on whether cable operators can be persuaded that the return on investment will be better than for a one-way system and that the greater capital risks are worth taking (Mason, 1977).

One of the most spectacular uses of cable has been to increase choice for home television viewers. In North America, the newest cables provide up to 120 channels, and cables with 36 or 48 channels are commonplace. Where does all the programming come from? The answer is that there has been a proliferation of specialist broadcasting. Stations aiming at relatively small groups, whether ethnic, religious, bound by language, interests or hobbies, now put out many hours of broadcasting each day. Cable operators charge these stations little or nothing to carry the signals, since they obtain cable revenues from those to whom the cable delivers. They can augment the number of channels by installing a satellite broadcast antenna to capture further broadcasts. By steering the antenna, signals from more than one satellite can be picked up (Bakan and Chandler, 1980). As each satellite may be broadcasting many or all of the channels being broadcast on another cable system elsewhere in the country, or even in another country, the potential for diversity is great indeed, although cable subscribers will have to pay more for some kinds of programming than others. In March 1981 no less than nine satellites were broadcasting on a total of over 70 channels beamed at North America. We may well wonder, along with Mahony, Demartino and Stengel (1980), what possibilities and challenges the combination of cable and satellite transmissions opens up for educational broadcasting in the United States.

The cost of installing and operating cable systems will fall, and their capacity to carry messages will rise, because expensive and bulky coaxial cable will slowly give way to fibre optics. An optical fibre is a hair-thin glass fibre, along which digitised information can pass extremely rapidly in the form of light pulses, each lasting seven millionths of a second. These pulses can now be generated by very small lasers which are manufactured cheaply in much the same way as the chip. A half-inch cable made of optical fibres can carry far more information than a four- or five-inch coaxial cable: a single pair of fibres carry nearly 2000 telephone calls simultaneously. Minute laser repeaters, installed within the optical cable, boost signals every 20 miles. Such cable systems have been installed on an experimental basis in the United Kingdom, the United States, Canada, France and Japan, and will become the new standard for terrestrial transmission systems. It is unlikely, however, that older cable systems, whether for telephone or television transmission, will be quickly replaced as there are considerable sums invested in them and it is costly to remove cables, particularly those underground. An interesting development in the United Kingdom is use of railways' rights of way for laying new cables, which can be easily placed alongside the tracks (Dineen, 1981).

The last transmission system we should consider in the context of new information technology is microwave broadcasting. The frequencies used fall outside the Hertzian spectrum and transmitters must have clear line-of-sight to the receivers. Microwave systems are particularly used to provide repeater chains between conventional television transmitters, but they are also used to carry telephone and data transmissions over long distances between cities. Microwave towers, each in sight of the next, are now familiar in town and country.

What is vital to note about all these transmission systems is that, more and more, they provide connections between a wide variety of input, processing, storage and output devices and systems. Broadband transmission systems are usually required to link those that deal in moving pictures, because these pictures must be transmitted as a very large number of bits of information. Narrowband transmissions can be used for conveying messages that require fewer bits. Both broadband and narrowband systems are becoming more efficient, some remarkably so. The technical problems of communicating over large distances, of broadcasting to large areas, whether by television or radio, and of linking many people are no longer waiting to be solved. The combined power of devices and systems linked up in fast-reacting networks has yet to be fully exploited, but it is immense.

Even the telephone system is being transformed. For example, the United Kingdom has already a few digital exchanges. These are replacing electro-mechanical versions that have many moving parts, each worn out a little every time a subscriber places a call (Street, 1981). In a digital system, callers' voices are represented by pulses, not by a varying electrical current as in the old analogue system. The new equipment is cheaper to buy, install and maintain, and takes up much less space. Callers will be able to obtain step-by-step spoken guidance in placing difficult calls, provided by an entirely automatic computer program. The digital system will give access to both voice and data transmission services, at high speeds and without the need for the traditional modem device to convert digital signals into analogue ones. Some 200 British towns and cities will have the system by 1990, representing five million connections. Telephone companies in North America, Japan and other Western European countries are moving quickly in the same direction, and hope to challenge the cable companies by providing a range of services, such as electronic mail (Maddox, 1981).

Electronic mail is already with us, particularly within individual large companies. *Communication News* for November 1981 reports on two systems installed by New York banking houses. Users type messages, with addresses, onto terminals. The messages are transferred via a computer to the addressee's terminal. He or she may retrieve messages by typing in an identification number. In one bank, there are now 350 users, 300 of them professional or managerial. By the end of 1983, 3000 staff will be using the system in this bank, but at the time of the report, 40 per cent of the messages replaced telephone calls, 40 per cent replaced memoranda and casual meetings and 20 per cent were judged to be new kinds of communications that had not occurred previously. In the other banking house, electronic mail is part of an integrated system, a paperless office. The system is integrated with word processors, adapted typewriters, telex machines and computers. Soon staff will also have portable terminals for use at home or when travelling. In this bank, managers were not told all the advantages of the system but have found out for themselves after basic training.

Output Devices and Systems

Next, there are the output devices and systems. Some are so familiar as to need little space here. Among the aural ones are the speaking end of the telephone, the earphones and loudspeakers that belong to radios and many other electronic devices, including now pocket calculators, clocks, microcomputers and educational games that speak or play music or emit other sounds. All of the last four contain voice or sound synthesisers, not tapes. In the jargon of the new technology, an aural display is part or all of the output. We are more accustomed to thinking of displays as being visual, but these devices provide analogic aural displays.

Many new electronic devices provide a visual display as part of their output. Visual displays are in either soft or hard copy. Soft copy is the term applied to a picture on a screen, or, for that matter, a set of letters and numbers on a screen. Soft copy becomes hard only when it is printed out, therefore we can say that teletype printers produce hard copy. A word processor produces first soft copy, which appears on its screen and can be manipulated in various ways, but then the printer attached to the processor can produce hard copy. Such a printer may be of several varieties, all the newer ones being largely electronic. Matrix printers have printing heads that consist of a matrix of, say, 9 by 7 pins that hit the paper in patterns corresponding to letters and numbers. Other printers use the old golf-ball or, more often, the new daisy-wheel, which has all the characters arranged at the ends of its 'petals'. Some form the letters through an electro-static process, using special paper. These charge the paper in a pattern of dots similar to those produced by matrix printers, then the paper is passed through a toner solution that causes black specks to cling to the dots. More expensive ones spray a very fine jet of ink, guided electro-statically, to form the letters. Still others use heat or electricity to 'scorch' dots on specially-coated paper. All of these printers are very much faster than a human typist. Another way of describing them is as serial, line or page printers. Serial printers are like typewriters and print only one character at a time. Line printers are faster, printing a line at a time at rates of up to 3,000 lines a minute, and page printers are the fastest. Perhaps the most impressive are the laser printers, working at 16,000 to 30,000 lines a minute in a wide range of fonts or typefaces (Jarrett, 1980). Printers are part of the new information technology: they have fewer moving parts each year and become faster and faster, with greater flexibility.

We should also mention phototypesetting equipment, which enables users to prepare text on a typewriter-like machine from which the output is a page that appears to have been typeset (Gates, 1980). Such machines are likely to change publishing practices.

Visual displays on television-like screens are vital for most computing, but particularly so for computer graphics. High resolution graphics is possible on screens that have more dots per square inch than those usually used. Computer-aided design equipment incorporates high resolution screens, introducing precision of control for designers and artists, as we have already noted. These screens are also becoming popular among those with micro-computers who like computer graphics as a hobby or an artform.

What is yet to come is high fidelity television broadcasting: it is noticeable that all television stations broadcast monoaural sound, unlike some radio stations. Predictions in the industry are that stereophonic transmissions will come soon, followed by high resolution on the screen. These broadcasts are technically feasible now, and one American satellite to be launched in the early eighties will have the capacity to receive high fidelity transmissions from earth, for rebroadcast to what will be initially very small numbers of high fidelity domestic television receivers.

One further kind of display: the kinaesthetic or touch display. A recently invented device is able to translate digital signals recorded on tape into a Braille display for blind people, while at the same time translating the same signals into an aural display through a voice synthesiser. Further use of the tactile mode is sure to follow, especially for handicapped persons.

Integrating Systems and Devices

From a layman's point of view, all these devices and systems for input, storage, processing and output may seem a bewildering array. We must note, however, the trend towards integrating them. At the most minuscule level, integration, ever-increasing integration, is the target of manufacturers of chips. Above all, they want to miniaturise so that more components, more switches and circuits can be produced in integrated form on a single chip. Why? The chief reason is economic. The cost of manufacture is likely to drop still further. There is also an important technical reason: reliability is enhanced by integration. Chips that have passed the quality controllers are unlikely to fail, and if they do they fail early in their lives. Their reliability is very much better than that of wired and soldered circuits containing valves and electro-mechanical relays.

Integration is also the target of designers and makers of devices ranging from pocket calculators to large communication systems. Their desire is to increase the capacities and capabilities of these devices and systems. By integrating within a pocket translator, say, an optical character recognition device, a processor and a voice synthesiser, they may be able to market a device that actually reads aloud, in another language, the words printed in a foreign newspaper or a book. Such a technological dream device would probably do little to solve major problems of translation, as in literature, but it might be valued by those whose tasks include scanning of foreign publications. In the meantime, Sharp markets a pocket translator with plug-in modules for eight languages (from English into

German, Dutch, Spanish, Japanese, French, Italian, Swedish and Portuguese). Each module carries 2,000 words and 152 phrases covering 14 of the most likely situations: air travel, customs, etc. The screen takes 23 characters; longer sentences roll across it at an easy reading speed. There is no voice synthesis, but that will surely be added soon.

On a much larger scale, systems are being installed to bring together a broad range of input, processing and output devices and to use them in conjuction with storage media and transmission systems to provide a widely distributed service, covering the whole of a single country or region. These major developments are dubbed 'The Network Nation' by Hiltz and Turoff (1978), who studied a well-known American project, the Electronic Information Exchange System (EIES) for scientific research communities, in which over 1,500 people were linked through a central computer.

Teletext and videotex (viewdata) are both systems of this type, intended for regional or national implementation. Teletext systems are much more limited than videotex, being dependent on broadcast signals, either over-the-air or on cable, which can be converted into messages for display on a television set. They were pioneered in the United Kingdom, under the names of Ceefax (See Facts) and Oracle (Optical Recognition of Coded Line Electronics), by broadcasting organisations whose example was soon followed in several other countries. Technically, the signals are broadcast in the brief interval between transmission of successive pictures. A fairly cheap adaptor is necessary on the receiver before it can display the messages. The number of 'frames' or 'pages' that can be transmitted is quite limited, although Morgan (1980a) indicates that this will change. The viewer, with a keypad, can call up pages containing news, the weather forecast, market reports and other items of broad interest. The over-the-air systems are one-way, since the viewer cannot transmit back to the broadcasting company by a similar channel. It is possible, however, to broadcast programs (software) in the form of coded signals to microcomputers, as British experiments show, including those on Oracle (Hedger, 1980). New cable-borne broadcasting systems may be two-way, of course, in which case they approach videotex.

Videotex or viewdata systems, also pioneered in the United Kingdom, use a different combination of technology (Woolfe, 1980). Messages are displayed on the television screen, but they are delivered via telephone line, telephone set, modem (to convert analogue signals to digital) and an adaptor. With a keypad to select items from menus displayed on the screen, a user can search a vast library of information, much of it regularly updated by 'information providers', and can respond to any page, as the systems are two-way. Prestel, the videotex system being installed in the United Kingdom, has over 200,000 pages in its central computers. Similar systems are under development with government backing in the Federal Republic of Germany (Bildschirmtext), the Netherlands (Viditel), Sweden (Datavision), Finland (Telset), France (Teletel and Antiope), Canada (Telidon, and various project names), Japan (Captain), Switzerland (Videotex) and the United States (various private schemes). All expect to offer a wide range of information services to users in commerce and industry, with some systems adding services aimed specifically at the professions and education. Woolfe (1980) names many potential applications for videotex in the home: amenity and service listings, news, sports fixtures, weather forecasts, home education courses, welfare and consumer advice, travel and tourism, health information, advertising and selling, reservations, banking, entertainment and calculations such as tax, mortgage and discounts. To purchase goods and services, users can use the response keys, with or without credit card numbers. To date, however, domestic users in the United Kingdom are outnumbered by commercial, industrial and other institutional users. The French Teletel system seeks to offer a similarly wide range of services: in 1981–2 about 2,500 households participated in a trial, with some households testing a 'smart card' for purchases, that is, a plastic card containing a microchip, and tens of thousands of these cards are being distributed for use in terminals located in shopping areas. In 1982, a special kind of videotex was installed in 300,000 French homes: the electronic directory service, as it has been called. Telephone subscribers have a new telephone, attached to a terminal with a keyboard and screen. With it, they are able to consult over 350,000 'white-' and 'yellow-page' telephone directory entries. Other services may follow.

In addition to such publicly available videotex systems, 'closed' systems, accessible only to a limited group of users but still using the public telephone lines, are being developed, such as Lawtel, a service for lawyers in the United Kingdom.

The overall picture in new information technology is one of increasing integration, as we saw in Chapter 1. National 'wired' systems, connecting homes and institutions to central computers carrying a number of information services may offer the best long-term opportunities to education, or small, 'stand alone', personalised equipment and information stores, readily to hand, may be a better prospect, but more of this in Parts Three and Four.

5 MAKERS AND SELLERS

Investment and Power

To understand something of the forces behind new information technology, we should look at the makers and sellers. There is no point in compiling a comprehensive catalogue, however, because it would be out of date before these pages could be printed. That kind of information is available from trade journals, of which there are many.

What strikes anyone surveying the market is that very strong political, industrial and commercial forces are involved. Koughan (1981–2) believes that 1981 was the year in which new information technology at last obtained full backing from American big business. He notes that very large companies, such as Piedmont Natural Gas (annual revenues $300 million), American Broadcasting Corporation, Sears Roebuck and IBM, led the way. Gerbner, also speaking of America, says, 'The new technologies will have a radical impact on our society. What we are seeing is a shifting of the structure of investment and power' (quoted by Koughan).

There is strong debate about who will benefit from such a shift. Will the consumer be the real beneficiary? Gerbner says everyone gains, but those in control gain a hundred-fold. Schiller (1981) takes the view that significant portions of the population do not gain at all. On the contrary, they are further deprived of opportunities, power and resources by new information technology. Koughan thinks that many experts doubt whether there will be enough consumer interest, but says they forget that the information and service providers have great interest in making new information technology systems work, and that these providers will subsidise the systems in order to get them going.

Schiller (1981) provides the fullest (and most critical) account of makers and sellers in the United States; he also dwells on the international impact of these companies. Similar accounts are not yet available for other Western countries or Japan, but Malik (1982) recounts a story which illustrates well the power of the wave of new information technology. In the late sixties, he says, the French politician Jean-Jacques Servan-Schreiber wrote a best-seller entitled

Le Defi Americain (The American Challenge) in which he proposed that the future of Western civilisation is intimately bound up with the computer and that European nations should therefore develop their own computer industry. Then President Giscard d'Estaing commissioned the Nora and Minc (1978) report, *L'Informatisation de la Société* ('Informatising' Society), and subsequently increased subsidies to telecommunications industries in France.

Servan-Schreiber next wrote *Le Defi Mondial* (The World Challenge), based on discussions among European politicians who called themselves *Le Groupe de Paris*. It sold in millions and was translated into 20 languages. On being returned to power in 1981, President Mitterrand, by no means a man of the same political complexion as Giscard d'Estaing, asked Servan-Schreiber to plan a new *Centre Mondial pour le Développement des Resources Humaines* (World Centre for the Development of Human Resources). Among those who have agreed to participate in the work of this centre are eminent computer scientists and academics from the People's Republic of China, Scandinavia, the United Kingdom and the United States, including one or two whose views are mentioned in this book, such as Papert and Beer. Much more surprising are the names of President Senghor of Senegal, Sheikh Ali-Khalifa Al Sabah (Oil Minister of Kuwait) and Sheik Zaki Yamani (Oil Minister of Saudi Arabia). The work of the Centre will be to take up the challenge, the world challenge, which is this, according to Servan-Schreiber: computer technology presents a fundamental threat to industrial society, East and West, and it must be met by a new alliance of Western technology, Middle Eastern oil money and Third World interests. Development of a 'culture-independent and fully portable personal computer', suitable for wide use in the Third World, must be the Centre's first goal.

Malik admits to being carried along by Servan-Schreiber's enthusiasm and says little about the possible success of such a centre, but perhaps this new constellation of interests cannot be ignored. If the Centre is successful, its work could have wide implications for education, not least in the Third World.

Makers and Sellers of Computing Equipment

Here the present dominance of American companies is well known and so is the continuing struggle of other companies against

American interests in most Western countries. Schiller (1981) provides some statistics: in 1980, American computing equipment worth $62.7 billion was installed worldwide, compared with Western Europe's $38.8 billion in the same field, while Japan and 'others' had $23.0 billion worth. In the same year, the microchip market was split similarly, with the United States at 67 per cent, Western Europe 10 per cent and Japan 15 per cent.

What is happening inside IBM, the American giant of the market and the largest computer manufacturing company in the world? It is changing the way it approaches the field of new information technology. Since 1981, IBM has reorganised into two groups, one dealing with large computers and their components, the other with smaller computers, office systems and communications. IBM is selling integrated information systems, with compatibility ensured throughout each system and between systems. Sales representatives stress applications for these systems rather than the hardware and software. As IBM is also moving into the microcomputer market, small businesses and domestic users are now its clients as well as large companies. Through MCA Discovision, in which it had part-ownership, IBM was briefly involved in videodiscs, too, but during 1982 its shares were sold, being purchased by Pioneer, the Japanese electronics firm.

The power of American and Japanese companies in new information technology is apparent in figures quoted in *The Times* (14 January 1982). Despite British expertise in electronic engineering, British manufacturers of new information technology do not hold much of the British market. In 1980 the trade deficit under this head was £300 million, and in 1979 83 per cent of the market went to foreign companies. Increased use of new information technology in the United Kingdom could increase the country's dependency on foreign makers and suppliers, although pressure is being brought to bear on the government to expand and protect the domestic market for British manufacturers. In the face of foreign competition, however, one British microcomputer manufacturer has outstripped all others in the United Kingdom. Crisp (1982) reports that Sinclair sold about 100,000 of the ZX80, and by March 1982 had sold about 250,000 of the ZX81, including many overseas. Both of these machines are relatively low-powered, although they can be enhanced.

Owners of Cable and Satellite Systems

Cable systems in North America generally are operated by wealthy companies linked to other mass media; financial control of these systems is highly centralised, being largely in the hands of market-oriented profit-making corporations. Krugman and Christians (1981) assert that in the United States cable systems are already integrated into the mass media structures of that country, with retransmission (for example, of television broadcasts) as the main service brought by cable to individual households. Cable operators focus on maximising profit and offer at present few locally originated services, although this may change if more local educational, civic and retail institutions decide to pay to use the cable.

Satellite systems are being linked into cable systems, financially as well as electronically. Large American companies such as IBM, Xerox, Exxon, Lockheed and American Telephone and Telegraph (AT&T) have interests in this field, as well as the European posts and telecommunication agencies (PTTs).

Sellers of Data

Many companies are becoming involved in providing, collating, computerising and electronically distributing data, that is to say, specialised information, ranging from telephone directories to chemical research abstracts. The United States is dominant in this field too: in 1979, 63 per cent of the records on databases throughout the world were in the United States, Lockheed's DIALOG being the largest anywhere with over 100 databases (Schiller, 1981). For example, three major American suppliers of online (readable on a terminal connected to a computer) economic and financial data are described by Houghton and Wisdom (1980). Data Resources, in Massachusetts, serves some 600 client companies with its own computer and private telecommunications network. Its database is made up from various American and international databases, and it offers an econometric model service providing forecasts for the United States, Europe, Canada and Japan. Another company, Business International, serves some 700 companies and governments. Its database on national accounts and marketing statistics includes 10,500 time series covering 150 measures of economic and marketing activity for 70 countries. The third company, Automatic Data Processing, has 60,000 clients worldwide and offers a wide range of services including databases for financial and banking institutions, foreign exchange rates, market shares and product performance. These three companies are not the only ones in the field, but they are typical and are potentially very powerful.

At a more general level, Woolfe (1980) identifies the institutions involved in developing and marketing videotex services (delivered by telephone line to a television screen) in Western countries. In Europe, strong government-controlled telecommunication monopolies or near-monopolies, such as British Telecom, are the principal agencies, although the private publishing industry is striving to obtain rights to develop and sell competing services in the Federal Republic of Germany, while it has already done so in the Netherlands. Even British Telecom is now threatened by competition from private companies with backing from banking, oil and electronic interests, following recent deregulation moves on the part of the government. In the United States, private companies are competing to provide videotex, ranging from American Telephone and Telegraph to the pilot system in Florida operated by Knight-Ridder, a very large newspaper company, and to Channel 2000, in Ohio, operated by a non-profit organisation. The Source, a videotex system designed for microcomputer owners (see Chapter 13), is owned by *The Reader's Digest*. American Telephone and Telegraph, one of the largest companies of any kind in the world, is extending its operations to Europe now that the American Congress has enacted the 1982 AT&T Consent Decree.

The borderline between videotex systems and other online information services that combine microcomputers and telephone networks is not distinct, particularly in the United States, and we may expect further convergence of these technologies. For instance, local area networks that use cables to link computers and terminals in many offices of a single company, thus providing 'offices of the future', are dominated at present by three powerful companies, Xerox, IBM and Wang, although in Europe the government PTTs (Posts, Telephone and Telegraph) are competing.

Makers and Sellers Interested in Education

Some powerful manufacturers of new information technology include education in their marketing, although many do not, preferring the more lucrative commercial and industrial markets. For example, IBM clearly has a foot in the educational camp through its educational publishing subsidiary, Science Research Associates, which now markets courseware produced by IBM for its own customers, to teach them how to use newly purchased equipment, plus programs for the IBM microcomputer. Honeywell recently announced (*Educational Technology*, vol. XXII, no. 2, February 1982) a software package for teachers and others who want to prepare their own courseware on Honeywell's DPS6 mini-computer.

Atari, a subsidiary of Warner Communications, makes these claims in its brochures for the 400 microcomputer:

> Learn everything from languages to chess and touch-typing, all at your own pace, from a teacher that never gets tired or impatient. Learning has never been more effective or more fun. Learn to invent your own games, create your own music and art, make your own experiments and discoveries. Or develop a deeper understanding of nuclear energy issues as you simulate the fascinating workings of a power plant.

Another powerful company, Apple, makes similar claims for its microcomputers in education and says that in the United States educational users are heavily committed to them:

> The beauty of Apple is that it lends itself to broad educational applications. With its colour graphics and audio capabilities, together with the educationally suitable accessories and wide range of programs, Apple helps to increase student motivation and improve knowledge retention . . . Apple leads the way in educational software in the USA . . . Already a range of programs related to the UK educational syllabus have been developed by the Schools Council Project 'Computers in the Curriculum' at Chelsea College.

The fact is that large companies like Atari, Apple, Commodore and Tandy can make agreements with groups producing the best courseware, such as Advanced Learning Technology (see Chapters 7 and 8 for details of some of this company's early work), as well as being able to buy licences to sell courseware adapted to their machines, as in the case of the Chelsea College programs. Textbook publishers in America, including large companies like Scott

Foresman, Houghton Mifflin, McGraw-Hill and Random House, have begun to sell courseware. Although in 1980 only one per cent ($10 million) of the American market for printed instructional materials was made up of courseware for computers, one prediction for 1985 is that this share will increase to $75 million, and by 1990 this courseware may overtake textbook sales (*Business Week*, 27 July 1981). Already we see Control Data Corporation, distributors of PLATO, marketing Micro-Plato, a version for use on a new CDC microcomputer.

In the United Kingdom, the government has lent its strength to a scheme (see Chapter 9) to put microcomputers into secondary schools. Two British companies, Research Machines and Acorn, were selected as official suppliers and Local Education Authorities can recoup half the cost of each machine from the government. Research Machines' 380Z led the field in 1981 (Brown and Stokes, 1981), but Commodore, Apple, Tandy and Sinclair microcomputers are being used in many schools in England, with Cromemco as well in Scotland. Textbook publishers such as Edward Arnold and Longmans are selling courseware. One of the more remarkable developments, however, is the Computer Literacy Project, launched in early 1982 by the British Broadcasting Corporation (another force to be reckoned with). The project includes a television series about computing and computers, loosely linked to a microcomputer made by Acorn, a substantial book written specially for the series, and a course on BASIC sold by the National Extension College, a non-profit organisation specialising in correspondence education. The series attracted considerable attention before it had even started, and by January about 12,000 orders for the computer had reached Acorn, far beyond what had been expected. The BBC Microcomputer uses a special version of BASIC with a full QWERTY keyboard, attaches to a domestic television set, normally uses a tape-recorder for memory storage, although a floppy disc drive can be added, and can drive a printer. The television series in its first showing (of several) reached 300,000-400,000 people, the book sold 60,000 copies, 12,000 microcomputers were ordered and over 1,000 people took the course (*Times Higher Educational Supplement,* 26 March 1982).

So much for microcomputers on their own: in developing video-disc courseware, two leading American groups are at the University of Nebraska and at the World Institute for Computer Assisted Teaching (WICAT), set up in 1976 in Utah. Bunderson (1981) describes some of WICAT's recent products, all developed for powerful companies, the government or the armed forces:

—A videodisc on electronic ignition systems for Ford Company mechanics.
—A highly interactive videodisc on developmental biology for college students, produced as a prototype for the National Science Foundation.
—A prototype for the US Army on artillery fire training.
—A series of interactive videodisc simulations for Smith, French & Kline Pharmaceuticals, covering medical diagnosis and patient management in gastroenterology. The series has been granted recognition for medical training by the American Medical Association.
—An interactive videodisc training course for the US Army on missile system circuits and trouble-shooting them. This includes a computer-generated simulation that can provide a million unique trouble-shooting problems.
—A videodisc for IBM, explaining and demonstrating to prospective purchasers a new system made by IBM.
—An interactive training videodisc for the US Army on the theory and fault diagnosis of certain Army radio sets.
—An interactive videodisc-plus-simulator system for the US Army on automotive and missile maintenance.
—An interactive videodisc for the US Army on aligning a commonly used field radio.

This list reflects some of the potential of videodisc technology. WICAT decided in 1981 to change its marketing focus from education to industrial training, but others are entering the educational field, as Chapters 8-12 show.

Brown (1982) says that British Telecom's Prestel section is now looking seriously at 'the hobbyist and educational computer fraternities as potential Prestel users'. Prestel is backing the telesoftware (transmission of computer programs, in this case by wire) standards published by the Council for Educational Technology and has announced a competition to design the technology to feed programs from Prestel onto the Sinclair ZX81 microcomputer. Again we see powerful forces, this time in British Telecom, behind this intervention.

6 BUYERS AND USERS

Market Sectors

As we saw in the last chapter, new information technology is being manufactured in Western countries by many companies, including some of the largest in the world. But who is buying and using the technology? What do they actually buy and is it what they want? For example, as far as domestic consumers are concerned, is there any strength in Weizenbaum's (1980) assertion that there is as yet no reason to believe in any substantial demand for home computer power other than from people who already use computers as professional tools?

We may ask these questions in relation to several markets or sectors of human activity: the military, commerce, industry, agriculture, government organisations (excluding education), and domestic consumers. These six sectors clearly do not include every application of new information technology. For instance, the leisure sector, especially sport, is rapidly increasing its purchases of the technology, and so is the medical sector. We can sense the strong trends, however, by looking at these six important sectors.

The Military

It may feel uncomfortable, in a book about education, to put the military first, but it is reasonable to suppose, if not easy to confirm, that the military sector buys and uses more new information technology than all other sectors put together. Despite some secrecy, we are aware that the armed forces in all Western countries purchase considerable quantities of the most up-to-date telecommunications equipment, with a wide range of computers to match. Modern defence and attack depend on extremely fast and accurate information. Military satellites, whether for 'spying' or for transmitting over great distances, are essential, together with the sophisticated telemetry required to launch and track them. Terrestrial communication networks dedicated to military use crisscross all Western countries. Navigation of naval vessels and military aircraft is based now on new information technology, with computers and satellites working together to provide precise 'fixes' of position. Telemetry guides missiles. Distant early warning systems, upgraded every few years, guard against unexpected attack. At a more mundane but still important level, information technology solves the military's logistical problems, such as knowing where spare parts are stored in various parts of the country, ordering food supplies or drawing up wartime contingency plans.

To meet its needs, the military sector is buying every kind of system and device mentioned in this book. It is working closely with makers, designers and producers of new information technology. In the United States, military funds support prototype development: the Spatial Data Management System (see Chapter 11), developed at the Massachusetts Institute of Technology for the United States Defense Advanced Research Projects Agency, is a case in point, and Ross, Kellner, Schmidt and Schubert (1981) report on a videotex system used under simulated conditions of war in major command post exercises in Europe. We noted, in Chapter 5, WICAT's work for the military, too.

Not everything that is designed and made for the military is of use in other sectors, but it is true to say, however much some of us may regret it, that, short of war, civilians often benefit indirectly and in the long run from demands placed on makers by the military and by the military paying for initial development. This is the case even for education: military experience in developing training courses based on new information technology is likely to benefit civilian training in due course. What many of us believe, however, is that the same funds diverted from the military to education would have far greater benefits, while reducing the risk of war.

As Schiller (1981) points out, increased military expenditure in the United States during the 1980s could benefit American leadership in the field of information technology, because the best way to increase military superiority is through enhanced communication, command and control, three functions that now require advanced information technology.

Commerce

Like the military, commercial interests want extremely fast and accurate communication, but they also need very large and accessible stores of commercial information, whether regarding commodities, services or manufactured products. According to Deunette and Dibb (1981), two-fifths of United Kingdom users of 'online' information, that is, live from computerised data banks, are from commerce or industry. Houghton and Wisdom (1980) conducted a survey of ways in which such data banks are being used in the United Kingdom and the United States. Most of their respondents were companies with more than 24,000 employees. No less than 52 per cent of the respondents reported spending over £20,000 a year on data bank services. These costs were justified, by the companies, in terms of obtaining information from a broad, accurate and up-to-date source in less time and more frequently than previously from other sources or by other means. Among the most needed types of information are data on economic indicators, statistical data on industries, financial data on companies and demographic data.

Companies are also seeking to improve communication between themselves and their suppliers and customers. Many feel hampered by the relative slowness and inefficiency of postal services in Western countries today, and impatient over the slow rate of modernisation of conventional public telephone networks. In the United Kingdom, once proud of its postal service, deliveries take longer than they did 25 years ago and despite a lead in telecommunications technology, the country is now committed to installing many more electro-mechanical exchanges based on analogue transmission, because installation of new digital exchanges cannot go fast enough to keep up with demand plus obsolescence of old exchanges. For commerce, this rate of change is too slow, and a private company was recently set up to offer rival services, using fibre optics and under the name Mercury, between major British cities.

The largest companies, usually with branches in many cities and sometimes in other countries too, particularly need new information technology to improve productivity and are willing to make very substantial investments in it, with an eye to long-term profit. Typically, they buy (or rent) a private system with appropriate links to public networks. For example, a bank installs a cable in, say, its head office building. Through this cable a large number of different devices are linked together in a 'net'. Their combined power is greater than the sum of their power, because each information function can be transferred instantly to an appropriate device, operating on a time-shared basis, or even to several devices working together. The 'paperless office' is an example of such a system, with electronic means of storing, selecting, manipulating and displaying information, all under the control of fewer people than were needed before and all requiring less space, particularly for storage. In large companies, these functions can be decentralised, too. They can be spread among many buildings or branches, provided that suitable links are available. These links are sometimes by microwave circuit or even by satellite. More conventionally, they are by telephone circuits. Fibre-optic cable and coaxial cable are becoming important for company-wide networks, especially when these can be within the same building. Both kinds of cable can carry broadband communications, suitable for television, as well as narrowband.

In these large companies, purchases of new information technology are accompanied by radical reorganisation of labour, with many secretarial and clerical posts being eliminated or transformed, and with new posts being created for operators of the new technology. These changes are dramatic in some cases. Unions are well aware of the problems and in many Western countries are negotiating with management to protect the interests of their members. Management's goal is to maximise profit through increased productivity; the new technology is particularly well-suited to the needs of commerce, where much information handling does nothing to add to the value of the product being traded but is essential to the conduct of business, as in the case of tax records.

Smaller companies are also buying electronic devices. New information technology has improved automatic vending machines, cash tills, money counters, mail scales, photocopiers and sur-veillance equipment. Inventory control and accounting for retail businesses are made simpler and cheaper through using micro-computers. Mail order businesses and opinion polling companies can streamline much of their administration. The list is almost endless: new information technology has come to stay in commerce. Many companies, with the help of specialist agencies (such as the London Micro Centre), are re-training staff to operate the new machines and there is no shortage of people wanting to learn.

Industry

Many industrial concerns, whether in manufacturing or producing primary materials, are buying and using new information technology for the same purposes as companies in commerce. To improve information flow within their organisations, they buy new communications equipment, ranging from electronic telephone answering machines to remote sensing equipment linked to computers for controlling the assembly lines. To reduce their invest-ment in expensive storage space for records, they buy and use new storage media, such as optical disc systems for engineering drawings (Adams, 1981). To cut their warehousing costs, they use computers to predict demand more precisely and can then reduce stock levels without risking loss of orders. For example, British Leyland, the car manufacturing company, installed an automated office system that incorporates electronic mail, filing, diaries, wordprocessing, voice messages and so on. It serves executives rather than being solely for secretarial use (Large, 1981).

New information technology is making an even more funda-mental contribution in this sector, however, because it is the basis for much improved 'process control' equipment. Development of this equipment comes under the general term 'robotics'. Industry is buying and using large numbers of computer-controlled devices which assist in or even take over portions of industrial processes. Within each of these devices, or connected to each, is a microprocessor using one or more chips, a miniature pre-programmed computer with the task of delivering commands in response to information it receives from, say, other parts of the assembly line or from the sensors attached to the tool it is operating. The example of process control made familiar by television is in car manufacture, where only a few men may supervise the work of robots on the assembly line. This example highlights the reorganisa-tion of labour that is being brought about by the new technology in industry as well as commerce.

Agriculture

Agriculture in Western countries is being industrialised as many small farms disappear and mechanisation becomes almost universal. We can safely assume that agricultural companies, ranging from those managing large ranches in Texas to those operating hothouse nurseries in the Netherlands, are already purchasing and using new information technology to increase productivity.

Farmers are using microprocessors to monitor climatic conditions and control irrigation systems, to check the water conditions in tanks on fish farms and to operate ventilation and cooling systems in battery sheds on poultry farms. On dairy farms, microcomputers store data concerning the life history of every cow and calculate precisely how much feed each should receive to maintain maximum milk yield. On farms devoted to fattening pigs and cattle, micro-computers are programmed to determine the feed schedule and even the date of sale or slaughter.

These are just a few examples. The Green Thumb project (described in Chapter 13), is another instance.

Government Organisations (Excluding Education)

Without exception, government organisations are purchasing and using new information technology, whether they are judicial bodies, or individual government departments responsible for, say, income tax collection, or regulatory agencies connected with, say, aviation. Government organisations deal primarily in information. They are seldom concerned with producing, manufacturing, buying and selling, except indirectly and for their own needs. (We are not considering here those parts of industry, commerce and even agriculture which are nationalised in some countries.) As the information they deal in has increased in volume and complexity, these government organisations have found themselves obliged to turn to new information technology. There are many examples, but we shall look briefly at three that are well known: the police, the tax authorities and air traffic controllers, and at a British report on using wordprocessing in government typing pools.

The police depend on information for solving crimes. Despite the protest of various groups (for example, the Technical Authors Group of Scotland, 1982), computerised data banks, containing much information about individuals, are being built up in all Western countries. As the crime rate rises, such banks are justified on the grounds that they may offer the only hope of constructing a case against an alleged criminal. In the recent notorious case of the Yorkshire Ripper, in the United Kingdom, it seems fairly clear that the murderer would have been brought to justice much sooner, before he had committed further murders, had computerised methods been used to collate evidence collected by hundreds of police put onto the case. Against this, we cannot ignore the dangers of ascribing too much authority to evidence lodged in such banks, of inadequately supported evidence being banked, of lack of privacy for individuals whose records are in the banks and of various procedures that might lead to the wrong person being charged. These hazards exist whether the case is criminal or civil.

The police, operating in the name of law and order, have secured for their use a wide range of telecommunications equipment, from high-powered two-way radios to computer networks. They have also discovered the advantages of videocameras and recorders in their work. We can expect them to continue to purchase and use new information technology, whether for field operations or for training, for compiling and maintaining criminal records, or for preparing documentation for the courts.

The tax authorities also need comprehensive records of the tax affairs of individuals and companies if they are to administer with justice the tax laws and regulations. Slowly in some countries, faster in others, these records are being computerised, with several potential advantages from the point of view of government. First, tax evasion may be reduced, since there is a better chance of all data being available to the authorities in assessing tax. Secondly, changes in tax law, which occur every year, can be taken into account more easily. Thirdly, the backlog of tax cases waiting to be dealt with may be cleared as the efficiency of the computerised system is felt. We should not expect governments to be too optimistic about these potential advantages, however, since it is clear that in all Western countries the tax laws are sufficiently complex, and individuals and companies are sufficiently skilful in evading tax, that even computerisation is not going to deal with all the problems of tax assessment and collection. We must rather expect that computerisation in this field will be a lengthy process, with frequent delays, and that manual procedures will continue side by side with the computer.

Air traffic control centres, much under pressure in many Western countries because of increased air traffic and the greater speed of jet aircraft, also use new information technology. The volume of data each controller has to handle is great, and the consequences of errors are so grave, that new systems to ease this load have been and will be introduced. Radar systems, telecommunication links between the control tower and pilots, recorders that run 24 hours of the day to record all the conversations on every channel, including those linking the control tower and ground staff, and plotting devices to reflect more fully the pattern of incoming and departing flights, these are all being redesigned to take advantage of new information technology.

Government departments in many countries operate typing pools. Can new information technology in the form of word processors raise job-satisfaction and productivity in these pools? In the United Kingdom during 1979/80 a small sample of Government typists tested word processors in a special trial. Among the conclusions: typists need more training, over a longer period, than was provided in this trial, but they like the machines and wish to continue working on them. Their productivity did not increase sufficiently to justify the extra cost of the equipment, in terms of salaries and prices at that time, although on certain types of work greater gains are likely than on others (Central Computer and Telecommunications Agency, 1980).

Domestic Users

People are purchasing new information technology for use in their own homes. Domestic appliances are now being sold with electronic programmers in place of mechanical ones. Washing machines, dishwashers, ovens and cookers, mixers and even central heating control equipment may have a silicon chip rather than mechanical switches and timers.

What is more important, however, is the development of the domestic market for electronic devices used for information reception and storage. Many of these are described in Chapter 4. They range from hi-fi radio receivers to television sets equipped with special adaptors to microcomputers and pocket calculators.

For example, Prestel, the British videotex system, may soon be brought into many homes, although Large (1982) reports that only about 10 per cent of the sets so far adapted belong to domestic users, the rest being in the hands of business, industry and other non-domestic users. This slow uptake is despite the fact that about 210,000 pages of information are available (February 1982) in the system. Some of the reasons are discussed in Part Two.

A similar system, Channel 2000, provided in 1980 as a pilot scheme to 200 homes in the town of Columbus, Ohio, was initiated and evaluated by the Online Computer Library Centre (OCLC Research Department, 1981) in association with a local bank interested in home banking services. Families were able to consult the city and county library catalogue and order books and other library items, delivered by mail. They could use the Academic American Encyclopedia, an 'electronic' encyclopedia (Greenagel, 1981) of 32,000 articles, one-third of which are updated each year. They could consult civic information (e.g., about local sports, taxes, services) and pay bills, check balances and review interest rates without going to the bank. For children, the system carried mathematics exercises for kindergarten up to sixth grade, plus reading readiness exercises for preschoolers. For the deaf, there was a special bulletin board. Those questioned in the evaluation were asked to say which services they found useful. The financial services were mentioned most often, followed by the library catalogue. The encyclopedia was mentioned much less frequently and the educational programs, probably not used or even seen by many of the adults, were hardly mentioned at all.

Despite these results, the encyclopedia is available on two-way interactive cable systems in six American cities, and will be marketed on videodisc, says Greenagel.

The domestic market for videocassette recorders, purchased primarily to provide entertainment, is growing rapidly. Spain, not widely considered to be oriented towards new information technology, was estimated to have close to 100,000 of these machines in 1982, while in North America and North-Western Europe 15-25 per cent of households rent or own one. In Japan, the figure is about 40 per cent, but is now increasing much more slowly. It seems doubtful whether these recorders will ever be in as many homes as radio and television.

Domestic purchases of microcomputers are going up, of course, although exact figures are unobtainable because sellers do not distinguish these sales from those to other sectors and it is impossible to refute Weizenbaum's (1980) assertion about demand being limited to those who already use computers professionally. All the principal manufacturers claim that their microcomputers sell in the domestic market, however, with companies such as Apple, Tandy, Atari and Texas Instruments to the fore in North America, and Sinclair and Acorn in the United Kingdom.

Education is one of the largest areas of government spending. It is beginning to buy and use new information technology. A survey of United States school districts, conducted in 1980 by the National Center for Education Statistics (1981), put the number of computers available to students at 52,000, with microcomputers outnumbering other types three to two. About a quarter of the schools then had a computer for teaching purposes, including about half the secondary schools and one-sixth of the primary schools. At that time, however, only about 18 per cent of the districts without computers planned to install one or more within three years; many others reported uncertainty over plans for computing in schools. A similar survey in the United Kingdom at about the same date put the number of microcomputers in schools at only 700. But in the short time that has elapsed since these data were collected, considerably more computers, chiefly microcomputers, have gone into schools. What is new information technology being used for in education? That question is answered fully in Part Two.

PART TWO: NEW INFORMATION TECHNOLOGY FOR LEARNING

Part One surveys new information technology in general. Part Two looks at its use, in the form of various devices and systems, in education, formal and informal, at all levels. Some very young children use it at home, young children at school. Some teachers use it at school and for training. University students use it and so do some adults participating in vocational and continuing education. Other adults use it for their own informal education.

Part Two contains many examples of applications during the last three years, but it touches only briefly on problems of using new information technology for learning, because they are dealt with in Part Three. Nor does it say much about the future: that is reserved for Part Four.

Chapter 7 deals with children of various ages learning at home, outside school. Chapters 8 to 12 cover various levels of formal education: the examples begin with devices and systems that 'stand alone', without wires or cables to distant places, e.g., microcomputers, interactive videodiscs, videodiscs, videocassettes and calculators. These are followed by 'wired' examples, e.g., mainframe and minicomputers, computerised databases, videotex, cable television and Cyclops. Finally, Chapter 13 deals with adults learning informally through new information technology.

7 CHILDREN AT HOME

Traditionally, children outside school hours are thought of as being out of education, unless they are doing homework, but new information technology may demand that we reassess the relationship between learning and playing. Pelton (1981) tells us the sobering news that two United States' toymakers, Mattel and Milton Bradley, are the largest buyers of silicon chips anywhere in the world. The prospect of our children or ourselves being overwhelmed at home by so-called 'intelligent' toys is not altogether attractive. Milton Bradley's *bigtrak*, for example, looks rather like a tank and can be programmed to roll through the house shooting up, say, Mother and Kid Sister. Its users learn something elementary about the concept of programming, but is this the only way new information technology will affect children's learning at home? Of course not.

Homes contain radios, television sets, telephones, audiocassette players and pocket calculators as standard items, these days. Children have relatively free access to such items for hours every day, and use that access for considerable informal learning, particularly from television. Teletext, microcomputers, videotext, videocassette records and players, and videodisc players are still fairly unusual in homes, but where they exist children are gaining access to them, again for informal learning.

We cannot dismiss children's use of the technology by saying that they are merely entertaining themselves. Hechinger (1981) tells the story of a child who had just started kindergarten and who was reciting the letters of the alphabet to his father. When his father complimented him on having learned so quickly, the child said, 'I learned it on Sesame Street, but my teacher thinks she taught me.' In fact, children are learning a great deal, not only from Sesame Street (the American educational television series for preschoolers). What they are learning informally through the technology is different from what children of the previous generation learned informally. How they are learning it is different too: to adults who observe their children, this informal learning appears extraordinarily random and episodic, without the coherence purportedly provided by the community for old-fashioned informal learning before the advent of new information technology. But first let us consider the youngest age-groups at home, children not yet at school, then we shall discuss the older age-groups.

The First Three Years

We know very little indeed about the impact of information technology, particularly new information technology, on children in their first three years, that is, up to the stage of speech development. Very young children respond to voices, to music and to moving pictures, but we do not know whether and in what ways their thinking is affected by the technology. Do they indeed come into contact with it?

By the age of two, children can safely operate some of the devices. For example, touch-sensitive switches on television sets enable two-year-olds to turn sets on and off. They can often select channels, too, and we can expect the behaviour from an average two-year-old to be sometimes more than mere random pressing of the channel selector buttons.

Similarly, a two-year-old may be able to press the buttons of a pocket calculator, but this is certainly random behaviour until the symbols acquire some meaning for the child. Some audiocassette players are simple enough for such a young child to start if he or she knows that there is a favourite story, song or piece of music on the cassette, although inserting the cassette may be too difficult.

Let us assume, however, that such young children do not normally operate the machines themselves but are listeners and viewers under the guidance of their parents or other adults. New information technology is certainly increasing the variety and amount of informal learning parents can provide for children in this age bracket. For example, a mother who finds that her young child greatly enjoys Sesame Street (aimed at a slightly older age group but reported to have great appeal to younger children as well), decides, copyright laws notwithstanding, to record the broadcasts for repeated replay. Once she has the tapes, she promises her child a viewing of Sesame Street as a reward, rather than placing him or her in front of whatever happens to be on television at the time. Similarly, parents with cable television, with access to many channels, select viewing for their very young children, as a reward or simply to keep them occupied. Parents value increased variety because it enables them to exercise their own values in selecting what they consider to be suitable rather than depending on patently unsuitable material such as old movies or 'talk shows', which, in North America at any rate, form a large part of television viewers' daytime diet.

It would be wrong to suggest, however, that new information technology is having great impact at this age level. Very young children are becoming accustomed to seeing the devices in their homes. Parents are beginning to use the technology for these children. Not much more can be said, because we do not yet have a perspective on this matter. Stories about very young children learning from microcomputers may not be wholly apocryphal, but researchers are not yet studying how or what these very young children learn in the average home from information technology. When they do so, they will encounter the usual problems in observing and measuring learning by this age-group, and will have to be very cautious in attributing cause and effect.

The Preschoolers

Preschoolers vary in age in different Western countries, some being as old as six, but usually they are aged three, four and five. The amount of time they spend at playgroups or other forms of pre-school also varies from country to country, indeed from community to community and from family to family. But what is the present impact of new information technology at home on these children? Here we know a little more and there is some recorded experience to draw upon.

Preschoolers in many homes have access to radios, television sets, audiocassette players, pocket calculators and the telephone, as we noted earlier. Parental guidance varies, of course, but many of these children rapidly acquire manipulative skills required to operate such machines. Where the latest technology is available too, they learn very quickly to carry out quite complex routines on, for example, keypads and keyboards. Even before they have learned to read, young children in this age-group like to 'play' with microcomputers, teletext and videotex, and they learn to call up particular displays such as the weather map on teletext (Chen, 1981). Operating a video-cassette player is not beyond them by any means, although adult attitudes about children's 'right' to do so with new and relatively expensive equipment may deprive them of opportunities.

Knowing how to press the right buttons is important for children at this age, as without that knowledge they will be at a disadvantage in future years, in school and afterwards, when they will be expected to know how to operate the technology. It is worth noting that children approach this learning task in a far less intentional manner than their elders, as Chen points out. By playing with the devices and systems they infer how to operate them, rather than reading instructions and deducing what they should do.

What is much more important, however, is what they learn and how. Children who learn much informally at home through new information technology seem likely to be high achievers at school. We cannot say that using new information technology to aid preschoolers' informal learning at home will actually cause high achievement at school, because the relationship is more complex than that. Children who achieve well at school tend to come from homes with many books, but books are only one factor among many that must be taken into account. The same is true for the new technology. Probably a cluster of factors, including important ones such as income group and parents' occupation, are associated with both provision of the technology at home and high achievement at school.

There is a discontinuity at present, a sharp and disturbing one, between what preschoolers are likely to learn at home through new information technology and what they learn in primary school. Homes with the technology may offer an environment that is much more information-rich than the average primary school classroom. Preschoolers spend enough of their waking hours in this rich environment to be able to learn a great deal from it. Unfortunately, schools cannot easily take into account the unstandardised curriculum that preschoolers follow at home.

To be more specific, what is it that makes up this unstandardised curriculum, mediated by radio, television and even microcomputers? From the radio and audiocassettes, preschoolers hear music, songs and stories, like their younger siblings, and they learn more from them because they are a little older. There is nothing particularly new about that. It has been happening in Western countries for about 50 years from the radio. The broadcasts, and more recently the cassettes, are about relatively familiar topics, often extensions of nursery songs and storybooks familiar to previous generations.

Television is doing far more than translating the familiar into the televised medium: it is also bringing to preschoolers a great deal that is unfamiliar. As a group, cartoon programmes are close to the familiar and so are programmes such as Story Time. Sesame Street is in quite a different category, however, as it presents a kaleidoscope of images in fast-moving short sequences, using techniques borrowed from television advertising. Some of these sequences aim to teach letters and numerals, which were very rarely taught at home through technology until this series was made. The same series brings a great variety of vicarious, mediated experience to the children who view it. It is this breadth of experience which distinguishes preschoolers today from those of the previous generation. They view broadcasts about nature (for example, wildlife series), about the social world far outside their own community, about journeys of exploration and adventure, and about war and violence. Their opportunities to choose these mediated experiences are far greater than those of their younger siblings, because they do not need adults to operate the television set and because their parents tend to exercise less control over viewing habits as the children get older. In fact, children's choice of viewing converges on adults' choice rather rapidly (Palmer and Dorr, 1980). These are significant changes in our society. Among the adults of the 1950s, how many would have thought that in 1968 millions of four-year-olds would be watching astronauts landing on the moon? How many would have predicted that in the 1980s television sets in American homes would be turned on each day, during the waking hours of preschoolers, for as many hours as the length of the primary school day?

Microcomputers may never become instruments of informal learning for preschoolers to the same extent as television, but enough microcomputers are now in homes for a little recorded experience to be available. A few parents have realised the potential of microcomputers for informal learning and have encouraged their preschoolers to use the machines for this purpose, beginning with games that teach the children familiarity with keyboard and screen, and going on to games and simulations teaching other skills and concepts. Some extraordinarily interesting programs have been written for this age-group: for example, Up-Down, Left-Right is a program, developed by Advanced Learning Technology in California, that teaches spatial relations to preschoolers; it makes full use of voice prompts and musical sounds as well as graphics (Piestrup, 1981, see next chapter). The same company has prepared a program for teaching four-year-olds to plot coordinates with negative numbers.

Electronic educational games deserve a mention here. Those at present on the market are intended for primary school children, but older preschoolers use them as well. Primary school children use them for reinforcing or even remedial purposes, to help them to spell or learn arithmetic, but preschoolers are only at the beginning of understanding what spelling is, or arithmetic. A five-year-old, perhaps impatient to get to primary school, may sit for hours with one of these games, fascinated by the combination of spoken word and visual display that is utterly at his or her command. What is being learned? We may think that it is not necessarily how words should be spelled, nor even the number bonds to 20, although the child may well pick these up, especially if a slightly older sibling is around to consult. Rather, the child may be learning at an intuitive level that letters are associated with sounds, that together they make strings of sounds that are words, and, similarly, that numbers have names and can be put together in several ways. These fundamental principles will stand him or her in good stead the following year at school.

It is worth turning our attention now to some examples of proto-types because these may indicate what can be expected more generally quite soon. The First National Kidisc is produced by Optical Programming Associates, in the United States, for (the relatively few) owners of interactive videodisc players (Lachenbruch, 1981). The Kidisc is recorded on one side only and takes 27 minutes to play through once at standard speed. It would not usually be used in this way, however, as it consists of many segments that can be played at any slower speed, including step-by-step, in slow motion or as stills. Segments cover topics such as making paper planes, learning national flags, sign language, what it is like flying, a visit to the zoo, jokes and riddles, making a xylophone from drinking glasses, origami (Japanese paper folding), dancing, secret codes, puzzles, athletes in motion, magic and games (Blizek, 1981).

Blizek describes how the idea for this videodisc came from a young boy (certainly not a preschooler!) who was given the opportunity to compile material from a film library: the lad put together sequences of explosions, car crashes and other exciting events. The First National Kidisc contains more educational material than that, and its compilers aimed at using all the optical videodisc functions. At first it was called 18 Things To Do On A Rainy Day. Much use was made of compression: that is, of sequences which would be incomprehensible if played at normal speed, but when slowed down they conveyed their messages well, as in the origami paper-folding example. Music for dancing is on one channel with visual sequences demonstrating the dances on the other. Once children learn the dances, if they wish they can turn off the picture and simply dance to the music.

The Petite Talking Typewriter, manufactured by Byron International and available for £40 in the United Kingdom, is a much less complex example of new information technology for young children to use at home. It has a memory of 160 words and as each letter is typed in the typewriter speaks it, clearly and distinctly. If the child spells the word correctly, the machine says, 'That is correct'. If the word is mis-spelled, the machine says, 'That is incorrect, try again'. After two mis-spellings the typewriter speaks the correct version. When ten words have been attempted, it tells the child how many were right. The typewriter can also be used in the normal way, unlike Texas Instruments' Speak-and-Spell, which helps children to learn how to spell by similar means.

Children used videotex in the Green Thumb project (Chapter 13), which involved 200 Kentucky farming families. This is a case of early exposure of children to such a system and one of the first studies of their learning from it. Researchers from Stanford University visited homes to find out how children are learning from this and other videotex systems in the US (KCET's system in Los Angeles, QUBE/Compuserve and Channel 2000 in Columbus, Ohio, or WETA's teletext experiment in Washington, DC), and interviewed children using The Source or Compuserve (see Chapter 13 also), but their findings are not yet available.

Time (21 September 1981) reports that Children's Television Workshop, creators of Sesame Street, have now perfected programs (selling at $50 for four) for Apple II microcomputers. No less than 70 of these machines and the programs are being used in Sesame Place, situated in Pennsylvania and the first educational 'playground' of a series to be set up under the auspices of the Workshop. Many of the programs are intended for older children rather than preschoolers. For example, children can learn spelling through a well-illustrated version of the game Hangman. With another the child engages in a kind of Socratic dialogue. The computer first asks (by means of words appearing on its screen) the child to think of an animal. Computer: 'Does it live on land?' Child: 'Yes.' 'Does it fly?' 'No.' 'Is it a wild animal?' 'Yes.' 'Is it a lion?' 'No.' Up to this point, the game is like Twenty Questions, but then it changes. Computer: Type in the animal you were thinking of.' The child types in t-i-g-e-r. Computer: I don't know the difference between a lion and a tiger. Press Go to help me learn the difference.' Onto the screen come four incomplete sentences: 'A tiger (1) has, (2) will, (3) is, (4) can.' The child has to complete one, and could write: 'A tiger has stripes.' Computer: 'Does a lion have stripes?' Child: 'No.' Computer: 'I'll remember that.' As the *Time* report says, the child has actually been programming the computer and vice versa. This is an example of children learning out of school and, where homes have an Apple II, at home.

Older Children

The Sesame Place example takes us on to consider informal learning by older children, up to adolescence. Clearly, children's capacity to use and, presumably, to benefit from new information technology increases rapidly as they learn to read and as their manipulative skills improve. On the other hand, formal education takes up five hours of each day, leaving them with less time for informal learning, and parents widely believe that entertainment is the dominant function of equipment such as television, radio, audiocassette recorders and even microcomputers. Shinohara (1981) tells how an experimental group of 30 children (ages 6-12) used the Japanese videotex system, Captain, for education at home. Some 8,000 'pages', with colour graphics, were prepared, covering arithmetic, social education, Japanese and science. The editors took into account the fact that children might be able to choose what pages they would see and that possibly nobody would know if they repeated pages. Mothers of the children were encouraged to watch with them, however, and both mothers and children were observed and questioned in the experiment. Among the findings: children enjoyed Captain and found it easy to operate, even in the lower grades. They did complain, however, of difficulty in backtracking. On average, they watched Captain for 90 minutes, although some stayed for five hours! Older children became bored sooner than the younger ones. As for the mothers, they were divided in their opinions: half expressed some form of disapproval and wanted their children to study from books. Some considered that their children's eyesight would suffer. (Had they ever prevented their children from viewing television for this reason?) Twelve out of the 30 said that their children seemed to be playing rather than studying. Captain is at present too expensive for many Japanese households, and this experimental curriculum would, in any case, have to be more closely integrated with that of the primary schools, says Shinohara.

Children at this age have few problems in learning how to operate new information technology systems; fewer than adults. Chen (1981) gives the example of a downtown Washington, DC public library serving black students after school: these students had no difficulty in learning, by trial-and-error, to use a keypad to operate a teletext system. Even those without good reading skills found teletext interesting. Adults nervously stood behind the youngsters, waiting for them to leave, and then copied what they had seen the children do, rather than first trying for themselves.

Is it the case that children are acquiring new mental sets, as well as new manipulative skills, through using the technology? Hon (1981) speculates that children are indeed doing so through games such as Space Invaders. Television-like screens have long been the place for 'presentations'. Competent presentations were judged, for example, by Children's Television Workshop in America, in terms of how attentive viewers were, and, occasionally, by how much they learned. Information-providers have taken a similar view: all they have to do is present information. This is no longer enough, says Hon, because children are learning to interact with screens. Space Invaders and similar games tell us something about the appeal of interactivity, and why these games holds humans' interest. Humans interact more eagerly with material that has been produced in much more complex ways than the presentations of old, which were linear like a story. The game Space Invaders engages humans' interest, by direct response, by being easily understood at the level needed to operate it and by offering a stake (in winning or scoring). But above all, it does so by offering control to the user, within certain limits. Hon's observations seem important for future applications of new information technology in education.

Along similar lines, Malone (1980) asks why computer games are so captivating and how this characteristic can be used deliberately to make learning with computers interesting. He reports three studies (admittedly using subjects learning in other places than home) that address the first question and advances some proposals in answer to the second.

In the first study, he questioned 65 students, from kindergarten to eighth grade, attending computer classes at a private school in

California (not a representative sample, although it did include 23 girls). He concluded that presence of a goal is the most important factor in determining which games students play. In the second study, he tested Breakout, a game requiring sensori-motor skill, in versions that varied the visual display, the motion of the simulated ball and the score display. His subjects were ten undergraduates and he concluded that presence of a visually-stimulating goal and a score to beat were the prime motivators.

The third study involved Darts, a computer game about concepts of arithmetic fractions. Three balloons appear at random places on a number line on the screen and players have to guess their positions in terms of whole numbers and fractions (e.g., Balloon A is at three-and-a-quarter). Players type in their answers as numerals and after each guess an arrow shoots across the screen at the position specified, popping the balloon if the guess is right. Players go on shooting until all the balloons are popped. Circus music is played at the beginning and a short song after any round in which all three balloons are popped with four arrows or less. The game teaches children to estimate distances on a number line and to express the answers as mixed numbers. From his results, Malone concludes that boys like the fantasy of arrows popping balloons but dislike the song, while girls' likes were the opposite.

Malone proposes that challenge, fantasy and curiosity are essential for intrinsically motivating teaching by computer games. Challenge depends on goals with outcomes that are uncertain because the difficulty level is varied; it may also depend on the goals being multiple, on randomness existing within the game or success following the discovery of hidden information. Fantasy, the opportunity for the player to fantasise, can be either extrinsic or intrinsic to the game, depending on whether it is closely related to skills demanded by the game. Curiosity can be enhanced by making learners believe their knowledge is incomplete, inconsistent or not sufficiently parsimonious. These are the principles to be applied if games aimed at providing informal learning are to be motivating.

Levin and Kareev (1980) give interesting accounts of micro-computer use by children in two computer clubs and at home, in Southern California. They note that entertainment provides the initial motivation for children. Soon, however, the children begin to learn cooperatively. For example, in the clubs there was a recurring progression as follows: (1) Four or five children would gather round an adult who demonstrated how the computer worked. (2) One child would claim a turn and sit at the keyboard. This child would be 'typist', typing in what the others suggested. (3) The group discussed (often without the adult except when help was needed) what to do. (4) In time, the size of the group would dwindle down to two, with children who had become more expert starting to work alone. (5) Once a child had become an expert in some particular area, other children would call on him or her before calling for the adult.

In a similar anecdotal report of observations of two boys aged six and seven living in a home where there was free access to a micro-computer, Levin and Kareev say that the boys enjoyed games, but did not take seriously the text editing the machine offered, preferring to write 'crazy stories' through hitting the keys more or less randomly. By contrast, they liked using the editing commands to amend their crazy stories! They were motivated enough to learn to read computer messages, program names and the like, and had to type in answers to play certain games. As the boys' first language was not English, however, there was an unusual factor in this 'field trial' and we cannot generalise much from it.

Adolescents

What can we say about adolescents using new information tech-nology to learn informally at home that does not apply with almost equal force to the age-group we have just considered? The computer magazines frequently carry stories about 14- and 15-year-olds who have become 'computer freaks' or 'whizz kids'. For adolescents, microcomputers hold a special fascination because with one it is possible to create a totally controllable world. If something goes wrong with the electronics, then perhaps the fault has to be repaired by experts, but if there is a programming error, that is detectable and remediable, usually by the adolescent who did the programming. For those of logical, mathematical and spatial bent, BASIC holds no terrors and requires little capacity to express oneself in English (or, in France, in French). Creative acts that formerly were beyond all but those most articulate in their native language now are possible, and the imaginative games programmed by adolescents on microcomputers are witness to the fact. Much of this activity is under the aegis of schools, however, and adolescents' use of most other forms of new information technology is more passive. They learn informally from television and radio, from audio- and videocassettes, from videotex in libraries and shop windows, from pocket calculators and cash tills, from electronic games such as chess and Space Invaders. Like their younger siblings, they are learning new mental sets from amusement arcades, television and audiocassette recorders. All these are part of their out-of-school world and must be taken into account in varying degree by educators.

Summary

Informal learning by children outside school is changing. They are learning more, and what they are learning is different from what it was 20 years ago. New information technology is in part responsible for these changes, and is likely to become more so. Educators in charge of formal learning cannot afford to ignore these trends.

8 IN PRIMARY SCHOOLS

The next few chapters describe ways of learning through new information technology at various levels in our formal educational system. First, what has been happening at the primary school level? This chapter begins with recorded experience of applications involving microcomputers (with a passing reference to mainframe computers) and calculators, then goes on to deal briefly with some videodisc and videotex applications.

Microcomputers

Recent British experience with microcomputers in primary schools is reported in two booklets from the British Microelectronics Education Programme (Jones, 1982a and Ellingham, 1982) that provide case studies in more detail than can be offered here.

At this level we begin to hear people talking about children acquiring 'computer awareness' or 'computer literacy'. What do these terms mean? This is a book which will raise its readers' computer awareness because it deals with the ways in which computers may have an impact on education. It is not a book which will help anyone to acquire much computer literacy, since it teaches little about how computers work and nothing about how to program them. Children's computer awareness is slowly increasing as microcomputers arrive in primary schools. Computer literacy will be acquired only by a minority, however, despite the urge to teach it in those teachers who bring computers into their classrooms. To acquire computer literacy children must learn by actual experience and practice in programming.

An early stage in computer literacy consists of 'keyboard literacy', acquired through playing with the machine, usually with games programs, just to get the feel of the keyboard and screen, and then to learn how to operate the various components. The next step is for children to use 'courseware', educational programs already devised, probably obtained by the teachers from a program exchange or from commercial suppliers. Only then are teachers likely to attempt to teach children to program.

Finkel (1981) reviews a computer literacy package published by Science Research Associates, a major textbook publisher in the United States. The package, Computer Discovery, contains a mixture of items, he says, of which only a handful are suitable for introduction at primary school level. Others, such as the Instructor's Guide, serve well to introduce teachers to computing, while much of the material is suitable for secondary level. At the primary level, Finkel considers the set of eleven programs entitled Robot is likely to be very successful from second grade (age eight) upwards in teaching programming on a suitable microcomputer (say, an Apple II or an Atari 800, both with magnetic disc, otherwise known as a disc-drive).

What about the stage between computer awareness and full computer literacy, when children can readily use the courseware? What can they learn of the formal curriculum from micro-computers? The primary school curriculum in all Western countries emphasises learning to read, to write in the mother tongue and to calculate. In some countries other school subjects, such as mathematics (in the broader sense than arithmetic), social studies, science, drama, music and art, get substantial emphasis, in others much less. Programming of courseware for computers has focused first on language and number, although programs for other topics do exist. As we shall see, courseware can also be divided on the basis of its teaching approach into three main types: drill-and-practice routines, tutorials and simulations. Games of one kind or another may be used in any of these three. Further, there are significant differences of pedagogy between followers of Papert's LOGO-based theories and those who adopt instructional strategies based more or less on programmed learning: more about this later.

What happens when young primary school children use a micro-computer for the first time? In a review of one school's experience, Conlin (1981) reports how an English infant (ages four-six) school introduced a PET microcomputer. When the staff first obtained it, they had little idea what to expect, but after using it to present simple exercises they decided to write programs to teach what they felt only the computer could teach. They completed 25 programs, with the help of students at a nearby secondary school and some friends and parents. The children, who work two at a time on the computer, have become 'keyboard literate' and completely at home with the PET.

Every child in the school now uses it. They begin at the age of four, usually with a simple measuring program requiring very little keyboard use. As they work in pairs they talk to each other about what is happening and appear to think of the PET as another child taking part in their game. The parents' reaction is mixed. When the staff showed the parents a videotape of children working on the PET, few parents present accepted an invitation to try the machine for themselves.

Perhaps a very simple introduction is all that is needed for young children (or their parents!). Yet this was not the case when Piestrup's (1981) program, Up-Down, Left-Right, was tested in a classroom at the Stanford University demonstration nursery school. Fifty children, including many foreigners, were involved over a period of three weeks. These children, who were aged three or four, used the Apple II microcomputer as one option among a number of indoor activities. The experimenter soon had them inserting discs, turning the computer on, and giving the right names to parts of the equipment. She also opened the computer to show them the area where the chips are housed and where each cable leads. The children were pre- and post-tested using modified items from the Random House Criterion Reading test. During the three weeks there was great interest in using the colourful and musical program Piestrup provided, and the microcomputer was welcomed by parents, children, the university and school administration, teachers and aides. Some children got as many as twelve turns on the computer but most had only one or two. Requests for turns came about equally from boys and girls, and from three- and four-year-olds. Very few left the computer voluntarily: in fact, it was in use continuously. One child, with help from the experimenter, wrote a list of names for those waiting their turn. Some children learned very quickly, usually by listening to the voice, watching carefully and moving slowly and deliberately through the learning sequence, says Piestrup. Other children hit too many keys too quickly so that they could not tell which key created which effect. Many of the children mastered the concepts being taught, as the test results showed, but this may not have been entirely due to the computer, since the teachers were also emphasising these concepts. Clearly many children took pleasure in using the computer to generate rainbows with changing colours and dancing rain. Butterflies and rainbows, both used in the program, were prevalent in the children's art during the experimental period. Piestrup says that these children enjoyed using the computer, were not intimidated by it and learned quickly not only the concepts being taught but also the necessary 'computer awareness'. Fisher (1982), working in an English primary school with a very much cheaper Sinclair ZX81, provides a program for infants that enables them to make objects appear and disappear on the screen through simple inputs. He says his children enjoy this too and become familiar with the equipment. The parents are interested, but he is not aiming to produce good infant typists!

In a Scottish review, Bremner and Prescott (1981) report primary school children's reactions to using a microcomputer for the first time. The children were eight to eleven years old and worked with programs specially prepared by the two researchers. The children rapidly gained confidence with the instructions, which were designed so that they could receive information from and impart information to the screen. In fact, they soon experimented with disobeying them. Straightforward arithmetic bored them quickly, but they enjoyed programs dealing with general knowledge and English. The researchers found that if more than one-third of a screenful of text was presented at once, children skipped or simply looked for the stimulus which would allow them to proceed if they gave a correct response. Children seemed to lose concentration after about 10 to 15 minutes at the screen unless the program contained considerable variety or some kind of scoring device to indicate performance on successive runs. Children liked competing against each other and against themselves.

Reports of American experiences with microcomputers in primary schools tend to be less critical. Wright (1981) describes how at the school where she teaches Tandy TRS-80s are used across the curriculum. First she deals with mathematics. The Tandy K-8 Maths programs and others are used by individual children and small groups, as part of a series of activities. Many children were previously content to work through paper-and-pencil drill exercises. With the Tandy programs, they want to find what level of difficulty is above their own, then they want to see how quickly they can respond and how the microcomputer will react when they type in answers. There is keen competition to use the computers, and Wright uses the privilege of working on the Tandy as an incentive to complete other work satisfactorily.

Logic games are used to practise problem-solving techniques (Wright gives no details). For History, children studying the Roman period use Emperor. It is based on maps and the aim for each player is to remain in control of a well-policed and stable empire. The game introduces a number of historical points about the Roman Empire, and as it requires manipulation of several factors, levels of decision-making are quite high but Wright says that the children understand surprisingly quickly. For Geography, there is The Horn, a race game for sailing ships between New York and San Francisco. Weather conditions and ocean currents are analysed to set course; with the help of graphics, ships' speed and progress are monitored. For English, the school found commercially-available language programs generally unsuitable. The logic games, however, require reading and are used for remedial work, in groups where children can discuss the problems posed. Children who have lost interest in reading want to read what is on the screen. By using the word processor program, they can write too. A line printer provides children with a permanent record of their writing, once they have edited it. A class newspaper is one product. In Wright's school about 30 children regularly give up their time to practise using the computers.

For learning the English language, there is actually no lack of drill-and-practice programs to improve reading, enunciation, spelling, correct usage and so on. Needless to say, the quality varies. Lubar (1980) describes a program designed to improve readers' speed and retention. Published by Edu-ware Services, a small American company, it is called Compu-Read and has six sequences or sub-programs. The first places random letters on the screen for a brief moment. The child must type the letters after they have vanished, and if he or she succeeds in doing so correctly, the next set of letters will remain on the screen for a shorter period, thus building up speed. If the child fails, the display time is increased next time. On completion of the sequence, the child gets a score, expressed in terms of the display time and as letters per second. Thus the reader competes against him or herself. The second sequence provides a similar routine, but uses single short words, not sets of random letters. In the third sequence, the computer displays a single word on the left of the screen and four words on the right, of which one is a synonym of that on the left. The reader must type in the synonym when the words have vanished from the screen. For the fourth sequence, the computer displays a sentence, then asks a question about either the subject or the object of the sentence, after it has vanished. The child chooses the right answer if he or she can. The fifth and sixth sequences permit the teacher to build up further files of new words for use by children in sequences the same as the second and third.

Lubar's report is uncritical, but we may well ask whether these exercises are likely to improve reading. Does research support the unimaginative teaching strategy employed in this package, which scarcely exploits the microcomputer's capabilities? Its chief virtue appears to be that it is presented as a game, permitting individual children who may have experienced reading failure to compete quietly and perhaps privately against themselves as they try to improve their own scores.

In Scotland, a small library of programs is now available for dyslexic learners in primary schools (see *Phase Two*, vol. 1, no. 3, 1981). The programs were developed by secondary school students under the supervision of a teacher of computing and with the advice of teachers of dyslexic children. Some programs are diagnostic, others are structured lessons that help dyslexics interactively. Among the diagnostic programs are ones for detecting left-right confusion, common letter reversals, left-right eye and hand coordination, sense of direction and spelling problems. The lessons range from simple games to spelling practice and mathematical routines and seem more likely to aid learning than the ones reviewed by Lubar above.

Another American set of programs is reviewed by Czechowicz (1981), who looks at English Basics Part II: Concepts in Language Arts. These are intended for teaching English language concepts to children in grades 3-6 (ages 9-12). He hesitates to recommend them on a number of grounds: (1) they do not assume that users will be naïve; (2) the accompanying materials are poor; (3) the programs do not branch to provide for individual needs; (4) students can inadvertently stop the programs or cause them to display the programming language in which they were written; (5) students cannot break off in the middle of an exercise; (6) the English content is weak and includes slang; (7) menus (of choices) should be informative, but are not; (8) the programs over-praise correct responses; (9) they make poor use of graphics and highlight wrong answers rather than the right ones, and (10) these are merely 'page turning' programs that could have been presented in book form just as effectively. Unfortunately, many of these criticisms can be applied to other programs, including some that have been praised. His remarks underline the inadequacy of much existing courseware: more about that in Chapter 14.

Attempts to assess whether microcomputers actually raise primary schoolchildren's achievement are rare. Attempts to compare effectiveness of microcomputers with that of conventional teaching are even rarer because of problems of uncontrolled variables. Thorwald and Hed (reported in *Educational Computing*, vol. 2, no. 5) arranged for some 70 third and fifth graders with low scores on the Iowa Test of Basic Skills to work with Micro-Ed remedial programs on PET microcomputers. The topics taught were punctuation, capitalisation and English usage. They claimed that average gains ranging from 18 to 27 months were registered by various groups on re-testing after seven months' learning. This is a case of improved student achievement, evaluated by standardised tests, among students who have used microcomputers, but the results must be treated with caution because in many such experiments special conditions make generalisation of findings unjustified.

These examples are drawn from recorded experience. Needless to say, many other programs are on the market or available through exchanges. Apple, for instance, sells courseware on enunciation which gives children practice in recognising initial and terminal sounds of three-letter words (necessary for correct spelling as well as correct pronunciation). Another Apple-marketed program is the logic game of 'Hunt the Thimble', set in a three-bedroomed house and suitable for six- and seven-year-olds. Apple also sells courseware on spelling, word recognition and word building. The game format rewards children with happy or sad faces, or moving objects and targets to fire at!

Computer assisted learning is still a long way from teaching children creative writing, as Sharples (1981) and Wall and Taylor (1982) point out. Many existing programs do little more than teach the accepted grammar or language usage in ways that probably inhibit creative writing. Few help children to develop their writing by planning a story for a particular audience, or to understand the structure of language. Sharples proposes a set of 'tools' that could be used, in a computer, to explore, construct and modify text. He suggests a stockpile of linguistic parts such as synonyms and definitions, a manual describing the function of each tool and a guide full of 'games, exercises and projects in story building'. His pilot project, employing a few such tools, was with six children (eleven years of age) in Scotland. For example, to help children escape from the limits of their normal writing vocabulary (adjectives like big, nasty, horrible, etc.), a thesaurus on the screen offers eight synonyms for each common word. Sharples says that children's responses varied. Two of the six showed little initial interest but eventually did well. The other four made very good progress indeed. Some of them liked working alone, others in pairs. Wall and Taylor's proposals for older students are discussed in the next chapter, but they consist of using a word processor program to help students to draft, correct and revise their English.

Thus far we have been considering examples of courseware to teach language skills. What about teaching arithmetic and mathematical skills? Is the recorded experience any less equivocal, since computers have always been associated more with numeracy than literacy.

This book does not set out the history of developments on computer-assisted learning based on mainframe and mini-computers, but it is worthwhile noting a recently published evaluation of two of the chief American projects in primary schools in the mid-1970s, before microcomputers were available: PLATO (Programmed Logic for Automatic Teaching Operations), based on the University of Illinois but now marketed by Control Data Corporation in a number of countries, and CCC (the product of Computer Curriculum Corporation, a Californian company). PLATO depended on large mainframe computers at the time of the evaluations, but CCC used minicomputers. Alderman (1980) says that PLATO, in a 1975-6 project, focused on mathematical concepts taught in American grades four to six, including whole numbers, fractions, decimals, graphs, variables, functions and equations. Each lesson followed a different format, often a game-like one. Three hundred children were involved and on average each worked for 50 hours at a terminal (keyboard and screen). Evaluation showed they had learned more than comparable children taught only by conventional methods, and that both teachers and children liked using the system. CCC provided drill-and-practice on topics ranging from simple number concepts to operations with negative numbers, covering grades one to six. Several hundred children spent 10-20 minutes a day on the computer using these programs, over a period of three years (1977–80). The results indicated that although these children performed better on tests than comparable children taught conventionally, the tests favoured them and the computerised instruction had not been well coordinated with classroom teaching.

Alderman's verdict was therefore favourable to PLATO's system but equivocal in the CCC case.

It is still rare to find more than one review of any particular package of programs, but here is one instance. Bejar (1980) describes the first edition of a package designed to give primary school children practice in solving mathematical problems. Published by Milliken in the United States, it was developed by the World Institute for Computer-Assisted Teaching (WICAT) in Utah for use on Apple, TRS-80 and PET microcomputers. There is a teachers' guide and a set of programs on tape cassettes or discs covering the main types of problems taught in grades 1-6 (ages 7-13). Forman (1981), reviewing the revised second edition (for grades 1-8), says that no diagnostic test is provided, teachers being expected to identify areas in which students require additional practice. Once the appropriate level has been specified by the teacher, the computer takes students through the problems step by step, with frequent questions. If they answer a question correctly, the computer encourages them, for example by flashing YES (no sound is used). If they answer incorrectly, they are told to try again, but after two incorrect answers the computer will move on to the next step after giving the correct answer. If a student is 'failing' a complete segment or level, the computer will return him or her to a lower level. If he or she is succeeding, the computer will take him or her on to the next higher level.

What do these two reviewers think of the package? Forman criticises some of the programs: for example, she points out that the number readiness program, at the beginning, requires reading skills that such young children may not have. On the whole, however, Forman praises the package, saying that it is suitable for routine use in supplementing with practice what teachers have already taught. Bejar comments that it is difficult to adapt the sequence used in the first edition to the teacher's sequence of topics, should this happen to be different, which it often is. There is no provision for skipping sequences or returning, other than in the way already described. Moreover, the teachers' guide does not provide cross-indexing with the most commonly-used American textbooks for mathematics in the primary school. Again, these criticisms apply widely to courseware at present on the market.

Gilmer (1981) reviews a program, Arithmetic Skills, that is one out of a package entitled Compu-Math. She describes how the program teaches addition, subtraction, multiplication and division, and notes that the classroom teacher can decide to some extent how the computer will teach. For example, the teacher can choose whether the computer will beep at the student and at what intervals. The teacher can also determine how many errors a student may make before he or she is sent back to earlier teaching. And the teacher or student can decide how many examples will be presented before the practice questions appear. Gilmer thinks that this program is a translation of conventional material and techniques to the computer, without the potential of the machine being properly tapped. She is critical of the content, and predicts that drill of this kind, using numbers separated from a problem context, will receive decreasing emphasis in the 1980s.

Four programs from Premier Publications, written by John Hooker, a teacher, and available for use on several makes of micro-computer, are reviewed by Futcher (1981). For addition, numbers to be added flash on the screen together or in sequence: children must add them and type in the answer. If they are correct, the computer sets more difficult sums. For subtraction, students are shown a number from which they have to subtract a string of numbers that appear in turn. Multiplication practice is provided by many standard questions, but to maintain interest children can also count the number of squares that appear briefly on the screen in two boxes. When the timer reaches zero, the squares disappear and the children must multiply together the two numbers. Division sums are offered in multiple-choice format: one of the answers given is the correct one and children must choose it, working against time.

These programs, although praised by Futcher, appear to be very elementary. They are typical of drill-and-practice programs, being similar to those originally produced for much larger computers. If teachers want their children to perform such drills on a computer, the children will probably be entertained and possibly educated. As in so many other cases, the only evidence that these programs increase children's achievement is the testimony of teachers like Futcher, who says, 'Staff and children gained from using them.'

Kendall (1981) reviews a similar drill-and-practice series, this time for kindergarten to eighth grade (up to 13 years of age) prepared for use on TRS-80 Model II machines. He is a little more critical than Futcher, but has much more (70 lessons on addition alone) to criticise. Kendall thinks the problems are graded carefully and he notes some useful prompts (e.g., a child taking too long will see a message urging him on). Unfortunately, there is no indication that the programs do much more than a textbook with answers at the back, or that drill-and-practice routines have been improved.

One further primary school example of a microcomputer program, this time a simulation used to teach history: Goodson (1981) reviews Oregon Trail, a program for studying migrants' problems as they moved westward on the Oregon Trail in the 1800s. Together with the students' manual, the program provides a number of activities for students relating to this migration. Students learn what supplies a typical family had on setting out, their cost and importance, but they are left to decide how to spend their money. Their choices turn out later to influence the outcome of unexpected events on the journey, which proceeds in two-week stages. These events are provided by the computer. At the end of each stage, students are told what supplies they have left, so they can make informed judgements when more unexpected events come upon them in the next stage. Goodson has some criticism of the graphics, particularly the hunting scenes, which are too slow, and feels that graphics are rather over-used. Sound is added (Home on the Range, not a typical 1800s song) as if for sound's sake, and is nothing but a distraction. In general, however, Goodson thinks this is a very good teaching simulation.

None of these approaches to using microcomputers in primary schools would be likely to meet with much approval from Papert (1977, 1980). Do they teach any better than pencil-and-paper? Do they make real use of the power of microcomputers to extend human thinking? Papert, a professor at the Massachusetts Institute of Technology, says that the computer provides a learning tool of great power because it enables young children to test their own theories about the physical or abstract worlds and to obtain rapid feedback. His turtle geometry enables children to create command sequences which generate pictures on the computer's screen just as if they were sitting on the pencil doing the drawing. The child must create a control program, and to do so must construct a model in his or her mind before seeing the result. If the model is right, the computer shows this clearly. If the picture turns out to be wrong, there is a strong motivation to correct the model and thence the program, to produce the right picture, says Papert. The language Papert uses for this programming is LOGO, which is not yet widely available on microcomputers. One of the reasons is that it requires a reasonably powerful machine, such as the Research Machine 380Z or the Apple II. With it, the child can work out the strategy involved in, say, adding two 2-digit numbers and write a program to do it. The language is simple enough for the emphasis to be on understanding the problem and thinking out the logical steps for solving it. Papert's approach thus contrasts sharply with drill-and-practice programs that do all the programming for students. LOGO expects them to program and Papert says that anyone listening to the conversation of children using LOGO will realise that they are unconsciously using concepts of deep significance in logic and computing. Incidentally, Milton Bradley's *bigtrak* (see Chapter 7) requires children to program it, somewhat after the fashion of Papert's turtle, but without demanding much conceptualisation from them.

Bourne (1981) reports that the Inner London Education Authority, largest in the United Kingdom, is investing £2 million in microcomputers, mainly for ten selected primary schools. What do teachers think these can do? He chronicles reactions at a conference. Some teachers said that children who had never shown much interest in classwork were prepared to do fourteen times what they had done before, 'thinking they were skydiving'. One teacher felt the machines added to his authority. But others were critical: with the present programs they could not justify the outlay, because these are not sophisticated enough. They questioned whether micro-computers are what London schools need most.

Calculators

Some controversy surrounds the question of whether such a rela-tively cheap device as the pocket calculator should be widely used in primary schools. This may seem surprising when we take into account government enthusiasm for much more expensive micro-computers that have yet to show their true versatility in classrooms. A somewhat exaggerated view is taken by Girling (1977), who suggests that 'At a time when a cheap calculator can be bought for the price of two good cabbages, we need to redefine our aims for numeracy.'

Baker, Easen, Graham and Tyler (1981) say that 'an underlying concern in the primary school is to provide a solid grounding in number work'. They believe that calculators can help children to learn and practise concepts and skills in number work and have prepared a short Open University course on the subject for teachers. They say that in the United Kingdom, Her Majesty's Inspectors of

Schools (1978) advocate use of calculators as teaching aids, while in the United States the National Council for Teachers of Mathematics (1980) makes a similar recommendation.

Baker and his colleagues identify 'the most commonly held fear about the use of calculators in the primary school — expressed by teachers, parents and children — (as) that they "rot the brain" '. This view can be refuted by research reports and examples of how calculators do quite the opposite. For example, they can be used to reinforce number bonds and to help understanding of place value and decimals, as the course shows. Beyond that, calculators can be deployed to help children understand problem-solving processes, both in mathematics and everyday matters requiring arithmetical solutions. Baker, Easen, Graham and Tyler also answer five common criticisms from those who do not like to see calculators entering primary schools:

(1) 'The children will not learn the mathematics they should if they have calculators to do it for them.' In fact, experience shows that children grasp the concepts better, in, say, long multiplication.

(2) 'Using a calculator will prevent children from acquiring basic skills wanted by employers.' Basic skills surely include number bonds, place value and decimals, in all of which calculators benefit children's learning.

(3) 'Calculators only help with arithmetic.' No, they go beyond, by helping children to focus on problem-solving processes rather than on calculation, by giving them confidence and motivation and enabling them to employ large numbers with ease.

(4) 'Children will not understand the basic algorithms of arithmetic if they are allowed to use calculators before they have mastered the routines.' Experience shows here that calculators, strangely enough, help the teaching of these algorithms enormously, because children come to understand what they are doing instead of following routines blindly.

(5) 'Children will become dependent on calculators.' Yes, they may depend on calculators to build up their confidence, but they will also become aware of calculators' limitations. In the past, only a few children actually ever became fully proficient and accurate at long division and multiplication. With the help of calculators, many more may become so. For the rest, it will be important for them to know how to use a calculator.

By the way, in case we are concerned about practical matters like batteries running out during a lesson, Sanyo make an 8-digit pocket calculator powered by room lights or sunlight. It looks like an ordinary calculator except that it has a small panel of solar cells just above the display panel for figures. The cells are a new type, simpler and cheaper to produce.

Videodiscs

Still at the prototype stage, videodiscs, especially interactive ones, may offer some benefits to primary school classrooms. Two examples will serve to illustrate this. ABC Video Enterprises in conjunction with the National Education Association and the National Foundation for the Improvement of Education, in the United States, is producing 20 optical videodiscs (SCHOOLDISCS) for players without microprocessor control. Children will be able to locate the start of particular segments, each disc having six ten-minute segments devoted to one of six subjects (arts, social sciences, science and mathematics, language skills, current affairs and in-service teacher training). Each segment includes 90 stills at the end, including bibliographies referring students to relevant reading (McEntee and Blum, 1981). In another videodisc, reported by Bates (1981), young Olympic gymnasts demonstrate tumbling skills, including the forward roll, the handstand, etc. The disc can be slowed down or stopped to show particular movements for children to practice. Needless to say, these discs are not being used widely yet.

Videotex

Finally, we should look at an example of videotex in use in British primary schools participating in experiments with Prestel. Thompson (1981) provides a list of topics available (at that time) for primary schools on Prestel:

00	ANCIENT MONUMENTS		Numbers of Farm Animals
	Ancient Monuments		World Wildlife Fund
01	ANIMALS	02	ARITHMETIC
	Animals	03	ART
	Care of Domestic Pets		Art
	Diseases in Farm Animals		Materials
	Dog Choice and Training		Exhibitions

This list reveals a few of the opportunities and problems facing the primary school teacher with a new Prestel set installed in the classroom. Some of the headings do not make sense therefore it is essential to consult the relevant pages before recommending them to students. In fact, this could be said of any of the pages, since any page may cover much or a little. For example, African Weather may lead on to pages and pages of information or it may merely offer the previous day's maximum temperature in a selection of African capitals. The pages must be consulted immediately before the lesson, too; to make sure they still exist, since the database is changing all the time (African Weather dropped out before this manuscript was finished!). Not surprisingly, perhaps, opinions regarding Prestel's usefulness to primary schools as a source of information for teaching are fairly critical, although schools using Prestel for telesoftware (electronic delivery of courseware via Prestel) say it is valuable for this purpose.

Summary

It seems clear from these examples that new information technology can be used by children for learning in primary school, but that we do not have enough good quality courseware nor cheap enough devices and systems. As yet the fund of experience is not large: it must be expanded.

9 IN SECONDARY SCHOOLS

Like Chapter 8, this chapter draws heavily on experience, reported during the last two or three years, in using new information technology in schools, this time at the secondary level. School systems vary from country to country in defining what is primary and secondary schooling, but here we take secondary schools as those serving children aged about 12-18. Experience in using microcomputers comes first again, followed by videotex and videodisc.

Microcomputers

Hubbard (1981) says that in 1980 a United Kingdom survey showed that there were more than 700 microcomputers in English and Welsh secondary schools, being used for about 14 subject areas, mainly computer studies and mathematics. This provision is increasing rapidly under two schemes to put microcomputers into British secondary schools, reports Cookson (*The Times*, 14 January 1982). The first, supported by central government funds, pays 50 per cent of the cost of a Research Machine 380Z or a BBC Acorn. The second, promoted by the manufacturer, provides a Sinclair ZX81 at half-price. By the date of Cookson's report, over 4,000 schools had ordered equipment under these schemes. But as he points out, one computer per school is not enough. Hardware must be backed up with more hardware, plus software (courseware) and training. The latter is being spear-headed in the United Kingdom by the Microelectronics in Education Programme, funded by government.

In France, there is a government-financed scheme to put 10,000 microcomputers into secondary schools by 1985. The Japanese have a similar scheme, already operating, and so have the Danes.

By contrast, the United States Federal Government, which does not control education (a matter for individual States), has found it difficult to arrive at a plan for financing either hardware for secondary schools or courseware development. The United States Office of Education, the National Institute of Education and the National Science Foundation have in the past funded experimental mainframe computer-based learning projects, but Melmed (1982) raises questions about the extent to which Federal funds will go towards providing microcomputers or the necessary software and courseware.

Nevertheless, recorded experience of applications already exists and there is a plethora of ideas about how to use new information technology. We can review examples from the literature, which are here arranged by school subject, as in the last chapter.

For example, in the field of English Literature, Lubar (1980) refers to the Talk and Teach programs published by Atari for use with their microcomputer. These programs are on cassettes which also carry a sound-track. Thus the computer talks to its students as well as displaying text and graphics on the screen. Among these programs is a series entitled Great Classics, including such titles as *Julius Caesar* and *Tale of Two Cities*. In about half an hour, each program tells the story of the play or book, with frequent pauses to display multiple-choice questions on the screen, aimed at testing comprehension. The students have to choose the right answer, and if they do, then the story continues. A wrong answer makes a buzzer sound, followed by a request to try again.

Lubar compares the programs with Classic Comics, which summarised famous plays and books in similar fashion, without the questions, for an earlier generation of Americans. Like the comics, these programs may encourage students to read the original, but Lubar does not think they will. Clearly the computer is not teaching literature. Perhaps the programs will help some students to grasp the story-line: they do not exploit the computer's capabilities.

The potential of microcomputers for teaching Creative Writing at secondary school level is discussed by Wall and Taylor (1982), who suggest five simple stages for classroom use of a word-processing program: (1) students compose stories; (2) teachers 'annotate' the drafts; (3) students revise their stories; (4) stages (1) to (3) are repeated as often as necessary, depending on the progress students are making; and (5) students print out their final drafts. Wall and Taylor mention a few ways in which the computer could help, but their (untested) model seems based entirely on automation of current student and teacher practices in creative writing lessons.

Meredith (1981) reviews *Practicando Español Con La Manzana II*, a program designed to give students drill in Spanish verb forms and Spanish vocabulary. Instructors may add to, delete or modify the content, within the framework supplied by the program. As supplied, it is pitched at the first three years of study of Spanish (as taught in the United States), and students may enter at their own individual level. If they make mistakes, they receive a good deal of help, ranging from simple correction to hints of various kinds to an offer to teach again that verb form. On the other hand, Meredith is critical of the program for not requiring students to understand the meaning of each question in Spanish before they can choose an answer. On a technical level, he thinks a range of tones could have been used to signal various kinds of errors, rather than a single tone. Black-and-white text is the only form of visual display. Spanish is not used for actual instructions, but it could be.

Reviews of other language applications at the secondary level are rare. For example, *Apfeldeutsch*, the Apple program for German language teaching, was tested in the United Kingdom at Ealing College of Higher Education, but no evaluation has been published yet.

What about History? *Educational Computing* for March 1981, carries a report from students of an Irish secondary school, who used a microcomputer to set up a database of census returns for 1901 in their district. They say they learned much about setting up such a database, involving 2,000 names, and they are now able to use it for studying local history. They wrote three kinds of programs to analyse the database: first, to count the number of people within various categories, such as religion, educational standard, occupation and workplace; second, to compute statistics such as average age, proportion of males to females, average number of persons per household; and third, to compile specialised lists, such as the ages of working children, whether or not servants were illiterate, and so on.

Business Studies may seem a more likely field for secondary school microcomputer applications. In Scotland, an international travel company set up a competition for secondary schools (the prize being free tours), to design and program a training game for travel tour operators (reported in *Phase Two*, vol. 1, no. 3, 1981). A microcomputer had to be programmed to produce all the balance sheets and market research information required for the tour operating industry. The game allows trainee tour operators, working in teams, to compete for advertising, hotel and resort selection, pricing policy, aircraft charters and retail outlets. Trainees work through both summer and winter trading cycles and have to allow for factors such as national and international economic variations. This is an example of secondary students, with their teachers' help, learning a great deal about a real-world industry at the same time as learning FORTRAN, a programming language.

By contrast, Music may not at first sight seem suitable for secondary school microcomputer applications, but Apple, one of the companies marketing courseware for microcomputers (in this case the company's own), sells a package aimed at helping students to learn how to write and play back their own electronic music, which can be reproduced on a stereo. The music staves are on the display screen. Notes are entered using the paddles. Programs provide drills in a number of musical skills, e.g., rhythm and ear training. Again, as yet, no evaluation of this package being used at secondary school level has been published.

Wittlich (1981), however, reviews Interval Mania and Arnold, two programs designed to teach sound-symbol association. Interval Mania teaches, through a game, aural and visual identification of melodic and harmonic intervals. The player can set the speed of the game. In visual mode, an interval is displayed on the screen, in correct notation, and the notes are played, the task being to identify the interval displayed. In aural mode, an interval is displayed on the screen only after the correct answer has been given to the interval sounded. After three wrong answers, the program 'teaches' the interval again. Wittlich considers that this program should succeed, but suggests a few minor improvements. Arnold, named after Arnold Schoenberg, provides practice in memorising melody. The exercises, of which there are 19, are of increasing difficulty, through five stages that introduce more notes and faster tempo as well as more complex melodies. Wittlich again considers the program useful, but is critical of the clumsy and slow method students have to use to enter notes on the screen (with arrow-keys and space bar).

Well-tested courseware packages have been produced for a number of secondary school subjects by the University of London (Chelsea College) and the Schools Council. For example, one Economics package, aimed at senior secondary students, requires no programming knowledge or previous experience on computers, but covers elasticity of demand, price fluctuations, agricultural commodity, price stabilisation, theory of the firm, the multiplier, fiscal policy, creation of credit, monetary policy and gains from trade. From the same source come Geography simulations and games: crop-planting, the SE Railway game, a joint stock companies trading game, a windmill game, simulations of drainage basin morphometry and human population growth, and, finally, statistics for geographers. A Geography Association project, being conducted at the University of Leicester, has produced four programs, all of which exploit the potential of microcomputers and deal respectively, with urban land use, land slopes, transport networks and location of settlements. They use varying approaches: for example, transport networks are studied through planning and plotting communications in a developing country, while settlement is studied through simulation within two specimen landscapes. Again, no evaluation of these programs has yet been published. For teaching Economics, a package from the Scottish Esmee Fairbairn Research Centre provides simulations of basic macroeconomic models and running the British economy, programs that were tested in secondary schools and revised before being marketed.

The Schools Council/Chelsea College (University of London) project is providing programs in Biology. The list of titles is being added to continuously, but includes programs on genetics and inheritance, predator-prey relationships, pond ecology, transpiration, counter current systems, human energy expenditure and statistics for biologists. For Chemistry, from the same source, there are programs on topics such as rates of reaction, manufacture of sulphuric acid, homogeneous equilibrium, lattice energy, electrochemical cells, gas chromatography and a chemical element game. In Physics, programs available include ones on photo-electric effect, mass spectrometer, gravitational fields, planetary motion, capacitor discharge, radioactive decay and gaseous diffusion (see Haney's review of one of these, below). Chelsea College also produced a program, intended for students from a wide range of ability, on home heating. It deals with energy loss and allows yearly running costs to be calculated, given a simple model of climate. New development work in the project covers topics in Science, History, Economics, Geography and Modern Languages (*Computers in the Curriculum Newsletter*, no. 2, March 1982). Textbook publishers Edward Arnold and Longman are publishing this courseware.

Haney (1981) reviews a Chelsea College program on particle scattering. He thinks this is a case where simulation on a microcomputer is ideal. The program is used by students to conduct a series of experiments, including one of their own design, but is not intended to teach everything about particle scattering. Indeed, students are to use the accompanying notes and should answer the questions in them before using the program. Haney comments that students will need to go beyond the notes if they are to get the best out of the program, and criticises it for long delays, reporting a 30-minute wait for the microcomputer to generate one particular graph. He adds, however, that the program is pedagogically sound, supporting rather than subverting experiment by students. Like other Chelsea College programs, this one was field-tested in selected secondary schools.

From America comes a review (Carpenter, 1980) on Chemistry programs published by High Technology and developed at Oklahoma State University. The five programs offer a series of laboratory simulations: (1) Acid-base titration to determine the concentration of an unknown acid. (2) Acid-base titration to obtain the gram-molecular weight of a fatty acid, and then to determine Avogadro's number by simulating a monomolecular layer of the fatty acid spread across a water surface. (3) Acid-base titration to obtain the molar concentration of an unknown weak acid, followed by three partial neutralisations in a pH meter simulation to identify the weak acid. (4) Ideal gas law simulation, demonstrating the kinetic-molecular theory of a gas, followed by a demonstration using graphs, of relationships between pressure, volume, temperature and number of moles of a gas. (5) Entropy simulations: first, two gases are allowed to mix; secondly, gas is allowed to expand from one chamber to another.

Carpenter's view of these programs is entirely favourable. The first two, on disc, employ high resolution colour graphics (see Chapter 4). The other three, on the other disc, use low resolution graphics, sound and the 'paddles' (levers on the computer, often used for playing games, because they can manipulate symbols on the screen). The programs are not expensive compared with the cost of laboratory equipment, and Carpenter says that they teach the concepts very effectively.

Caspers (1981) reviews five Science programs from the Minnesota Educational Computing Consortium. Odell Lake is a game-like simulation of certain aspects of freshwater lake ecology, leading to discussion of food chains. Quakes puts students in the role of seismologists trying to plot the epicentre of an earthquake. Ursa teaches the polar constellations. Fish is about the circulatory system of an animal with a two-chambered heart. Minerals is a program teaching students how to test and identify certain minerals. Each of the five programs requires about 30 minutes on the microcomputer from the average student. Caspers does not criticise them in detail; he clearly considers they are useful.

Koetke (1981) reviews a program, Tribbles: an introduction to the scientific method, which starts by presenting students with a puzzle, and, through a computer simulation, guidance in solving the puzzle. Tribbles are alien organisms on another planet, Conway, and the puzzle concerns populations and life cycles of these organisms. The program is based on the game Life (see *Scientific American*, October 1970). The program explains and demonstrates seven steps: (1) defining the problem, (2) distinguishing between assumptions and observations, (3) making observations, (4) verifying observations, (5) tentative explanations, (6) making and testing predictions and (7) revising an explanatory system. In one to two hours, students gain a good appreciation of these steps through the simulation, says Koetke. He is critical of the program, however, and of the accompanying manual. The latter is at too high a reading level and is written too tersely for most students, unless they already know the Life game from the *Scientific American*, in which case they may not need this program. The simulation makes poor use of the microcomputer's capabilities, although it keeps students interested and Koetke thinks they will learn something of the scientific method.

Shaw (1980) says that Chemistry teachers using microcomputers do not need much technical knowledge of computing, although they must be able to use a keyboard and be ready to memorise short standard operating routines. In return, microcomputers help them to teach what could not otherwise be taught, or to teach better what was being taught already. Microcomputers provide for creative interaction between the student and the program. A good program requires the student to examine a problem, plan an investigation, respond to computer prompts and interpret computer-generated results. Microcomputers oblige students to engage in high-level intellectual activity.

Shaw points out that most schools do not have sufficient or appropriate apparatus for teaching all aspects of chemistry in their syllabuses. Nor may they want to permit students to use expensive and sophisticated items, or, in some cases, to carry out dangerous experiments. Moreover, some experiments must be conducted over a long time-span, longer than can be conveniently accommodated in school laboratories. Practical skills acquired by students may also be inadequate for certain experiments, leading to interference from factors they have not learned to control. Microcomputers can be used to simulate experiments so that all these problems are eliminated. Students can vicariously experience the consequences of errors of judgement, inappropriate experimental design and dangerous procedures. Shaw claims that 'They can be presented with a relatively open-ended enquiry but be able to pursue this rapidly, safely and in-depth in their own time and at their own pace. They can repeat sections at will and pursue their own lines of thought . . . Without a doubt there is considerable motivation inherent in the challenge presented by simulated experiments and investigations. Some of this may originate in the . . . rapid feedback which students receive about the consequences of their decisions.'

There is, of course, the danger that students will confuse the simulation with reality, says Shaw. 'The computer does not allow genuine experiments to be performed and any attempt to make out that it can, such as using a simulation as experimental evidence for the theories and assumptions on which the simulation is based, would be dishonest.' He gives details of simulations for the Haber process for ammonia manufacture, for sulphuric acid manufacture, for 'The Alkali Industry Exercise' and for 'The Energy Exercise'.

Shaw also writes on model exploration. Chemistry introduces mathematical models such as the distribution law, homogeneous equilibria, solubility product, common ion effects and their applications, rate equations, the Nernst equation and the Born-Mayer equation. The emphasis is usually on their qualitative aspects rather than on quantitative predictions of a system's response to changing conditions, because of the many and often complex calculations required for the latter. Hand-held calculators are not up to dealing with these problems, but microcomputers may be. The Born-Mayer equation for ionic crystal lattices is examined in this way, in one model exploration Shaw quotes.

Computer science itself, including computer literacy, is now being taught in United Kingdom secondary schools, using micro-computers. Coll (1980) gives figures for candidates taking Ordinary and Advanced levels (ages 16 and 18 approximately) in the United Kingdom in Computer Science: at Ordinary level the numbers rose from 3,217 in 1976 to 11,635 in 1979; at Advanced level, from 1,512 to 2,323. Applications to study computing as a major at university rose over the same period from 11,091 to 22,000. Coll criticises the 1980 syllabuses for being too theoretical and for not offering students enough hands-on experience. At his school (an English public school, therefore far from typical), every student is introduced to BASIC at the age of 13, then to word processing and data retrieval. The next year they are taught the fundamentals of electronics, including circuit building. These two years are a good basis for further work, in Coll's opinion.

Many programs have been written, in a number of countries, for teaching Mathematics, of course. Most of them offer drill-and-practice routines, as we saw for the primary school. For example, Kelly (1981) reviews Geometry and Measurement — Drill and Practice, a set of 30 programs to provide practice for students in this field. It does not introduce the concepts, but leaves this to the teacher. Some of the programs are more suitable for younger children, such as one on the clock, but drills on polygons, length, perimeter and area, angles, circles and volume and area seem appropriate in secondary school, even if they do not reach the level of Euclidean geometry. Since the programs use random-number generators to produce new problems, no two students will have the same problems to solve. Kelly criticises the way in which the programs deal with wrong answers: after two or three tries, students get the right answer, but there is no remedial teaching. Unfortunately, wrong answers disappear off the screen as students proceed, leaving little incentive for them to examine their errors. Kelly's view is that drill-and-practice programs of this kind must be balanced by others that make more imaginative use of microcomputers' capabilities.

By contrast, Phillips (1982) developed three short programs for secondary school students to help those who misinterpret graphs. Many people have trouble with graphs, some even interpret them as pictures. Phillips uses the microcomputer to introduce greater variety than is usually possible, and to shift the emphasis from plotting graphs to reading them, on the grounds that people normally read graphs but do not plot them. He says that we are accustomed to reading off measurements in one dimension, as when we measure with a ruler or read a speedometer, but Cartesian graphs are two-dimensional and must be understood as such.

His first program, Air Temp, is a program that shows mercury moving up a thermometer on the screen, as it would during the morning of a typical June day in England. Next, the depicted thermometer is shifted to the right in stages, to signify changes as they occur each half hour through the day. Then a scale is added on the time axis. These three steps can be repeated, thus showing students something which cannot be represented easily on a blackboard or even with film or video.

Eureka shows what happens to the water level in a bath when it is filled, when a man gets in and when the plug is pulled out. On the top half of the screen these steps are shown pictorially, while at the bottom the computer draws a graph. When they have watched Eureka, students consider what might happen to the graph if there were a different sequence of events: say the man is called to the telephone while filling the bath, or the bath overflows. Each student draws the relevant graph and discusses it with a classmate.

Island is about what happens on a calm day when a forest fire spreads across an island uniformly covered with trees. As fire spreads (on the screen), the computer plots a graph of the number of trees destroyed each minute. The shape of this graph depends on the shape of the island, which can be varied, and on where the fire starts. Students can be asked to forecast the graphs that will result from different shapes and starting points, and their forecasts can be checked by the computer.

Again, this is a case of the computer doing what it can do well, to teach concepts that are difficult to teach by other means. Papert might well be more sympathetic to such programs, but he would still criticise the drill-and-practice routines represented by some of the examples quoted in this chapter.

In England, the Schools Information Retrieval (SIR) project, based on Research Machine 380Z microcomputers, is being tried in six schools and an adult education college. Staff and students can search a demonstration database of about 500 items on the subject of modern environmental problems. What they find is, say, 15 items concerning (1) air pollution in (2) London, or four items concerning (1) solar energy for (2) house heating in (3) France. Each item provides a bibliographic reference, taking students to reprints, books and other documents within the research collection provided as part of the project. Staff and students can use the same software to create their own database, however, and this is important both for teaching them information retrieval skills and for students to learn about the subject matter. One or two interesting problems occur. As in using any reference system, less able children have some difficulty in deciding which keywords to use and lack the reading skills to scan efficiently. On the other hand, children who cannot spell may use the 'truncation' facility: if they type in the first two or three letters of the keyword they have chosen, then an asterisk, the computer will list all keywords with that beginning and the children can easily choose which one they want. Teachers report that less able children are strongly motivated by the system and usually master it sufficiently to be able to claim with pride that they can do what children without a computer cannot. Students of all abilities use the system for homework. An intriguing extension of the project is a floppy disc version of a catalogue for schools of source materials on British industry. This disc is used in conjunction with the SIR software.

Payne (1981) reports on a similar project in four English secondary schools and one in Scotland. Students aged 14 to 18 and their teachers are able to use Research Machine 380Z microcomputers to set up databases and indexes relating to all the teaching resources available at each school for a particular subject or course (in one case, 'Modern world problems and solutions'). About 300 records (summaries relating to separate items in the school's bank of resources) can be stored on one floppy disc, and these files are created by students and staff, who edit each record by using the screen and keyboard. A student wanting to use the index types in keywords and the computer responds by typing out all items with those keywords. Geography and Biology teachers have been involved so far, and the system enables them to identify quickly what is available in the school. They and the students also get experience in on-line searching, a useful information skill.

Videodisc

We have two examples of videodiscs prepared for use in secondary schools. Bates (1981a) reports on the videodisc *Mejore Su Pronunciación*, which is aimed at teaching Spanish-language students to improve their pronunciation of certain sounds. Students have to choose which of two pronunciations is correct; the videodisc repeats the correct one. A typical segment: a restaurant with two people ordering a meal using words with the 'a' sound. The English translation is on the second track if needed. Bates queries the use of videodisc, because videotape could be used similarly and perhaps even audiotape could teach most of what the videodisc aims to teach.

A much more impressive example is described in *Videodisc News* (October 1981): an MCA Discovision videodisc aimed at teaching the physics of sympathetic vibrations through the example of the Tacoma Narows Bridge collapse. In 19 'chapters' it is able to provide several levels of explanation depending on the mathematics background of the student using it, up to and including university standard.

First the student is taught, on the disc, how to use the player. Then the disc moves on to show archival film, taken by a chance observer, of the oscillations building up in the bridge during a storm and its eventual collapse. At this point the student has nine simulations to choose from, dealing with effects on the bridge of three different wind speeds and three gust frequencies. After working through one or more of these, the student views an introduction to standing waves and completes an experiment by collecting data from nine rope oscillations shown in slow motion and drawing conclusions about the effects of tension, length and linear density of rope on standing wave frequency. Finally, the disc provides information about the bridge's design to explain why large amplitude standing waves built up on it, leading to its collapse. This disc was developed at the University of Nebraska with funds from the National Science Foundation and is widely acclaimed.

Videotex

In the United Kingdom, telesoftware is sent by videotex. Computer programs stored on the Prestel (videotex) computer can be accessed, retrieved and stored by any school (primary or secondary, but most are secondary) which is a registered Prestel user and which has a Research Machine 380Z disc-based microcomputer (Coates, 1981). The system is fully automatic. The user calls the appropriate Prestel page number and the program is retrieved, delivered and stored without further intervention. A 5K program can be transferred in about 2.5 minutes, at a cost of 15 pence at peak time, less at other times.

The system can be used to transmit software in any language, although only a few are being used so far. It has automatic error checking so that problems from line noise are eliminated. Because updating is easy on Prestel, the program supplied should be the latest version. A Prestel response frame makes it possible to order documentation and related learning materials. As many as 25 institutions (not only secondary schools) are taking part in the 1982 trial, and have access to about 50 tried and tested programs.

Secondary schools within an experimental scheme established by the Council for Educational Technology in England and Wales are using Prestel in the school library for two main purposes (Thompson, 1981 and 1981a). First, it enhances the teaching of various subjects by making available up-to-date information, e.g., financial statistics in the teaching of economics and business studies. Secondly, it helps teachers and students to acquire information retrieval skills through using a new information technology, videotex. With regard to the first, however, Thompson admits that the amount of Prestel information likely to be useful to teachers and students is at present limited and often presented in unsuitable formats because it is aimed at other users. In this trial, the schools found that information available on Prestel was not what they wanted: it simply was not relevant for most subjects, except for economics and business studies (only taught at higher levels and in a few British schools). Inadequacies in indexing were a serious barrier, although the technical system is easy to use. Running costs, particularly telephone and computer costs, were seen as too high. Thompson comments that Prestel is certainly not suitable for primary schools yet. But teachers are willing, he says, to tell information providers what kind of information is needed by schools.

Fort (1980) reports on an evaluation of Prestel as used in three schools plus a few government Occupational Guidance Units and Careers Offices to provide vocational guidance information from the United Kingdom government-operated Careers and Occupational Information Centre. Considering the fact that users' comments were generally favourable, the terminals were sparsely used (on average, four and a quarter hours a month). Teachers or students were able to consult the database in several ways: one of the most popular was by keying in the student's best school subject, when Prestel provided a list of occupations that required qualifications in that subject. The Prestel service is fairly primitive, however, compared with vocational guidance systems developed for use with mainframe computers. American systems are described by Shatkin (1980) and analysed by Katz and Shatkin (1980), while recent British experience is summarised by Watts and Ballantine (1981). An enquirer using one of these systems, which operate through a network of terminals linked to the mainframe computer and placed in large numbers of schools, colleges and career guidance centres, is able to ask more sophisticated questions and receive fuller information in reply, than via Prestel. Work is being done to develop such systems to provide not only occupational data but also job placement information.

Summary

This chapter has offered many examples of students learning through new information technology at the secondary level. We can say there is much development activity, with a wider provision of courseware than at the primary level, but we cannot say much yet about its contribution to improving education at this level because evaluation has not been a prominent feature of these early projects. The hardware is still not cheap enough and teachers are still having difficulties in integrating these methods into their classroom routines.

10 IN TEACHER TRAINING

This chapter shows what kind of initial and in-service training is being done to take account of new information technology in schools. It does not describe applications of devices and systems. All the countries discussed in this book must look to such training, but as yet little recorded experience is available and no evaluation of effectiveness. A good deal can be said about plans for training related to microcomputers and associated devices. We have one American example of in-service teacher training using interactive videodisc technology. There is also something that can be said about British attempts to train teachers in using calculators for teaching in primary classrooms.

Microcomputers

Those who wish to train teachers in how to use computers in education have first to convince teachers that these machines are not simply yet another educational gimmick. This task is made more difficult because the courseware available looks too much like poorly-designed programmed learning, and because strong doubts exist among teachers about whether a machine can educate (as opposed to instruct). Probably the most convincing demonstration is not of machines, but of children's enthusiasm and concentration while using good programs.

What about training teachers to select good programs? Hartley (1981) criticises training courses for teachers that introduce them to microcomputers, to types of programs and even to elementary programming, but fail to discuss teaching of particular subject-matters. He asserts that it is unrealistic to expect that many teachers will learn to write programs and spend precious time testing and debugging them, but at least teachers should be trained to select programs on educational grounds. What are some of these grounds? Hartley provides several:

(1) Does the program provide feedback for incorrect answers,

explaining how they can be corrected and giving students time to appreciate the explanation and make corrections before it goes on?

(2) Does the program provide students with a learning laboratory (on LOGO lines) or is the model it employs hidden from students?

(3) Does the program allow progress by performance (if you answer correctly, you move up or on) or does it leave students to use the program as they will, with no records kept?

(4) Does the program, if it is for teaching problem-solving of a particular kind, provide help, explanations and evaluation of students' answers when they need these? Can they back-track, get summaries of progress, have access to files of additional facts, and so on?

In fact, teacher training is a very important component of the 1981–4 Microelectronics Education Programme for England and Wales, which is aimed principally at secondary schools and some colleges (Fothergill and Anderson, 1981). The Programme covers four domains: (1) electronics and control technology; (2) the computer as an instrument (computer studies, computerised instrumentation, computer art and music); (3) computer-assisted and computer-managed learning; (4) information technology associated with business studies (electronic office, word-processing and information retrieval). Fothergill and Anderson believe that in-service training of teachers should relate to each of these domains, and, in 1982, topics are being identified in each domain by advisory groups. The stock of training materials now existing is being assessed before short-term projects are commissioned in which training and classroom materials will be developed.

Teachers are to be trained by the Programme to one of three levels: awareness, expertise and advanced. Awareness, perhaps at about the level afforded by this book, will be taught through one- to three-day courses aimed particularly at principals, careers teachers and teachers of subjects in which microcomputers are not apparently useful, such as languages. The next level, labelled expertise, will generate deeper understanding and teach skills needed to apply and adapt the technology effectively in the classroom. It will require week-long courses. The top level, advanced, will teach applications to the teaching of specific subjects, plus skills needed to lead the innovation process. This level will be reached by teachers who attend longer courses of up to three months' duration. The Programme will train mainly to the middle level, because it will bring interested teachers nearer to being able to contribute through day-to-day applications, thus building up a pool of experience. By the end of 1984, 40 to 50 per cent of secondary school teachers in England and Wales should have completed at least one course offered by the Programme, which is setting up a network of training and information centres, each serving a cluster of local education authorities. Schools that receive a computer under government funding schemes must agree to send two teachers for training. Similar training is being set up in Scotland, as Walker and Megarry (1981) report in their account of the Scottish Microelectronics Development Programme.

An important element in in-service (and possibly initial) training of teachers in using microcomputers in British schools will be the Open University's courses, prepared under contract to the Programme. The first materials are being distributed in 1982 and will be followed by further modules in 1983–4. Overall, the materials will raise awareness, provide basic knowledge and skills training, stimulate project work and curriculum development and encourage self-reliance and self-help. The introductory module aims at raising awareness among all involved in education of the potential significance of microelectronics in the school. It provides opportunities for them to gain personal experience of using one or two items of microcomputer-based educational software and asks them to think about how to develop the knowledge and experience they gain. As Wills (1982) suggests, teachers may first learn to use the hardware and software; next, they may learn to amend 'skeleton' software, inserting their own data; and only later, if at all, learn to design and write their own programs.

Later modules will help staff to support their own teaching and administrative activities with microcomputers, to bring into the curriculum new practices or topics resulting from the availability of microelectronics, to prepare students for changes which microelectronics will bring in their lives, and to understand the limitations of the technology.

The Open University course will complement other activities in the Programme by developing in teachers three sets of skills: (a) cognitive (understanding microelectronics, its uses and limitations), (b) practical (using microcomputers and developing software) and (c) professional (undertaking curriculum development and introducing new teaching practices).

In addition, a number of United Kingdom universities and

colleges offer full- and part-time courses for teachers who wish to use microcomputers.

At Stanford University in California a new Master's degree has been launched in the School of Education. Interestingly, it is intended for people who already have a background in computing and who wish to move into the educational field, rather than for teachers who want to learn about computing. Students taking the degree, which is mainly a taught degree, like other American postgraduate degrees, are obliged to take advanced courses in computer science, curriculum development and educational evaluation. It seems likely that similar courses will be offered by other American universities in an effort to bring more computing expertise into education in that country. No such degree is yet available in the United Kingdom.

Interactive Videodisc

So far this chapter has discussed microcomputers only, but clearly there is a need for teacher training in using other forms of new information technology, such as interactive videodisc. Bates (1981a) reports that Michael Streibel at Pennsylvania State University has produced an interactive videodisc for the State Department of Education, to familiarise teachers with microcomputers and interactive videodiscs while at the same time providing them with a 'viewing catalogue' of broadcasts to schools by the television network of the Allegheny Educational Broadcast Council. A teacher using the system at first sees a succession of still pictures and hears the voices of two media librarians describing the purpose of the system. Next, the system switches to computer control and the user is asked to type his or her name on the keyboard. The computer uses that name thereafter, thus adding a sense of personal interaction as it gives instructions for continuing or backtracking.

The computer offers a catalogue of programme types. The teacher responds by telling the computer what grade level and topic will be taught, and immediately the computer lists appropriate titles, from which the teacher chooses one. An extract from that programme is then played from the videodisc. The routine can be repeated to preview other extracts. Before the teacher signs off, the computer asks which programmes will probably be used and why, storing the teacher's answers for later analysis if required. Finally, the librarians come back on the screen for a closing sequence from the videodisc.

This is an apparently teacher-friendly system, in prototype. It does raise some serious questions, however, such as: (1) Surely the catalogue dates very rapidly? (2) Why not use an addressable VCR tape that could be rerecorded for updating? (3) Are teachers satisfied with seeing such short samples of broadcasts (better than nothing)? (4) Is this a cost-effective solution to a pressing educational problem?

Calculators

The Open University offers a short self-study 'course', to train teachers in the use of calculators by students in the primary school (see Chapter 8). An Open University research study showed that many teachers are not yet aware of the potential of calculators in the primary school and instead see them as a threat to children's acquisition of skills and understanding. The Open University's researchers have evidence that calculators can increase stimulation, motivation, confidence, diagnosis, practice and reinforcement of skills, used as a tool during mathematical investigations. Specifically, they can be used as a teaching aid, to initiate and reinforce understanding of number concepts and operations with numbers, as an aid to learning mathematical processes, by encouraging children to make guesses, estimate, generalise and check results, and as a calculating aid, to liberate children from the need to work only with very simple numbers.

But teachers are concerned about the effects of calculators on children's work with basic number facts. The course helps them to obtain reassurance by trying out calculators, under the guidance of the course package, in the ways just described. They need evaluation skills to make good judgements about the impact of the calculators, so these skills are taught too.

Summary

From these selected examples, mostly British, of teacher training in using new information technology for learning, we can see how much teachers need to learn to take advantage of the new machines. Similar training is now being offered in teacher training establishments in most Western countries, but should any country oblige all its present and future teachers to take such training? Probably not, yet teachers now in initial training will be in our schools until about 2025, by which time new information technology will surely be in wide use in education.

11 IN HIGHER EDUCATION

Universities have been using mainframe and minicomputers to aid teaching and learning for about 20 years at Dartmouth College in the United States, for example, and more recently in the National Development Programme for Computer Assisted Learning in the United Kingdom and at the Open University. Universities were able to obtain these computers, which also served research, at a time when other educational institutions could seldom afford them. Ample literature exists describing and evaluating projects associated with these computers (see Luehrmann, 1971; Hooper and Toye, 1975; Hooper, 1977; Suppes, 1981; Wildenberg, 1981). This chapter looks instead at microcomputer and interactive videodisc applications, then at computerised databases used for teaching and research. University students have made little or no use of videotex and teletex system, although Chapter 12 contains examples at community college and postgraduate continuing education levels.

Microcomputers

For many students entering university in the 1980s their first acquaintance with computing is through a microcomputer. They need to gain computer awareness and perhaps some literacy, enough to use microcomputers for their studies. Universities and colleges are trying to meet this need. For example, San Francisco State University provides microcomputers on campus and also makes it possible for students to add to their mathematical literacy. Finzer (1980) gives details: the Center for Mathematical Literacy contains a library of programs available on disc or tape for use on PET microcomputers in the University, including some in the Center. The programs include video games, simulations, strategy games, games of chance, word games, number problems and games, programming languages, graphics, geometry, probability, physics, algebra, statistics and logic. Students (and some staff) of the university who do not feel familiar with computers can thus choose a suitable program with which to find out what PET microcomputers can do and how they are operated. There is some evidence that, as microcomputers are more widely used generally outside the universities, more students are taking up the opportunity to use them. The numbers may well be greater in systems like that at San Francisco State than for university computing services based on time-sharing of a minicomputer, since microcomputers can be more easily decentralised and are often simpler to learn to use.

Besides using microcomputers to pick up computer awareness or even computer literacy, some university students (and staff) are using what Lefrere (1982) refers to as 'electronic editing systems', which can be based on microcomputers. Such systems provide more facilities than word processors, and authors, whether students or teachers, can learn to write better with assistance from editing aids for composition, reorganising copy, correcting spelling and so on.

Computers, including microcomputers, are vitally important in higher education because they make possible a wide range of teaching simulations. Matthews (1981), in reviewing Wildenberg (1981), asserts that computer simulations and modelling can teach university students of science and engineering things which they need to know and which cannot reasonably be taught in any other way. Most of the examples mentioned by Wildenberg depend in some way on computer graphics and many are concerned with visualisation.

For example, the laws of physics are now described by sets of deterministic equations, governed by the laws of probability, as in the case of Ampère's law, but the complexity of relationships represented by these equations limits analytical treatment to simple instances. The complexity is a barrier to a full physical appreciation of the implications of the equations. Computers can carry out simulated experiments, based on solutions of the equation in their most general form, that help students towards this appreciation. Even more valuable are visualisations where the laws are unknown in detail, as in biological systems, or where the laws may be simple but the systems complex, as in chemistry or engineering.

The conventional analytical approach to problem-solving can be contrasted with one based on a solution algorithm such as Euler's rule for solving differential equations. There is no easy logical step, says Matthews, between the differential equation for harmonic motion and its prescribed solution. Euler's solution, however, is related in a simple logical manner to the physical processes of harmonic motion. Writing down the algorithm actually helps students to understand these processes and leads to computer programs for modelling them. We can see a parallel here with Papert's view of the computer as a tool for exploring (see Chapter 8).

Banks (1980) cites a further advantage of computer-based simulation. Some chemical reactions are so slow that it is difficult to study them in a laboratory with students: the reaction of ethyl bromide with sodium hydroxide takes two days in a laboratory but can be simulated in a few seconds on a microcomputer.

Interactive Videodisc

Microcomputers control interactive videodiscs, of course, and one of the most remarkable examples of development work on interactive videodisc technology for learning in higher education is described by Bolt (1979). This is the Spatial Data Management System (SDMS) built at the Massachusetts Institute of Technology as an experimental project for the United States Department of Defense. The system is a working prototype with many potential applications in education, although its cost is high. It brings together sound, visual and tactile means of communicating in unique ways under the student's control, for the purpose of exploring spatial environments.

Spatial data management is a new term. To manage data spatially, the user goes to where the data can be found, electronically speaking, rather than calling it up by naming it. Bolt gives us the example of our home libraries, in which we go to the book we want rather than looking it up first in a card index and then searching the shelves for a book with the right number on it. He says, 'We find items on the basis of a more or less definite sense of their location in a familiar space, which space may be actually present or remembered.' This human ability can be exploited in information handling. It does without symbol systems, and it does not need keyboards, which cannot give the user 'a direct, palpable sense of spatiality'. The SDMS provides, between the user and the machines, links that can take advantage of human spatial ability; it is a 'multi-dimensional window into data', a system for displaying information to the user in many ways.

The SDMS has a screen covering most of one wall, and pictures are projected onto this screen from behind it. Facing the screen is a comfortable chair in which the user sits. In each arm of the chair is a small pressure-sensitive joystick and a touch-sensitive pad. On his or her lap, the user has an electronic writing pad with stylus, and a microphone is mounted on the top edge of this pad. On either side of the chair is a small screen, touch-sensitive. Four loudspeakers are mounted around the screen and another four are on the wall behind the user. Bolt states,

> We have tried to create an interface which is not a tiny, narrow-band 'porthole' into an information bank, that bank itself an abstractly addressed set of intangibles. Rather, we have attempted radically to recast the setting as an 'informational surround' wherein the user is directly engaged with data bodied forth in vision, sound and touch, data inhabiting a spatially definite 'virtual' world that can be interactively explored and navigated.

When the user is seated, he or she can call up on the right-hand small screen a bird's-eye view of the information field to be searched. This field is not defined by lists of descriptors, however, but by miniature pictures of the documents, maps or other items in that field. A small portion of what is on the right-hand screen is also displayed, much magnified, on the wall screen. By using the right-hand joystick, the user can guide him- or herself around the field; on the wall screen, images will appear giving the impression that he or she is passing in a helicopter-like flight over the surface, in whichever direction is desired, faster or slower according to the amount of pressure exerted on the joystick. As the 'flight' occurs, the images change on the wall and a square of light on the right-hand screen indicates where the user is. Bolt says that travel of this kind is too slow for veteran users, who can instead 'teleport' to given places instantly, simply by touching the desired spot on the right-hand screen. In searching the landscape, users need only slight visual cues, rather than detailed ones, to determine the direction they wish to take.

Sound is also a navigational aid in SDMS. Voices off become louder as the explorer approaches the associated item: a telephone rings louder and louder as the user gets closer to seeing it on the wall screen. One of the touch-sensitive pads can control its volume.

During a flight across a landscape, the user can 'descend' by zooming in on the picture displayed on the wall screen; that is to say, the picture gets more and more enlarged. He or she can zoom out too. The magnification changes in a somewhat uneven way because the data for the pictures are stored digitally, and each picture is composed of small squares, as on low resolution screens used by microcomputers. But at several stages of magnification the picture suddenly becomes clear, not 'blocky', as a consequence of the technology being employed (Bolt provides details).

Once a user had found the item he or she may peruse it in various ways depending on its nature. For example, a book can be perused on the wall screen, simulated exactly even to the pages turning over. By touching an item in the table of contents, displayed on the small left-hand screen, the user can call up a finer breakdown of that item, as well as seeing the start of the relevant page on the wall screen. Bolt denies that the intent is to give 'a nostalgic impression of the ways books used to look, like the electric fireplace with plastic back-lit logs'. Rather, he says, the page-by-page simulation is easier to read than constantly scrolling text, and the book can be readily supplemented by movies or a sound commentary.

The user can also call up pictures of various devices, including a television set and a pocket calculator. He or she can zoom in on the television set until its screen fills the wall screen and can then call up one of a stock of television programmes or switch into broadcast channels, over-air or cable. The pocket calculator can be put onto one of the small screens and used to calculate by touching appropriate keys as shown on the screen.

A further provision is for the user to control time, as it exists in the virtual world of the screen. A display on the left-hand screen must be touched in appropriate places to slow down, speed up or reverse the sequences being seen on the wall screen.

How does the SDMS work? It is a combination of computers, an optical videodisc player and other microelectronic technology. Each side of each videodisc provides one environment to explore, coded into 54,000 frames. Each frame can be manipulated electronically too, as in the zooming procedure. Using one of the demonstration videodiscs, we can see the North-eastern United States as if from a satellite, and then travel through a succession of highly realistic images to the city of Boston, where we can view, from various angles, some 200 architecturally interesting buildings in one part of the city. On another demonstration videodisc, we are invited to take a tour of the town of Aspen, Colorado. As our car moves through various streets, we 'look' forward, backward or to either side. At intersections, we decide which way to turn. If our drive is during the summer, at the touch of a button we can see the same scene in winter, when Aspen is snow-bound for several months.

SDMS may well seem to us, in the early 1980s, to be either an

expensive toy for automating what does not need to be automated or a pioneering project in higher education that explores spatiality to an extent that was impossible before new information technology. Bolt indicates that further research is in progress: for example, to make the system more aware of how the user is behaving in his or her own personal space. Can the system become aware of the direction of the user's gaze, for example, or of his or her speaking or gesturing? And if so, how should the system respond? SDMS is, in fact, at the forefront of studies of man-machine interaction and of artificial intelligence. It probably has important long-term implications for education, if only we could perceive them. Our initial reaction may be that it is dehumanising, or that it will be principally useful to trainers of secret agents. But will it eventually help to make education less mechanised, since it shows signs of being able to bridge the communication gaps created between humans by heavy use of digital modes in education? SDMS depends instead, almost entirely, on the analogic and iconic.

Another, but less dramatic, American interactive videodisc development project uses a Thomson-CSF player, an Apple II microcomputer and an HP2000 minicomputer (Sustik, 1981). On the videodisc are 1,000 black and white images of woodcuts and engravings by Albrecht Dürer and Raimondi from the Bartsch collection in London. To search the collection, users can either use the Bartsch number or select by artist, date, medium (woodcut or engraving), state (if the print was completed in stages), theme or words in the title. Series can be found as well as individual images. During a short ten-day trial in late 1980 in an American university, users were critical of the system, however, saying they could not compare two images at once (important in art history) and the image quality was poor compared with slides. Searches were sometimes slow because it was a time-sharing system and they could not be interrupted once started. For some, 1,000 images were too few. In general, art historians were antipathetic towards the technology and did not feel the money had been well spent.

An evaluation of interactive videodisc use for teaching college-level developmental biology at a university in Utah and in a community college in Texas is reported by Bunderson, Olsen and Baillio (1981). The disc itself was developed through three phases: in Phase I, film segments supplied by McGraw-Hill were incorporated within a general strategy of teaching by rule, example and practice of the rule, all on the disc and without use of a microcomputer. Phase II took a more varied approach, using a branching format (similar to branching programmed learning) that enabled students, with a microcomputer, to choose their own routes. It also showed students their score as they worked through the disc and judged their answers to questions imbedded in the teaching. In Phase III, again with a microcomputer, simulations and games were added, as well as more content, better displays of students' scores, more sophisticated answer judging, a glossary and much more complex learner-controlled branching. The videodisc taught about DNA structure and function, and about the transcription and translation phases of protein synthesis, topics commonly occurring in biology syllabuses at this level. Students took about two hours to work through the three lessons on the disc. Results of tests before and after studying showed that students (47) using the interactive videodisc learned more in less time than similar students in conventional classes, but this outcome must be treated with some caution because variables are difficult to control in such experiments. Student reaction to using the videodisc was generally rather favourable, although this particular videodisc did not present a wide variety of biology teaching strategies. The disc dealt with what is largely a theoretical aspect of biology, a fact reflected in its low film content (four sequences of a minute each) and high text content.

Computerised Information Databases

University libraries are leaders in using new information technology to assist students and researchers. For example, most North American university libraries use the services of the Online Computer Library Center, known widely as OCLC, which began its life assisting Ohio colleges and now has 2,400 participating institutions. Over 4,000 terminals in these institutions are connected by a private network of 150,000 miles of telephone lines. The central computer holds entries for more than seven million titles, attached to over 90 million locations, i.e., a title may be held by several libraries, all of which are listed. Every week, another 25,000 titles enter the system, mostly from member libraries, and 4,000 interlibrary loans are initiated within it. Many of the loans are between universities. OCLC was established to provide libraries with a centralised acquisition and cataloguing service too. It offers an excellent research tool to university scholars and researchers, including students.

Commercial computerised scientific database services such as DIALOG (provided by Lockheed) are now firmly established and essential to higher education, particularly for research but also for postgraduate teaching. The DIALOG databases, located in California, are accessible by data transmission lines, via cable and satellite, from many countries. An example at the user end: the Gray Freshwater Biological Institute of the University of Minnesota uses a computer terminal to search library and other databases and to request interlibrary loans. The Institute particularly needs up-to-date information in its field, drawing on over 1,500 journals, far more than the Institute can afford to subscribe to (VanGrasstek and Rubens, 1980).

Other countries are struggling to keep up with the American lead in computerised information databases. For example, Marx (1980) reports that the French Ministère des Universités established the Agence Universitaire de Documentation et d'Information Scientifique et Technique in 1978, to serve in particular the 50 French universities. Under this agency, twelve bibliographic databases and ten data banks have been set up, each in a different institution, usually a university. Similarly, Nayakama, Tezuka and Toyama (1980) say that the Japanese Ministry of Science, Education and Culture decided in 1979 to establish an Inter-University Science Information Network, using a number of large computers already in universities and linking these to libraries, research institutes and other university computing centres. This scheme reflects a pattern being repeated in most Western countries.

Summary

New information technology is being used by students in higher education. Courseware is improving in quality and variety, but is still inadequate in quantity. Teachers in higher education appear willing to allow students to use the technology for learning. Funds for hardware, software and courseware are generally more readily available at this level.

12 IN VOCATIONAL AND CONTINUING EDUCATION

'Vocational' education has different meanings in different contexts, but here we shall take it to mean education or training aimed particularly at fitting an adult to pursue a livelihood. 'Continuing' education is much broader, taking in education and training after first 'vocational' qualifications have been obtained.

Vocational and continuing education agencies are already taking advantage of new information technology to provide services to old and new clients. This chapter provides examples of applications based on microcomputers, interactive videodisc, videodisc, videocassette, Cyclops (audio-visual tutoring by telephone), mainframe computers, videotex, cable and open-circuit television.

Microcomputers

The widest use of microcomputers for vocational and continuing education so far is in Business Studies. Many packages are available, for various makes of microcomputer, to teach basic business practice, including accounting. Similarly, packages to teach computer programming are widely available. Specific recorded experience is difficult to locate, however, although Shotwell and Associates (1981) report that an American telephone company uses a microcomputer-based training programme to teach telephone installation. Trainees study for about 20 hours, four hours being on the (Apple) microcomputer, which simulates graphically the process of installation.

An interesting list of the advantages of using simulation in training is reported by Hollan, Stevens and Williams (1980). They point out that many of the normal physical constraints inherent in an actual plant are removed, time can be speeded up and slowed down, event sequences can be replayed, casualty procedures too dangerous to attempt in a real plant can be readily practised. Ideally, a simulation is accompanied by a computerised tutor to answer questions, provide hints and give explanations required to develop a deep understanding of the system being simulated. In their project, integration of such a tutor with a simulation is being attempted. They began by looking at how expert operators talk and reason about steam plants. These people seem to have a qualitative model in their heads, not a mathematical one, for the propulsion plant. The project will probably produce a simulation that can be taught via a microcomputer. This will lack the high fidelity of some United States Navy simulations, but it will be much cheaper and much more portable.

Interactive Videodisc

For vocational and continuing education, videodisc and micro-computer can combine powerfully, as in an example provided by Bates (1981): an interactive videodisc, entitled Flight Training, which teaches trainee pilots the landing procedures for a private light plane. Segments cover visual cues, instruments, the approach and landing. The computer shows instrument readings and asks the trainee what part of the landing he is in. To go on to the next segment the trainee has to answer correctly. Although it would take only twelve minutes to play the disc straight through, trainees are not expected to use it in that way, but to learn slowly, segment by segment. It is next best to a simulator, which is much more expensive.

Another example of trainers taking advantage of interactive videodisc technology: Hessinger (1981) reports on a new interactive optical videodisc developed by the American Heart Association to teach cardio-pulmonary resuscitation (CPR). Trainees begin by watching a doctor on the screen, who tells them about CPR with the help of stills and demonstrates the motor skills required. They answer a test at the end of the doctor's 'lesson', using a light pen to spell out words (by pointing at selected letters on the screen) instead of a keyboard. Next, trainees use a manikin to practise CPR. The manikin has sensors, wired to the microcomputer, which 'tell the doctor' whether the trainees are carrying out CPR correctly, and the doctor coaches those who make mistakes.

Videodisc

Bates (1981) also reports on a videodisc entitled A Pulmonary

Problem. Trainee doctors use it with one sound track, patients with another. Depending on their choices when answering questions about which of two procedures for treatment is correct, doctors or patients will see various segments of the video track, which will teach them how to diagnose the problem and then how to treat it, as doctor or patient.

In the same account, Bates describes a totally different training videodisc: The Missing Food Coloring, which uses very few spoken words therefore could be used even to train the deaf. The disc sets the problem, for retail store managers, of where the food colouring is in a supermarket. The trainee is offered several choices of sub-problem, then gets a choice of possible solutions to work through. If the trainee thinks the colouring is on the wrong shelf, the videodisc helps by searching all the shelves. If he or she wants to ask people in the store, these people will speak directly back, to camera. And so on. Bates said that the flow-chart behind this disc was very carefully planned to allow for many alternative routes. The general principles employed could be applied to many problem-solving situations for trainees.

Those who seek to educate themselves by using libraries may now benefit from a consortium of major international publishers of scientific information, which has a document delivery service, ADONIS, supplying on demand copies of scientific articles. The service puts onto laser-read optical videodisc more than 200,000 articles each year, and, using high-speed printing technology, supplies libraries in many countries (*Observer*, 13 February 1982).

Videocassette

An outstanding example of videocassette technology being used in this sector is provided by the Association for Media-Based Continuing Education for Engineers, a consortium of 21 universities teaching engineering, with headquarters in Atlanta, Georgia, which distributes over 500 engineering courses, particularly for continuing education, on videocassette. Most of the cassettes were recorded during lectures in one of the 21 universities, although some were recorded specially in studios. A one-hour videocassette costs the purchasing institution about $50 and must be used within a specified period.

Cyclops: Audio-visual Tutoring by Telephone

The Open University in the United Kingdom is trying out an audio-visual tutoring system, called CYCLOPS, that uses telephone lines to connect students in study centres with a tutor elsewhere (Sharples, 1982). At each study centre students have a television set linked through a special box and a modem to a telephone line. A loud-speaker telephone is connected to a second telephone line. The tutor has similar equipment. Both students and tutor may 'draw' on their screens with a light pen, and the tutor may also connect to the system an audiocassette tape-recorder. On the cassette, he or she can pre-record pictures, including ones incorporating slow motion, and sound. These audio-visual messages can be played to students during the tutorial.

Early evaluation of this teaching technique shows that, apart from any technical difficulties caused by the equipment, tutorials need to be very carefully planned. Since students cannot see each other in the various centres, nor the tutor, the usual cues for controlling conversational interchange are missing, much as they are in telephone tutorials and teleconferencing, which have been studied for some years. The first 15 minutes of a tutorial are particularly tense, says Sharples, as students try to relate to disembodied voices, but here CYCLOPS can help, because students can be encouraged to sign-in on the screen. Tutors are developing ways of overcoming the loss of facial cues. The system holds promise for widely-scattered student populations, however, and the Open University is continuing the trials.

Mainframe Computers

It is worth mentioning the somewhat patchy experience in America in using mainframe computer-assisted instruction at the community college level, where much vocational and continuing education occurs. Alderman (1980) evaluates PLATO (see Chapter 8), a computer-assisted teaching system, as it was used in community colleges in 1975–6 to teach mathematics. The lessons were written by staff, with the help of an authoring language provided with the system, and were mostly of the drill-and-practice type with some remedial teaching. The programs most used covered whole number arithmetic, decimals, algebraic expressions and other basic skills.

Staff sent groups of (adult) students to work on the computer at various times during the conventionally taught course, but the average time each student spent on the computer during an academic term was only four hours.

The evaluation indicated that these students' scores were no better than those of comparable students who had no access to the computers. Staff retained autonomy in the system, which may have influenced the amount of time students used it as well as resulting in favourable attitudes on the part of both students and staff towards it.

In a similar evaluation of the Timeshared Interactive Computer Controlled Information Television (TICCIT) system, installed for the same academic year in a different group of community colleges, Alderman states that the TICCIT mathematics lessons, produced by the Mitre Corporation, consistently employ a rule, example, practice sequence. Students were obliged to use the system for 30-40 hours per term, and those who completed the computerised course had higher scores than those taught conventionally. Many did not complete the work, however, because they made such slow progress through the computerised lessons. Students (again adults) reacted unfavourably to certain aspects because they felt they needed greater individual attention and more elaborate content explanations from teachers.

Videotex

Videotex is being used, too, although not very much, for vocational education. Gates and Maslin (1980) report an evaluation of British students' reactions to programmed learning via Prestel. The text dealt with lithographic printing techniques, in which retraining is often required. Forty students participated, being letterpress operators, students in printing schools, editorial staff and paper salesmen. The text, originally produced and tested in printed form, was modified to fit Prestel and to take advantage of Prestel's facilities such as colour graphics. Students said they enjoyed learning via Prestel, and their test results showed increased scores.

Videotex system are suitable for carrying guides to vocational training courses, as Hubbard (1981) suggests. Using the response buttons, students will be able to ask for a specimen test, to see whether they already know enough, or for teaching material to be delivered by mail. If the teaching material is in the form of computer-assisted learning programs, these programs can be delivered to students' microcomputers via the videotex system.

Cable and Open-circuit Television

Dallas County Community College District offers telecourses. These consist of series of up to 45 television tapes, accompanied by a study guide, textbook, teachers' guide, examination papers and often other materials. The television series may be leased for open- and closed-circuit broadcasting, and also for cablecasting. Under separate arrangements, they may also be purchased. Among the telecourses leased and purchased by other community college systems are courses in business education, American history, American government, earth sciences, environmental studies, English language and literature, the humanities (Instructional Television Catalog of Dallas County Community College District, 1980). Many similar examples can be quoted from the United Kingdom, the Netherlands, France, the Federal Republic of Germany, Japan, Canada and other countries that are using teaching-at-a-distance methods based partly on television (Neil, 1981; Hawkridge and Robinson, 1982).

Summary

This chapter shows that vocational and continuing education is making use of new information technology. The recorded experience to date is fragmentary and we cannot easily judge whether it has been successful, yet this sector seems likely to move rather quickly towards using more of the technology. Money for vocational and continuing education is scarce, the demand for it is increasing as jobs become obsolete more rapidly and the students are often widely scattered. The Open University's recent experience in this sector supports the view that cost-effective, decentralised training is what is needed. New information technology may have considerable potential here.

13 IN INFORMAL LEARNING BY ADULTS

The boundary is blurred between those who learn formally, by taking courses in institutions of higher, vocational or continuing education, and those who learn informally, without such support. But just as children learn informally at home, adults are learning informally at home, too, in libraries, at work or in some other place. This chapter lists examples of new information technology being used in such contexts: microcomputers, videodisc, calulators, videotex, computerised databases, cable and network television.

Microcomputers

As microcomputers penetrate the domestic market, we can expect them to be used a great deal by adults learning informally about many topics, not least computer programming. For example, according to Sternberger (1981), American owners of Apple II microcomputers can use them to learn about the stock market by linking them to a central computer. A typical owner can set up on his or her microcomputer a list of stocks and shares (whether he or she owns these or not). With the Portfolio Evaluator program, suitable for that machine, the owner can tabulate or display the figures graphically. Using a telephone network (Tymnet) to link the Apple to the Dow Jones News Retrieval Service, he or she can obtain the latest prices for these investments, thereby observing market trends. The program tells the microcomputer to signal when the price on a particular stock reaches a predetermined level at which the owner may wish to sell. The Portfolio Evaluator program cost $50 and the service costs $45 per hour in the daytime, less at night.

Another American system requiring users to own microcomputers as well as telephones is The Source, operated by Source Tele-computing Corp., based in McLean, Virginia, and now wholly owned by The Reader's Digest Association Inc. It started in June 1979 and now claims thousands of subscribers nationwide in the United States. Microcomputer owners use their telephones plus a specialised network for data transmission (Tymnet) to gain access to the computerised database in McLean. The service is not free, but users are charged local telephone rates, not long-distance, if they reside in or near any of 350 population centres served. They also pay a charge (in 1982, $4-$40 per hour depending on the time of day) for being connected to the central computer. If they wish, users may set up their own 'files' on The Source's computers, for a further fee.

What is available for learning on The Source? There are computer programs in various programming languages, business and financial services, United Press International wire service (news), the *New York Times* consumer database, an electronic mail system to other users, cheap voice messages of up to a hundred words sent anywhere in the country, database search services (including abstracts from 27 leading business journals), health and medicine information, personal financial information services, travel and leisure pursuits information, a buying service (including an electronic book-ordering service), games and educational services. The latter include teaching a child to count, tell days of the week, learn the alphabet, do simple arithmetic, learn to use the keyboard and spelling. For older children and adults there are French, German, Italian and Spanish vocabulary drills, Esperanto, algebra, geometry, social science, vocational guidance and business analysis and planning. Information available under other headings, such as science and technology, is probably of some educational value. For example, the set of programs for computing statistics may be useful in learning about statistics.

No evaluation of The Source has been published. The size of screen for the display is rather small, leading to considerable pruning of information. Highly selected information is not always useful: for example, being told the top ten books or records may well be what we do not want to be told. The costs are rather high: it is easy to spend $50 a month as a domestic user. This covers (in 1982) minimum charges of $10, plus three to four hours connected to the more comprehensive (Source*Plus) service, described above, at the cheapest time (midnight to 7am) and at the slowest speed. Use at other times of the day, or at the faster rates, is much more expensive but The Source had 11,500 subscribers in 1981 and probably has many more now.

Compuserve is a third American service, offering microcomputer owners similar information to that available on The Source: the entire text of eight major newspapers, including *The New York Times* and the *Washington Post*, sports news, weather forecasts, an encyclopedia, electronic mail, securities quotations, etc. Compuserve is owned by H.R. Block, a very large firm of tax consultants who wanted to make use of their computers during the night and at weekends. Chen (1981) says that Compuserve is now being offered over cable in the QUBE two-way system in Columbus, Ohio, and that, although the trial has only recently started, games, electronic mail and the newspapers are proving most popular among Compuserve's services.

While it is true that many adults are learning informally from microcomputers in their own homes, the People's Computer Company, using microcomputers situated in a public library in a Californian town, offers informal learning opportunities to adults every weekday afternoon and one evening a week, setting an example that other libraries may soon follow. Adults can gain computer awareness or literacy; they can find out what a computer is like to work on, with an assistant to hand if needed, and they can learn to program. They can obtain advice on buying a computer, should they decide to have one at home for their own use after experimenting on ComputerTown's. The services are free, being funded in part by the Federal Government and in part by the municipality.

Interactive Videodisc

Lachenbruch (1981) writes that at the Massachusetts Institute of Technology, the Architecture Machine Group (responsible for the Spatial Data Management System described in Chapter 11) has prepared a bicycle repair manual on optical videodisc. The videodisc player is attached to a special colour television set with a touch-sensitive screen and to a microcomputer. If the user touches any part of the bicycle shown on the screen, a moving picture shows exactly how that part works, in slow motion or speeded up. The user can zoom in or ask for more information on any part. This is a potentially very useful application, because in many training courses it is essential for trainees to understand how parts of machines work, without these machines always being available or disassembled.

Calculators

Adults need help from new information technology, according to a

British study of their mathematical literacy, yet have difficulties in using it. A sample survey carried out by Gallup on behalf of the Advisory Council for Adult and Continuing Education in 1980 found that although nine out of ten British adults interviewed in the street can do a simple addition sum without making a mistake, only seven out of ten can do correctly simple sums involving multiplication, percentages, subtraction and division or understand graphs. Needless to say, because the questions were asked on the street, hardly anyone among the interviewees used a calculator to find the answer. In a related study, based on lengthier interviews, Sewell (1981) reports that many British adults feel inhibited about using mathematics, athough some mathematical skills (estimation and approximation, for example) are widely used, often clumsily. Many were also unable or unwilling to use a calculator; on the other hand, some of limited mathematical ability considered their calculators invaluable, enabling them to function competently and confidently. Interviewees reported particularly that they have problems with percentages, ratios, graphs and charts, timetables, metric units and metric/imperial conversions. We may note in passing that all of these problem areas can be dealt with fairly well by microcomputers.

Videotex

No reports are available on domestic use of Prestel, the British videotex system, for informal learning by adults, but, in Kentucky, Green Thumb was a 1980–1 pilot project for 200 farming families (Case and others, 1981). A computerised database of information intended to be useful to the farmers and their families was stored and updated at State and County levels, and each family had free use of the system for 15 months. A family could call up information from the database by using a special adaptor (the Green Thumb Box), the telephone line and television screen. We may ask what information was available, bearing in mind that this was a service funded from public sources (State and Federal agriculture departments and the National Weather Service), not by a private company? For the farmer there are updated crop and market reports, weather forecasts (including tornado and severe warnings), data on plant diseases, entomological information, animal husbandry, pest management and horticultural guidance. For the family, 4-H (agricultural) club news and recipes for the kitchen. One local phone call obtained a maximum of 64 'pages' of text, which were temporarily stored in the Green Thumb Box, for perusal at leisure. Weather and market information were the two categories used most by farmers, but they ranked newspapers, radio and buyers as more important sources of market information than Green Thumb, and radio and television as more important sources of weather information.

Libraries are beginning to use new information technology to provide additional services to their readers, many of whom are adults learning informally. Butterworth, Keenan and Arundale (1982) report a 1981 survey of British libraries' use of new information technology. Only 32 libraries out of 203 surveyed then said they were using videotex, but another 21 were considering use, and 28 reported use of online retrieval. Convey (1981) comments on the installation, promotion and use of an online searching service in the Lancashire public library system in the United Kingdom. Following over 50 demonstrations involving in all more than 800 members of many potential user groups, the service is now part of the routine operation of the library system, with terminals located in easily accessible places in each library that has one. One-third of those using the service during its promotional period had not previously used the library system at all. Now that there is a charge for the service, usage is lower but new users are still arriving from commerce and industry, the health services, local government, and education as well as private citizens learning informally.

Cable Television

According to a report in *Channels* (vol. 1, no. 5, December 1981 – January 1982), the New York-based stock brokers, Merrill Lynch, conducted in late 1981 a nationwide investment seminar using new information technology. The seminar was televised from New York via satellite, but not on channels available to the public viewer. Instead, 17,000 viewers gathered in 30 convention halls and seminar rooms in as many centres, and possibly two million watched at home, being subscribers to certain cable systems covering about 60 population centres. The seminar was on the 1981 tax law, and included the President of the United States speaking live from the White House. Merrill Lynch participants used the company's own new studio, near Wall Street. Viewers were able to phone in questions. The journal, *Channels*, comments that here is one large corporation taking new information technology very seriously, admittedly because its customers (learners) are sophisticated and want to have the latest information quickly.

Network Television

Should we look to network television's most popular broadcasts as a source of informal learning by adults? Probably not in the US, UK and Federal Republic of Germany, although the answer depends to some extent on what we count as informal learning. A typical week's listings in September, appearing in the magazine *TV World*, shows that among the top 20 US broadcasts, only the programme 60 Minutes came close to being such a source. Among 30 top-rated British broadcasts, three documentary-style programmes on BBC2, which normally commands rather smaller audiences than BBC1, were clearly sources of informal learning, but probably no others. The German listings showed a similar pattern. Perhaps it is too much to expect network television to capture such very large audiences of informal learners, and instead we should note the success of many series aimed at this group, often combining print with television, or print with radio. In every country discussed in this book, broadcasting organisations have collaborated with educators, as in the case of TELEAC (Stichting Televisie Academie) in the Netherlands, Bayerisches Rundfunk in the Federal Republic of Germany, NHK (Nippon Hoso Kyokai) in Japan, and, of course, the BBC in the United Kingdom. From the BBC, the Computer Literacy series (described in Chapter 5) is a typical example.

Summary

New information technology is already in use by adults who want to further their education informally. This may be the sector of education in which expansion is fastest, since it does not depend very much on government funding. In terms of numbers, adults make up the largest group and many of them, particularly those who are retired from work, wish to learn informally. New information technology is waiting for adults to use it extensively for informal learning.

PART THREE: PROBLEMS AND CONSTRAINTS

Part Two provides a snapshot, with numerous examples, of new information technology being applied in formal and informal education at all levels. Evaluation of applications in the last few years is not far advanced, however, therefore many of the descriptions in Part Two are uncritical, despite being based on recorded experience.

Part Three redresses the balance, because it focuses entirely on problems and constraints. Anyone reading only Part Three might come to the gloomy conclusion that education probably will never take advantage of new information technology. Yet these problems and constraints must be faced squarely.

Part Three begins with a discussion of major educational problems (Chapter 14), then moves on to discuss social and political problems (Chapter 15), economic problems (Chapter 16) and, lastly, technical problems (Chapter 17).

14 EDUCATIONAL PROBLEMS

In education, many people whose opinions are widely respected are resolutely opposed to new information technology. They believe they have sound educational reasons for rejecting it. They think it will be bad for education. What are these reasons? Five problems that are often raised are dealt with fully in this chapter, while other chapters touch on further issues in this debate (for example, Chapters 18-20).

Problem 1: No matter how versatile the hardware technology may become, education depends on high quality software and courseware, which will not be available in sufficient quantity and variety.

Problem 2: Information technology in education will lead to over-reliance on mediated learning, as opposed to enactive learning (Olson and Bruner's terms, which are explained below).

Problem 3: Teachers will be unable and unwilling to make the necessary role-changes demanded by the introduction of new information technology into educational institutions on a large scale.

Problem 4: Information technology will increase educational elitism, widening gaps between the more and less able in schools.

Problem 5: Our formal educational systems will be fundamentally weakened in the long run by greatly increased public access to information technology outside the systems and particularly by commercial exploitation of information technology for education and training.

Quality, Quantity and Variety of Software and Courseware

Software is the term used for the programs that control computers (see Chapters 3 and 4). Courseware is a wider term, applying to all teaching materials that store information in forms that are compatible with new information technology. An example of software is the Wordstar program, prepared for use in microcomputers and with which this chapter was written and revised. Examples of courseware appear throughout Part Two, ranging from educational films and tapes broadcast over cable television to interactive videodiscs for the Spatial Data Management System and to the multimedia (print, television, radio, etc.) packages used by Open University students. The term courseware can be applied to instructional materials even when there is no formal course to be taken.

Critics of new information technology point out, with some justice, that the courseware available so far for use in the new machines is inadequate in quality, quantity and variety. Many of their criticisms can be levelled with some force against old information technology (such as textbooks), but that fact does not render these criticisms less valid.

The quality of courseware is inadequate for several reasons. First, the scope of the content is frequently misjudged. This scope is determined more by factors relating to the technology, such as memory capacity or its ability to present information in digital, analogic or iconic mode, than by careful analysis of the field of knowledge being taught or, indeed, of the previous knowledge and needs of students. Thus a videotape may teach a topic in poorly related fragments, among which important pieces are missing, or it may contain bias which goes uncorrected because to include alternative views would take too long to present, or it may take too broad (or too narrow) a view for its supposed audience. Compilers of videotapes do not focus sufficient attention on what is to be taught; instead, they concentrate on applying technical standards born in the film industry. Writers of computer courseware, many of them without training in education, still less classroom experience, devise materials that may be elegant in terms of use of computer technology but abysmal as teaching because the writers do not know the subject. Secondly, even when the scope is more or less right in educational terms, the sequence of the content is poorly conceived and unrelated to what is taught in schools and other educational institutions. We saw this criticism cropping up in Part Two in relation to microcomputer courseware, but it applies with equal force to educational information stored in videotex and teletext systems. The fact is that defining scope and sequence of content is a difficult task, as Rowntree (1981) and Melton (1982) show. It does not interest many producers of courseware, who in any case often lack the knowledge to undertake it themselves. Thirdly, the content is often quickly outdated. In many fields, new knowledge is accumulating so fast that half the content of a new course or package is out of date within five years, yet to update every five years is too expensive for most sectors of the courseware production industry, even for the textbook publishing section. Fourthly, despite the technical interests of producers, in many cases the presentation is not up to standards students have come to expect through media such as television, with the consequence that students reject the courseware as shoddy. Fifthly, the content and presentation do not take sufficient advantage of the medium (including capabilities of the hardware, such as a microcomputer), leaving teachers and learners feeling that they could have used less costly means to achieve the same ends. There is, of course, the risk that any attempts to remedy the fourth and fifth deficiencies will succeed only at some cost to the scope and sequence of the content, or to its timeliness.

The quantity is inadequate too, if we are looking for full coverage of curricula by any one medium. Even in very large projects such as PLATO (Chapters 8 and 12), the total amount of courseware available is insufficient. In many disciplines, only fragments of the syllabus can be covered through using new information technology. This is particularly true in using microcomputers, where for any single make the catalogue of courseware for a particular age-group in school is still small, covering no more than a few hours a week. Much the same can be said about television or videotapes or radio or audiotapes, despite the fact that these media are longer established. Fortunately it makes good educational sense to use a variety of courseware for different media, therefore what is not available through microcomputers may be on film or audiotape or in print. Yet the integration of courseware for these different media is weak or non-existent. Teachers and students must make their own connections.

Lastly, the variety of courseware available is inadequate. The present diversity of providers, mostly commercial companies, makes for technical incompatibility, one source of complaint. But the principal complaint from educators is about the lack of sufficient variety of courseware to meet individual learners' needs, whether perceived by teachers or learners themselves. If there is only one courseware package on macroeconomics for use on Apple microcomputers, for instance, that is very restrictive, as it gives access to only one view of macroeconomics. Similarly, fast learners are usually obliged to use the same courseware as slow learners, because producers provide for the middle of the ability range to maximise sales. The textbook publishing industry has faced up to such problems, but producers for the new information technology have not, by and large.

These criticisms are rife among teachers, at all levels. Their edge is sharpened today by common knowledge of the fact that teachers and students are partly, sometimes totally, excluded from courseware production processes. Outside the United Kingdom it is particularly noticeable that television and radio broadcasts, films, videotapes and videodiscs for education are often made by people with different training and values (see Hawkridge and Robinson, 1982). Courseware for mainframe computers comes from consortia of psychologists, teachers, computer scientists and others, based in universities or companies (for-profit and not-for-profit). Courseware for microcomputers comes in part from individual teachers (and occasionally students), working on their own or in small teams, particularly in universities, and in part from commercial software companies. Within the United Kingdom, teachers have been drawn into courseware production more extensively, for example, through the Schools Council projects.

Teachers also question the quality of courseware because they are out of sympathy with some of the dominant pedagogical models being used in its production. This is particularly true for courseware produced for computers. Teachers dislike the 'programmed learning' model underlying many computer-based packages, with good reason. The packages are frequently mechanistic drill-and-practice routines ostensibly employing Skinnerian operant conditioning. Students find them boring. Teachers challenge their validity in educational terms.

Even packages that are more tutor-like do not appeal to many teachers, because they suffer from the same disadvantages as 'branching' programmed learning texts: the diagnostic tests that lead to branching are poorly designed, the branches are not necessarily those that students need to take to increase their understanding, and the programs are far from 'student-proof'. Burton and Brown (1979) discuss some limitations of computerised tutoring systems. Such systems may be able to guide students' discovery learning, if they can be made robust (in the sense of not breaking down intellectually!), friendly and intelligent enough. But Burton and Brown agree that tutoring requires greater subtlety than has yet been achieved. What is needed in, say, an educational game is enough tutoring to (i) stop students from forming grossly incorrect models of the underlying structure, (ii) help them to see the limits of their strategies, and (iii) help them to discover the causes of their errors. The computerised tutor must know when to intervene and what to say. Clearly the computer must be programmed in such a way that it 'knows' a good deal about the individual students whom it tutors. It must know what students already know about the domain of knowledge underlying the program; this implies some sort of diagnostic procedure that goes on while each student is playing. Ideally, it must also know how students form abstractions related to the game, how they learn and when they are likely to be most receptive to advice. Programming a computer to know all this requires theory yet to be developed.

Artificial intelligence, the science of making machines do what would require intelligence if done by men, according to O'Shea and Self (1982), may provide some of this theory. As these researchers point out, 'artificial intelligence programs are often involved with processes such as remembering and accessing relevant knowledge; using this knowledge appropriately (for example to reason and to form plans of action); revising and extending their knowledge; searching in some more or less systematic way for a solution to a problem; recognising similarities and drawing analogies between things, and attempting to understand some aspect of their surroundings, for example, something communicated to them, perhaps in English'. All of these processes are relevant to tutoring, as O'Shea and Self explain through the example of MYCIN, a program that performs medical diagnosis of bacterial infections in the blood and suggests appropriate treatment. Such programs are mere prototypes, however, very expensive to develop, and very few are yet available.

Lesgold (1981) proposes four categories of computer-assisted learning that will exploit the technology in various ways. In doing so, he also identifies a number of constraints.

(1) Programmed Learning: As noted above, techniques employed in programmed instruction are used now in computer-assisted learning. The authoring languages, often specific to particular computers, are unsuitable for designing novel teaching uses of the computer. For example, it is difficult to add 'sophisticated hint or tutorial systems', says Lesgold, although improvements could be made using more elaborate technology: a graphics package such as TELL-a-GRAF shows a large variety of type fonts and sizes, can

colour or shade regions in many different ways and can be used by a courseware author without too much training in its operation. It does require considerable computing power, however, beyond the present resources of most educational establishments. Even where computer-based systems are built to prompt authors (usually by organising in some way the steps authors need to take in designing instruction), these systems must operate unobtrusively. If they respond slowly or are difficult to understand, authors simply stop using them.

(2) Educational Games: Programmed learning does not put students in charge of their learning as much as educational games do. Authors of these games have two aims: to provide practice of skills, in a form that motivates students to practice, and to motivate exploration leading to discovery of principles. A repertoire of motivating 'special effects', visual and aural, possibly similar to those used in machines in amusement arcades, can be provided as part of the stock-in-trade of an author's computerised workstation. Noises, flashing lights and other visual effects may be added to the game, although they increase its cost. Similarly, a 'Hall of Fame' can be added, being a list of the highest scorers so far among players of the game. Lesgold recognises, however, that authors of games are seldom working in heavily capitalised laboratories; more often they are classroom teachers with very limited facilities and with little hope of obtaining a better 'authoring environment'.

(3) Tutorial and Coaching Systems: In these, a 'tutor' monitors the interaction between students and the rest of the system, and decides when and how to intervene. At a primitive level, such systems contain what Lesgold calls 'canned hints' which appear when students press the HELP button. Often these hints are not particularly helpful, since they are entered in standard form and may be quite irrelevant to the problem being experienced. More intelligent tutoring requires considerably greater complexity, as we noted above. In many games, for example, a hint is only appropriate if the system knows what the student is doing, can identify optimal moves and can decide what to do to improve the student's performance. The system must diagnose and decide, before it advises. Work in the field of artificial intelligence holds out some hope that systems with these capabilities can be designed (see, for example, O'Shea, 1981),

but clearly they are at present out of reach for the average teacher who wants to prepare some courseware.

(4) Computer as Laboratory: Here the computer offers an environment in which students can freely engage in many different activities, under tutorial guidance. Lesgold speaks of 'open-ended environments', although in fact there are limits to what can be done within each. He identifies BASIC, LOGO and Smalltalk (see Chapter 3) as the programming languages authors use in establishing such environments. BASIC, he says, is not up to the standard of modern microcomputers, which offer more memory and speed than the systems for which BASIC was written. BASIC is not very suitable for preparing teaching programs, yet hundreds of teachers are writing programs in this language. These teachers are likely to resist introduction of newer and better languages. By contrast, LOGO is a language oriented towards children's learning, although it is designed to be written by adults. It is available for use with only three makes of microcomputer, says Lesgold, compared with BASIC's ubiquity. Smalltalk was originally a language for teaching children about computers, but it is being transformed into 'a system to serve the creative spirit' (according to one of its designers) and therefore entirely comprehensible to that individual. In practical terms, however, Smalltalk is unavailable as yet, being still within Xerox's research laboratory, and Lesgold points out that it is not, as it stands, very accessible to children or even to adult authors.

Lesgold envisages two other general constraints and suggests ways in which computers themselves might be employed to overcome them. First, sceptics (parents, teachers, administrators) will want to know what is going on as a student sits learning from a computer. The computer might provide, on request, a layman's explanation. Secondly, researchers will want to know what is going on, too, in order to test learning theories and develop new models of learning, but they will be faced with an almost impossible task of dealing with very large amounts of data resulting from the interactions. The computer might operate as research assistant, collecting, collating, analysing and interpreting the data.

Finally, Lesgold identifies forces militating against standardisation of authoring languages. He regards some standardisation as probably desirable but not urgent:

The capital investment required to produce low-grade software for instruction is currently extremely low. There are many cases of people buying microcomputer systems for a few thousand dollars and using them to develop and even to reproduce and distribute instructional software. Such users will not be pleased with . . . standardisation that might, for example, remove their low overhead by requiring use of a language that can only be compiled on expensive hardware. Larger producers may prefer such a language precisely because it will drive out cheaper software.

Lesgold goes on to note that copyright, patent and trade secret laws (in the United States) offer little protection to authors' rights, therefore commercially-produced software often contains features that limit its portability, thus hindering standardisation still further.

It is clear that designing, developing, testing, producing and distributing high quality courseware is difficult and expensive. Before new information technology came over the horizon, experience gained in several North American and European countries in preparing teaching materials for new secondary school curricula showed how difficult and costly these processes can be. Similarly, mainframe computer-assisted learning projects in the 1960s and 1970s indicated that one hour's worth of high quality courseware could be produced only at a cost far above what was first estimated, and that this courseware was both ephemeral and non-transferable to other systems. Clearly, large sums of money and expertise will be required to match the technical capabilities of new information technology with high quality courseware. The millions spent so far have not been enough.

So cynics say, reasonably enough, that suitable courseware does not yet exist for microcomputers. Without suitable courseware, they say, the hardware is almost useless. But what standards are being applied to microcomputer courseware? That question is addressed in America by the *Journal of Courseware Review,* published by the Foundation for the Advancement of Computer-Aided Education in California. The Foundation was set up in 1981 as a non-profit corporation with the support of several microcomputer manufacturers. Its predecessor was the Apple Foundation, which came into being in 1979 perhaps because one of the principal microcomputer manufacturers, Apple, realising that it would be difficult to sell hardware to schools without suitable courseware, launched it to promote development of high quality programs. The Foundation, in response to suitable proposals, makes grants of cash or equipment to American educational institutions interested in writing programs. By July 1981, grants had been awarded in the fields of art education, business education, computer literacy, engineering, foreign languages, health and medical sciences, history, library science, mathematics, music, reading and spelling, science and special education.

In the first issue of the journal, Hakansson (1981), designer of the computer hall at Sesame Place (see Chapter 7), suggests that we should judge microcomputer courseware as we would any other educational material, but with several additional criteria. The programs must run, that is to say, they must work from beginning to end. They must be easy to use, prompting the user when difficulties occur. The content must be educationally sound, no matter how fascinating the hardware or the presentation. To be educationally sound, says Hakansson, the programs must have appropriate goals, be matched to the age-group that will use them, do their job at least as well as other media (print, television, etc.) could, and be interesting. The programs must also be well enough designed that the student is in charge, not the machine. This means, for example, that the pace must be adapted to the student. Finally, the programs should use the capabilities of the computer in such a way that text, graphics and sound support each other in teaching. These criteria seem eminently sensible but more general than the guidelines published recently by the National Council of Teachers of Mathematics (Heck, Johnson and Kansky, 1981) and not as practical as the first information guide produced by the British Microelectronics Education Programme (Jones, 1982), which is full of advice for primary schools intending to use microcomputers.

Another new American journal serving a similar purpose is entitled *School Microware Reviews*. Merrill (1982), commenting on the first edition, which was limited to courseware for four American microcomputers, says it offers rather short but good-quality reviews.

For the United Kingdom, Hartley (1981) underlines some of the lessons learned from the British National Development Programme in Computer Assisted Learning. He says that the role of computers should result from analysis of teaching and learning situations, particularly where other methods are not succeeding, not from use of programs to cover topics chosen almost at random from the curriculum, and he advocates that computers should be used in various ways as appropriate (adaptive tutoring, simulation, databases, question banks, problem-solving, etc.).

Hartley also notes the 'woeful lack of published experience and programs of quality'. A Leeds-based project funded by the Social Science Research Council in 1980–1 asked which programs caught teachers' attention, which did not and why? What programs were used and how were they used? What influenced the teachers' decisions and what were the effects on classroom activities and learning? For the project, programs were obtained from many sources and microcomputers were made available. The findings showed that initial enthusiasm was dampened when teachers saw the programs, which were considered not central to the curriculum, too time-consuming for use within the time scheduled for the subject or in need of amendment before they would be suitable. How did teachers organise their classes with microcomputers to hand? Typically, they split the class in two: one half would work without computers on a related topic, while the other half shared three or even six microcomputers. Teachers had to work very hard answering questions encouraged or caused by the programs. As Hartley says, teachers are often unaware of how unambitious programs are in the questions or tasks they put to students.

Brahan and Godfrey (1981) compare courseware for computer-based learning and on videotex. They suggest that the former started, in the 1950s, by using frames like programmed learning, but then expanded to act as tutor, exerciser, simulator, calculator, mediator, manager, information source or some combination of these roles. Since courseware costs are high, possibly videotex offers a cheaper alternative, since it was conceived for mass markets. It is designed to provide selective access to information, unlike computer-assisted learning. Videotex systems, however, usually have only a keypad, not a keyboard, thus limiting user inputs. More important than that, the structure of the videotex database is unsuitable for education. It would be more useful if it would permit different user views, through a mapping of data and their relationships according to individual user requirements. Videotex would have to be upgraded for education; this may be more feasible on a system like Telidon with good graphics. Thompson's (1981a) findings from the trial of Prestel (videotex) in a few British schools confirm this: he says that up-to-date information, often cited as a feature of Prestel, is not required for many subjects, since often principles are being taught rather than current states. As a general information source, Prestel is inadequate compared with other sources, mainly because its information is incomplete, e.g., the British Rail timetable book is complete, but Prestel's rail information is selected. Prestel's indexing system is hard to use and students cannot easily retrace their steps to information once found unless they have noted the 'page' number (this may be true of other media, but the large database is daunting on Prestel). Teachers feel it takes too long to get to know the database and appreciate its uses, and they do not adopt Prestel for their own teaching unless they have had a good introduction, but to provide this introduction is costly.

Over-dependence on Mediated Learning

The second fundamental problem perceived by many educators is that we simply do not know enough about the interrelationships of learning from different media. Perhaps this concern only reveals that written and spoken communication, the old forms, are still the ones in education that are rewarded most, as Ahl (1977) suggests, but at a practical level it reveals itself in demands for studies like one now being conducted jointly by Stanford University in California and the Hebrew University in Jerusalem, to examine the impact of television on reading development over a period of three years. The results will be known in 1983–4.

At a theoretical level, the possibility of over-dependence on mediated learning is underlined by two American scholars, Olson and Bruner (1974). They draw distinctions between learning through direct experience (enactive learning) and learning through media (mediated learning), which they believe are substantially different, with different potential roles in the intellectual development and acculturation of children. They assert that school experiences largely comprise of learning out of context and through media that employ symbols. At its most naïve, the underlying psychology of schools holds that knowledge equals words, and words can be told, therefore children can acquire knowledge from being told. Teachers know. Children do not and must be told.

Such a naïve view may be held in its entirety by very few teachers, but Olson and Bruner say that there has been 'a certain blindness to the effects of the medium of instruction as opposed to the content . . . and . . . a de-emphasis of and a restricted conception of the nature and development of ability'.

Direct experience provides information about the world and about the activity by which that information is gained. The former counts as knowledge, the latter as skill, or ability. Mediated experience does the same, say Olson and Bruner, but the skill acquired is in using the medium, not in carrying out the unmediated activity. For example, by living in a country one can directly experience what it is like to walk its streets, hear its language or see its beauty spots. To learn about the same country through viewing films, listening to tapes or reading books is clearly not the same kind of experience. It is vicarious or mediated.

Olson and Bruner do not suggest that education should do without mediated experience. Humans rely on symbolically coded experience, and literacy and numeracy are cornerstones of formal schooling. Rather, 'different forms of experience converge as to the knowledge they specify, but they diverge as to the skills they develop'.

In an earlier publication, Bruner, Olver and Greenfield (1966) propose three modes of experience: enactive (direct), iconic (related to models) and symbolic (words, numbers and other symbol systems). Their use of the terms iconic and symbolic is slightly different from the definitions offered in Chapter 3, but is exemplified when Olson and Bruner point out that, 'You may learn that the stove is hot by touching it, by seeing someone recoil from touching it and by being told that it is hot.' In the first, the teacher provides direct experience, in the second, a model, and in the third, tells (provides facts, descriptions and explanations). Teaching through direct experience, by observation or by symbols requires varying roles of the teacher.

Within each mode different learning experiences demand different codes, too. Thus within the symbolic mode, various media employ various codes. For example, production codes used in television are not the same as written codes used in print. A producer will zoom in to catch a slight expression on a speaker's face, thereby signalling to the viewer the importance of catching that expression. A printer will use italics for emphasis. Knowledge is constantly being reorganised, say Olson and Bruner, and translated into symbol systems (see Salomon, 1979, for a full discussion of symbol systems in various media).

Olson and Bruner's views are further explained by their tabulation of relationships between cognitive development, categories of information-obtaining behaviour and what they call 'technological realisations'.

Figure 14.1: Acquisition of Knowledge and Skills Through Different Kinds of Experience

```
COGNITIVE DEVELOPMENT    │ CATEGORIES OF BEHAVIOUR    │ TECHNOLOGICAL
                         │ FROM WHICH INFORMATION     │ REALISATIONS
knowledge │ Skills       │ MAY BE EXTRACTED           │
----------│--------------│----------------------------│------------
                                          Direct      │
  chair     sitting      Contingent    <              │
    ¦       drawing       experience      \           │ -Laboratory
    ¦       describing                     Directed   │  experiments
    ¦          ¦                           (instructional) -Simulations
    ¦          ¦                                       │ -Educational
  objects   locomotive                                │  games & toys

  events    prehensive                  Observation   │ -Films & ani-
                                          /           │   mation
  space     linguistic   Observational  /             │
                          learning                    │
  time      mathematical              \               │
                                        Modelling     │ -Demonstra-
  causality iconological              (instruction)   │  tion

                                      Communication   │ -Print
                                       /              │ -Drawings
                          Symbolic    <               │ -Models
                          learning     \              │ -Graphs
                                        Instruction   │ -Maps
----------│--------------│----------------------------│------------
```

Source: Adapted from Olson and Bruner, 1974, and reproduced by permission.

Figure 14.1 shows, on the right, some of the media considered by Olson and Bruner to be roughly appropriate to each of the modes of experience. They suggest that laboratory experiments, simulations and educational toys are all suitable for simplifying direct experience for children. Observational learning, based perhaps on demonstrations, can be easily provided by technological media, which can highlight critical points, slow down the motion (or even stop it), and so on. Yet nobody learns to ride a bicycle by watching a film: everyone has to get onto the saddle and try it.

We may well ask whether the new information technology eases the task of teachers in bringing to life in the classroom the ideas of our culture. Finzer (1981), in writing about microcomputers, notes the gap between the image in the teacher's mind and the image on the screen. In a typical primary school classroom, he says, the cupboards are full of 'tools for teaching', such as paper, pens, chalk, calculators, Cuisenaire rods, flash cards, books and so on. A teacher will go to the cupboard to obtain some of these objects for use in a lesson. But when a teacher wants to put a lesson on the screen of a microcomputer, there is no similar cupboard readily available. Instead, he or she may have to explain what is to be taught to somebody else, probably a computer programmer, and has to make do with a very limited knowledge of how the computer can actually help children to learn that set of concepts and skills. The computer programmer, on the other hand, lacks a full understanding of what is to be taught.

This gap between the image in the teacher's mind and the image on the screen determines, in part, the quality of programs available for children. When it comes to learning, most of these programs are inferior, says Finzer bluntly, to printed material, films, manipulative materials and investigations of the real world.

What is needed to close this gap? What should be inside the computer cupboard? He suggests there should be easily identifiable simulated objects for use in teaching. Manipulation of these objects should occur graphically on the screen, with no intervening codes of letters or other symbols, and it should be easy to see the immediate effects of manipulation.

Papert (1980) has no patience with those who fear the influence of computers in education. He says, 'The computer is the Proteus of machines. Its essence is its universality, its power to simulate. Because it can take on a thousand forms and can serve a thousand functions, it can appeal to a thousand tastes.' He asserts that we must rid ourselves of current notions of computers if we are to make full use of them educationally. At present, the computer is being used to program the child. Papert has a vision of the child programming the computer and in doing so acquiring 'a sense of mastery over a piece of the most modern and powerful technology' as well as establishing 'an intimate contact with some of the deepest ideas from science, from mathematics and from the art of intellectual model building'.

Although in Olson and Bruner's terms a child using one of Papert's computers would be experiencing mediated learning, Papert seems to see it as enactive experience:

It is possible to design computers so that learning to communicate with them can be a natural process, more like learning French by living in France . . . learning to communicate with a computer may change the way other learning takes place. The computer can be a mathematics-speaking and an alphabetic-speaking entity. We are learning how to make computers with which children love to communicate. When this communication occurs, children learn mathematics as a living language. Moreover, mathematical communication and alphabetic communication are thereby both transformed from the alien and difficult things they are for most children into natural and easy ones.

Papert speaks of the QWERTY phenomenon. The first form of the new technology tends to have a momentum beyond what is justified by the quality of its design. QWERTY layouts should have been discarded long ago, he says, and he cites BASIC as an example of the same phenomenon. BASIC is not a language suited to educational purposes, as we know: it employs too small a vocabulary in its effort to be simple, but Papert argues that a larger vocabulary, capable of fuller expression, is what children should learn. BASIC actually suffers from having rather an elaborate programming structure, so that only the brightest and most motivated children and teachers continue to use it.

Other American scholars express different concerns: Pelton (1981) thinks that information technology may separate education from nature (not that he defines nature), and remove from schools their present socialising function. Postman (1979) believes that television damages children's ability to think clearly and robs them of a normal childhood. He considers that in American children there has been a shortening of their attention span, erosion of their linguistic powers and of their ability to handle mathematical symbols, and increasing impatience with deferred gratification. He quotes some figures: between 6 and 18 years of age the average American child spends roughly 15,000 to 16,000 hours in front of a television set, whereas school probably consumes no more than 13,000 hours. He says that television is having a homogenising effect on society, reducing differences between children and adults, whether in language, interests, dress and amusements. Television communicates the same information to everyone, he argues, regardless of age, sex, levels of education or life experience. Schramm (1981) wonders whether television is encouraging a taste for information rather than a taste for knowledge (see Chapter 1 for the distinction between information and knowledge), and whether people are using it to get the latest 'word' rather than the deepest explanation. It is hardly surprising that the United States government is asking questions such as: 'Is the present hardware suitable for application to education? How does technology when introduced change the curriculum? Can technology provide teaching beyond the classroom teacher's capacity?'

Teachers' Role-changes

The third problem is again bound up with teachers' attitudes rather than those of parents or the general public, yet it is a problem common to many fields of innovation. Teachers' unwillingness or inability to change roles when new information technology is introduced is paralleled by similar attitudes among industrial workers, office staff, farmers, priests and many others. The general problem has been widely studied by scholars in communication and sociology (for example, Chin and Benne, 1969; Havelock, 1971; House, 1974; Rogers, Eveland and Bean, 1976).

Teachers have roles as providers of knowledge, diagnosticians, tutors, judges of achievement, disciplinarians and so on. While the roles for an individual teacher vary according to the level at which he or she teaches and the way in which teaching is organised, that teacher is normally expected to be in control, not the students. New information technology may change that situation, putting students in control and asking new roles of teachers as technicians, selectors of courseware, individualisers of instruction, managers, schedulers and advisers.

For example, Maddison (1981) writes about the problems of using a microcomputer in class teaching in schools. He points out that most schools will have only one computer, at least in the near future. Although this can be linked to a large monitor for all the class to see, the computer's unique ability to interact with students may not easily be deployed under this arrangement. On the other hand, the teacher-class relationship may be temporarily transformed into a teacher-class-computer triangle, with the teacher freed for the moment from the role of judge of students' performance. Or the computer may provide additional examples, diagrams, or other source material, all summoned more or less instantly.

There are practical difficulties, as Maddison says, such as scheduling use of the school microcomputer, moving it or the class around, protecting students against accidents with trailing wires, placing the monitor where it does not obstruct other facilities, such as the blackboard, yet where it can be seen and read. Teachers must add to these problems the delays that occur in changing programs, especially those on cassettes, and the fact that often whole lessons or series of lessons can be jeopardised by having computerised learning as an integral part, should something go wrong.

Maddison's comments have a ring of reality about them: teachers could be in for a rough time while wrestling with a microcomputer, cassette player and separate television monitor. If the class of 30 teenagers decides to be unruly too, a teacher trying the microcomputer for the first time could be put off permanently. Why bother to make the role changes? Is the new information technology worth so much extra effort in the context of class teaching? Why not leave it to the boffins?

American experience in this respect may differ from British. Levin and Kareev (1980) report, 'The most striking observation was that the introduction of the computer into the classroom *did not* disrupt the other classroom activities.' They note that the teacher explained the computer to the (fourth grade) children on the first day, then it was placed in a corner, with a list of most frequently used commands attached to it, and it became one activity out of many to which children were assigned during the school day, usually in pairs. The children showed no signs of 'computer anxiety' and the teacher was willing to leave them to regulate their own activity on it. Within a few days they were reserving times on a list they maintained themselves for the teacher, and changed places at the computer without being told.

Increased Educational Elitism

Some educators see a danger of new information technology leading to a new form of educational elitism. They say that some children, but not the majority, will gain computer literacy and take advantage of whatever becomes available to them through the technology. Evans (1981), a British expert on computers, acknowledges that the danger exists. Some children take to computers for sheer pleasure, exploring them endlessly, he says. Groups of such children emerge in schools that possess microcomputers, and they often become expert programmers. As teaching computers appear in large numbers, there may grow up an elite of children who feast on what these machines can provide, outstripping quickly the other children. Is the only precaution against this danger likely to be that governments will try to provide teaching computers for every child, thus offering equal educational opportunity? Evans thinks that children who have found learning difficult may be helped by the 'lucid, non-patronising and endlessly patient' machines, but the danger does exist that a new elite will be rapidly created. It is a social and political question (see Chapter 15) whether schools should aim to offer the best to as many children as possible, even if all cannot benefit equally.

Weakened Public Educational Systems

Concern about elitism is linked to concern about the potential of new information technology to weaken public educational systems. There are two groups of critics here. The first, perhaps with an eye cast at what is happening to public broadcasting systems, note that new information technology is expensive, perhaps too expensive for public educational systems to adopt on a massive scale. They assume that commercial interests will set up private educational establishments, not necessarily run on the same lines as conventional schools or colleges, to offer technology-mediated education to those willing to pay, thus creaming off substantial numbers of able students from the public system and reducing political and financial support for that system. They note the problems faced by local education authorities in major American cities, such as New York, where middle-class parents have opted out of many schools in the public system. They foresee the possible demise of the public system following taxpayers' revolts and a decline in student numbers, and predict that new information technology will accelerate this demise.

The second group of critics believe that new information technology will be cheap and will so increase opportunities for learning, whether for general education or for vocational training, that existing educational systems will be irreparably damaged, even rendered obsolete. Learning will be moved, to a far greater extent than at present, from schools and colleges to homes and places of work. Face-to-face instruction will become a rarity, they say, and that will be bad for education, for reasons explored above. Just as critics of information technology in industry fear displacement of traditional industrial institutions, so these critics fear displacement of traditional educational institutions. Public education may become a ghetto of some kind, poverty-stricken and without the capital investment in new information technology that the private sector can afford.

Summary

In this chapter we have looked at five fundamental problems in taking advantage of new information technology for education. They are not the only ones. The first two (production of courseware and the balance between direct and mediated learning) are in particular commanding the attention of researchers. The problem of teachers' role changes is an old one receiving insufficient attention from teachers themselves, or from politicians, researchers or administrators, despite the fact that changes in teaching and learning in the medium and long term depend on recognition of the need for and training in role changes. The last two problems (new elitism and weakened public educational systems) are of substantial interest to only a few researchers and politicians, and unfortunately are dismissed by many as scaremongering and speculation. Chapters 19 and 20 return to some of these issues.

15 SOCIAL AND POLITICAL PROBLEMS

Educational systems exist within social and political systems. Commercial bias is inherent in new information technology, which is also bound up with national prestige, but people are generally ambivalent towards technological innovation. There is a tendency for inequities to be increased rather than reduced by the technology, for the 'communication effects gap' to be widened. These problems occupy the first half of this chapter.

The second half of the chapter looks at problems more specifically related to applications of the technology in education. Public versus private sponsorship and control is a vital issue here, but there are other social and political problems apparently inherent in the technology when it is used in education, such as the fact that younger learners more easily adapt to it than older learners.

Commercial Bias

New information technology, for the time being, is more a phenomenon of capitalist economies than of 'centrally planned economies', such as those of Eastern Europe. There are signs that the latter will be forced to enter the race, probably on unfavourable terms as they will be to some extent dependent on capitalist companies. But at present new information technology carries with it the social and political values of commercial sectors in those countries where it is being developed and introduced. New information technology is a vehicle for commercial profit, sometimes very substantial profit. For instance, capital invested in some cable television systems in North America has yielded a first-year return of 100 per cent.

Schiller (1981) reinforces this point, saying that, in the United States, the most important information industries other than education are those involved in acquisition, transfer and protection of property, such as banking, credit, brokerage, insurance, accounting, legal services and advertising. 'The onrush of computerisation in general in the United States is inextricably tied to the kind of economic and social activities generated overall by the economy . . . the dynamics of the system compel the introduction of advanced electronic calculation . . . What is at issue is the systemic development and utilisation of computer power to facilitate an economic order which is inherently exploitative and wasteful of human and natural resources, domestically and internationally. This order, at the same time, possesses tremendous power and is remarkably capable of attracting and pulling other countries and peoples into the orbit of its operations.'

Schiller also believes that an international three-cornered fight for new information technology markets is going on between the United States, Japan and Western Europe, with the United States dominant. The final outcome is of course unclear, with Japan recently declaring as its national goal a doubling of its share of the market by 1990, but Schiller predicts that dependency on American technology and expertise is likely to increase worldwide, resulting in greater fragility and instability in individual nation's economic systems. (The Third World's fears are expressed by Mankekar (1981), who notes that the New Information Order, portrayed in the report of the International Commission for the Study of Communication Problems (1981), is likely to penalise Third World countries.)

Arnold (1981) argues from a similar point of view in criticising the British videotex system, Prestel, which he thinks is unlikely to benefit private individuals. Prestel, he says, depends on cooperation between organisations operating in different markets, on different timescales, with differing resources and different goals. The Post Office was faced with the problem that in 1978 domestic subscribers averaged one and a half calls per day, thus not providing much revenue, yet capital investment was required at the then rate of £900 million per annum. Prestel was originally seen as having potential for increasing revenue from domestic users in hours when the system was not heavily loaded, but equipment manufacturers do not have a great interest in Prestel because it is merely a sideline.

Do consumers have an interest? Arnold says that the Post Office hoped that demand would expand in proportion to the effort expended, but recent market research indicates that only a quarter of the consumers in subsidised trials are likely to keep their sets afterwards, compared with 54 per cent of business users, and 30 per cent of connections are to the Post Office and firms in the television industry. Arnold's view is that Prestel sets are too expensive for domestic users to buy, let alone run, although adaptors at cheaper prices may bring down the price of sets through competition. Rental companies are beginning to offer special packages, but these are more likely to include videocassette recorders and teletext than Prestel, which is still relatively expensive. Arnold thinks that consumers do not have a use for text services. Prestel costs much more to get than teletext, which is free once you have the adaptor or modified set, even if the information is much more limited. Prestel is a typical case of technology push rather than market pull. Prestel is a Concorde, which brings us to the problem of national prestige.

National Prestige

National prestige is at stake in the field of new information technology. This is particularly true in France, according to Hutin (1981), where the image of French technology would be greatly enhanced by an economic revival led by information technology, particularly in the face of international competition. Such a revival is not guaranteed, however, because although technological advance is likely, use of this technology is in doubt. As a national priority, France is more than doubling the number of telephone lines in four years, from 6 to 14 million, and by 1992 the number should be 34 million. Telecommunications will be taking four per cent of all national investment, a vast amount when compared with investment sums going into the daily press (less than 0.3 per cent). It is likely, Hutin believes, that the money will not be well used and that it will produce gross imbalances within the country. He does not see this investment as being on behalf of the people but to please the administration. It will be controlled by technocrats and businessmen, not by ordinary people. The databanks, particularly American-owned ones, will not store what is not profitable to sell. Information will become mere merchandise. People will become alienated by working from screens rather than paper, and the press will be damaged beyond repair. Simon (1981) presents a less pessimistic view, stressing the potential benefits of the new technology, but there is no doubt that French national prestige is at stake.

Similar comments can be made about other Western countries, not least the United Kingdom. While national prestige may be a force for good or ill, in the context of new information technology there is certainly a danger that development will be pushed out of balance to preserve national prestige, at least in the short run. This has happened in other fields, such as aeronautics, where less was at stake and where the scope of development was smaller. New information technology systems are massive and require very large capital investment, therefore they soon acquire momentum and grandeur. They cannot easily be allowed to fail.

Ambivalence Towards Technological Innovation

This book is not the right place for a treatise on the phenomenal ambivalence of humans towards technology, but we cannot ignore the fact that this ambivalence exists and is shared by those concerned with new information technology in education. Its roots are deep in our history. One recent example will suffice to show how strong it remains. Donahue (1980), in an article that concludes by saying we must embrace technology, points out that technology has brought us 1,100 known carcinogens for workers to die from. In the hands of some companies, it creates stress at work, puts people out of jobs, disrupts the workforce and wreaks havoc in individuals' lives, yet we are being told we must use it to survive.

The 'Communications Effects Gap'

This term, coined by Tichenor and others (1970), refers to the gap between those who possess knowledge and those who do not, a gap which is widened, according to Tichenor and his colleagues, by the effects of mass communications. This hypothesis has not yet gained strong support from field studies, possibly because of the difficulties of conducting such studies. Others argue that mass communications can close the gap because new information media take less processing skill than books, magazines and newspapers. But use of all information media is intercorrelated and the most active users of each new information medium tend to be the active users of previous information media, as we definitely know from the field studies. The 'Matthew Effect' is prevalent: to them that hath shall be given. We cannot say firmly that radio and television have narrowed the gap. Information-poor people seem, on the whole, to choose not to hear or see information broadcasts. The information-rich do so. Public funds spent on videotex or any other new information technology should increase social equity, not reduce it, yet videotex in its present forms offers little hope for narrowing the gap, since it requires not only literacy but also new skills that combine reading with some understanding of computer-stored information files. The fascination that computer games hold for all is the only contrary evidence, but it is not convincing.

Schiller (1981) notes pessimistically that:

The justification of the new communication technology rests heavily on its promise to reduce inequalities and extend educational, cultural and human opportunities, locally and internationally. The institutional arrangements that are being established, however, work toward an altogether different outcome. Under the stimulus of market criteria, the new information technologies . . . wind up facilitating the activities and extending the influence of the already-dominant elements in the social order . . . the practice of treating information as a commodity . . . promises to exacerbate old inequities in new ways.

There is no such thing, according to Schiller, as a 'bountiful and benign information system'.

Evans (1981) has much more positive views on the general effects on political and social life of the microelectronic revolution. He sees, among many things, an end to wars, poverty, crime and ignorance.

Schramm (1981) takes the line that

Individuals are going to have more control than before over the information that flows around them . . . more power to call for the information . . . they need . . . to maintain communication with individuals elsewhere . . . to make use of files and databanks and libraries . . . more individual control over information resources no longer far away, no longer restricted from their use.

Hoggart (1982) asserts that new technology in Britain will do little or nothing to break down the class structure, and points out that specialist journals for the meritocracies, 'each with its own filtered and angled approach to its treatment of more general issues' are part of a subterranean trend that favours the meritocrats. But Bowes (1980) advances ten positive suggestions for making the machines more friendly, thus possibly enabling the information-poor to catch up:

(1) Make the machines look like things we already know, such as typewriters.
(2) Break down into small easy steps the complex decisions required in searching for and selecting information.
(3) Use several sensory channels, e.g., audio, graphics and text.
(4) Design the machines to be forgiving and able to help users who make mistakes.
(5) Reward the user and give him a sense of control by building into the machines indicators that they are working properly.
(6) Design the machines to respond fairly quickly, but not too quickly.
(7) Make the machines reliable and consistent in operation.
(8) Allow the user to control the rate at which he or she and the machine interact.
(9) Allow the user to find out where he or she is within a series of steps and to retrace these steps if necessary.
(10) Put the user in control of the machine, not the machine in control of the user.

Public *v*. Private Sponsorship and Control

Let us turn now to social and political problems of new information technology being used in education. In a centrally-planned economy, perhaps in a country of the Soviet bloc, new information technology in education would be sponsored (and controlled) by public bodies: national, regional or local. In all the countries that this book focuses upon, mixed economies prevail, even in the United States, with public and private institutions taking roles in most forms of enterprise.

In the field of new information technology, as we saw in Chapter 1, governments (public sponsors) are stepping in. They are promoting the technology, even to the extent of providing large sums of money to subsidise manufacturers and distributors, who, in their turn, are putting pressure on governments so to act. In education, governments are taking direct action, through legislative, financial, regulatory, advisory and persuasive means, aided and abetted by commercial interests.

Chapter 16 deals with economic implications of this kind of collaboration between public and private interests. Here it is worth noting some political pressures that are being felt in education. For example, in the United Kingdom, political pressure is behind the decision to include in the national scheme for funding micro-computers for schools those of British manufacture only. The French Government has a similar nationalistic policy (Simon, 1981). A consequence, which can be seen as good or bad, is that courseware developed in other countries is excluded from use in schools unless private funding provides for imported equipment.

By contrast, the United States Federal Government is probably in something of a quandary. Its stance towards communications for some years has been one of decreasing intervention and of deregulation, as we have seen in other chapters. Traditionally, it does not intervene in education, which is a matter for individual States and local authorities. Yet it would like to see new information technology serving education. There is some evidence that manufacturers would like to see the Federal Government subsidising the technology in some way in schools, colleges and universities. They would also like the Government to assist in establishing national standards for hardware and software in the education field, and contributing to the immense costs of courseware development. At the same time, they wish to avoid government control as much as possible: probably companies like Texas Instruments are in a quandary, too, when they examine the education market.

A specific problem of public *v.* private sponsorship concerns copyright. Governments will be obliged sooner or later to take more interest in this issue. In the United Kingdom (and in most countries that are signatories to the Berne Convention), copyright law fails to recognise the special needs of education. Students and teachers want copies and recordings, whether from printed material, tapes, broadcasts or elsewhere, and should be able to have them, legitimately. Making copies and recordings has become very much cheaper since the advent of new information technology, yet the law predates these developments, giving a high degree of control to the author or originator.

What are the consequences of the inadequacy of this law and the administrative arrangements that flow from it? Undoubtedly, much copying goes on that is strictly illegal. Perhaps worse, much valuable educational material is underused in schools and colleges because of the legal constraints. For the United Kingdom, the Council for Educational Technology advises that the law be changed to clarify what amounts to 'fair dealing' (legal copying) for educational purposes; to provide for blanket licensing of educational copying, controlled by a single national agency, and to set up a tribunal to deal with problematic cases. These changes would not wholly deprive commercial interests of profits, but, if adopted, would serve the public interest better.

Social and Political Bias Introduced with the Technology

Bias, subtle or blatant, intentional or unintentional, may be introduced at the same time as applications of new information technology in education. What kinds of bias?

First, we have already noted an age bias: the young take to new information technology more easily than the old.

Secondly, evidence exists from many sources of a sex bias: males take to it more easily than females. For example, Chen (1981) mentions the observations of the Head of Children's Services at a Washington, DC public library where a teletext receiver is installed in the foyer. The keypad is on a pedestal about four feet high, preventing younger children from using it. Adolescents are the principal users and often are observed by adults standing behind them, trying to work out how to use it. When the adolescents leave, the adults try for themselves. But what is remarkable is the claim of this observer that she has never observed a female using the system. This sex bias has also been reported, for example by Resek (1981), in secondary schools, where girls do not use microcomputers as much in class and avoid joining the 'computer club' because it is male-dominated. As yet there is no systematic evidence on the causes of this bias: some teachers blame the long-standing prejudice (possibly abetted by males) against mathematics among females. Clearly this bias holds the seeds of a long-term problem.

Thirdly, there may be a cultural bias. Some cultures, such as the Anglo-American, may take to it more easily than others because their cultural and linguistic structures are more adaptable to information processing than others. If we are to believe Schiller (1981), new information technology is essentially the product of American capitalist post-industrial society. But witness the herculean efforts of Japan to overcome problems posed by their character sets (Chapter 3).

Fourthly, there may be a social or class bias, in that lower-class students have more difficulty in learning through the new technology than those from middle and upper classes. We looked at the wider problem earlier in this chapter: in education, it is underlined heavily.

More subtle biases, which we might call psychological or even ideological, exist in how information technology is used and how courseware for it is designed. Some of these can be detected in a report (Malone and Levin, 1981) of an American conference, sponsored by the Carnegie Corporation, on 'cognitive and social design principles' for microcomputer-assisted learning.

Malone and Levin note that successful use of microcomputers in education depends on cognitive and motivational processes of learning and on the social structure of the educational setting. Levin describes how when children work on computers they draw on 'social resources', that is, the advice of their peers. Much cooperative work occurs, particularly as novices learn procedures. He puts forward five guidelines:

(1) Learners should assume more responsibility for the task to be mastered as they progress, although initially the computer should take the initiative.
(2) Programs should encourage and enable children to help each other.
(3) Children should participate actively in the learning.
(4) Children should have available a variety of 'microworlds' in which to exercise the skills they want to acquire, so that they can choose one that engages their interest.
(5) Even novices should be helped to get interesting results without too much difficulty.

These guidelines are based partly on experience, no doubt, but also incorporate a particular model of learning, which assumes, for example, that cooperation is desirable and that active participation enhances learning.

In the same conference report, Lesgold claims that massive amounts of drill and practice are needed to acquire basic skills, and says that practice should be motivating, appropriate and with immediate feedback (again, a particular model underlies these claims). Motivation depends to some extent on a child being able to recognise success, he says. DiSessa, on the other hand, espouses a different model, Papert's LOGO programming, in which children have a sense of control, set their own goals and form deep links with material they learn. But Collins believes that most children read and write to please teachers, not themselves. They can be encouraged to read and write for themselves if they are given computer games where they have to read or write to play. Children can also use new information technology to communicate with friends, classmates and even children they do not know, in much the same ways as adults. Dugdale, commenting on programs, says that they should engage students in productive thought and activity, rather than show off the capabilities of the hardware or the author; they should draw on the inherently interesting characteristics of the topic, rather than hiding it under graphics, animation and music unrelated to the learning task; and they should make students participate, rather than letting them watch and listen.

The good sense of these conference remarks does not entirely mask the social, political, psychological and ideological issues that are behind them. For example, to what extent should children choose for themselves in educational settings? How much intrinsic motivation should be built into courseware? What is the right balance in education, between children being taught to compete or to collaborate? In Japan or France or the United Kingdom the answers to these questions will differ from those suggested by these American experts, and new information technology for education now being designed and introduced in each country will contain different biases.

Finally, we may agree with Dwyer (1977), who declares that efforts at perfecting technology cannot change the fact that different learners learn different things from the same information. Connoisseurs of opera do not learn the same things from listening to a recording of Verdi as do those who seldom listen to opera. Learners, as well as teachers, have their own social and political biases.

Summary

We cannot ignore these problems that surround new information technology yet, according to Bowes (1980), little research is being done to find solutions to them. Educators will have to move to take advantage of new information technology without the benefit of such studies. We know very little about the likely social and political impact of new information technology in education.

16 ECONOMIC PROBLEMS

As Scriven (1981) points out, the voice of reality speaks through cost analysis. Information resources may become widely available at relatively low cost, but they will not necessarily be educational resources. The latter may only become available at relatively high cost, in which case information technology will soon be discredited in the world of education. Pocket calculators at less than £3 apiece will not be enough.

In this chapter we shall look first at economic problems relating to national information technology systems. If such systems are established, education may well benefit by 'riding piggyback' on them. Then we shall look at educational systems and at cost issues within them, with examples of costs of the new technology in various forms.

National Information Technology Systems

New information technology, despite falling costs, is not cheap to install on a national scale, yet its benefits are likely to be realised most where national networks exist and where synergy can develop through combining different devices and systems. The advantages of being able to use a domestic television receiver with various attachments for a wide range of information purposes are clear. Similarly, businesses will benefit from having a full range of the equipment they need to receive and process and send information.

By contrast, countries which install only one or two components of the new information technology will probably gain very little benefit. They will not see the development of synergy, that is, the combined effect of many components, which is probably greater than the sum of their individual effects. National governments in the West are becoming acutely aware of this likelihood, and are striving to find the resources to foster installation of national systems, either under direct government subsidy and control or through private enterprise or, occasionally, through some combination of government and private initiative (see, for example, Simon, 1981, on the French initiatives).

There is considerable debate at present about whether new information technology is a case of 'market pull' or 'technology push'. Market pull exists when potential buyers are expressing what they perceive to be their needs, and are calling for these needs to be met, in this instance by new information technology. In commerce and industry in Western countries, the profit motive drives managers to search for means of improving productivity. Productivity depends on many factors, but can scarcely be improved without information. Therefore market pull operates. The call is for cost-effective means of dealing with increasing information flows and rising demand for storage. Companies large and small, for example, are complaining of being swamped by paperwork, and want to use their resources more productively when dealing with information.

Technology push occurs when makers and sellers of the technology are expounding the capabilities of their products and services in the hope of creating a market and enlarging it. They want to persuade potential buyers that their needs include ones that can be met, in this instance, by new information technology. Of course, we know that buyers sometimes feel they are being pushed too far, while sellers consider that some potential buyers cannot judge their own needs. Allegations that new information technology is the subject of too much push and not enough pull may have some justification. Without doubt, as we saw in Chapter 5, immense capital sums are being invested in the technology and investors will seek a return. On the other hand, we know that before innovations of any kind are widely adopted there has to be awareness-raising. Many countries are at that stage now. Hooper (1980) said of viewdata (videotex), for example:

> The technology of viewdata remains obstinately ahead of good examples of its cost-effective application. Even after three years of trials in the United Kingdom with Prestel, there is still a general feeling that viewdata is a technological solution looking for a problem to solve. Prestel is itself a classic example of technology push rather than market pull.

The question that remains is: Can nations afford new information technology? There are two points of view. The first is more pessimistic. If a country wants the technology, something else will have to be sacrificed, and government will probably have the task of deciding what it will be. Since resources are limited, shortages will occur elsewhere if new information technology takes a large share. The second and more optimistic view proposes that the technology should be installed as quickly as possible because it will help to generate greater wealth, enlarging the pool of resources to an extent greater than its own cost. This view is complemented by the implied threat that any nation not investing in the technology will fall far behind in competitive world trade.

What seems likely to happen is that governments will intervene, as they are already doing in some Western countries, to ensure that new information technology becomes the basis for national and international telecommunications. Intervention may take several forms: as we saw in Chapter 15, in the United States it is by a policy of deregulation, while in France it is through financing of a quasi-government agency and in Japan it is through government directives and encouragement to private companies.

Schiller (1981) criticises what he sees. He says that the new technologies are best understood in terms of long-established market-based criteria. He asks us to be aware of state subsidies to private undertakings, risk-avoidance by these undertakings coupled with insistence on special premiums for risk-taking, claims of public benefit for what is private enrichment and shifting of considerable and never-calculated costs onto the shoulders of the working population. He asserts that underlying the whole is promotion of private accumulation of corporate capital, regardless of the public good. His remarks are based particularly on the United States but could apply elsewhere in Western countries.

As countries upgrade their telecommunications and become 'wired nations', large markets are created for many of the new information devices and systems we have looked at in earlier chapters. Even where telecommunication links have not yet been upgraded, markets exist for microcomputers, videocassette players and other relatively self-contained devices.

What are the problems of these markets? For our purposes, the most important one to note is the extent to which they are specialised. Products and services developed for one sector of industry, for example, are not likely to be of much use in another sector. Many systems have to be built to order and consist of a carefully selected set of devices, with programs that are either written specially or adapted. Another problem is that changing needs require changing systems, and the rate at which equipment in these systems is likely to become obsolete is likely to be high. Instead of a company writing off its investment over 20 or 30 years it has to do so over four or five. A third problem, related to the first two, is that standardisation is proceeding rather slowly in the new information technology industry, meaning that interchangeability of hardware and software is likely to be low for some time, adding to costs.

Cable systems offer a case in point: Mason (1977) discusses the cost constraints that cause cable system companies to pause before investing in two-way cable rather than one-way. Although fibre optics may render obsolete the 1975 data that support his 1977 arguments, he claims that for a cable system serving 78 per cent of households in a given district, capital costs are four times as much for a two-way system, programming costs about the same and operating costs three times as much. He also points out that the revenue per household drops as coverage approaches 100 per cent. This is mainly because the more inaccessible households are more expensive to reach. On the other hand, Chen (1981) reports that the QUBE two-way systems operating in Cincinnati and Pittsburgh have achieved close to 90 per cent coverage of households in their districts, following the success of the Warner-Amex QUBE two-way system in Columbus, Ohio, where some 30,000 middle-class users are on the cable. A new two-way cable system in Dallas, again to be operated by the Warner-Amex combine, will offer 60 channels for $4.95 a month per household, a price low enough to attract custom from poorer households as well as richer ones.

Cost Issues in Systems for Education

If we assume that nations can afford new information technology, to an extent and on a scale that makes a significant difference to their ways of carrying on industry and commerce, may we also assume that they will be able to afford it for education? There are good reasons for believing that the answer, even in Western countries, will be no. First, we should look at national expenditure on education, world-wide. Up to the first major oil crisis in 1974, expenditure on education, in real terms, steadily increased in most countries (Eicher, Hawkridge, McAnany, Mariet and Orivel, 1982). Some countries each year after that date cut back their budgets in real terms. Others managed to sustain increases, but more moderate ones than before, up to about 1978. Since that date only the rich oil-producing countries have continued to do so. All others, including the Western countries on which this book is focused, have spent less on education each year, when inflation is taken into account. Notable examples abound. Education cuts have been particularly marked in higher education in the United States, the United Kingdom, Canada, Australia, the Netherlands, Denmark, the Federal Republic of Germany and other Western countries. At primary and secondary levels in the United States, the State of California has set a deplorable precedent: a taxpayers' revolt is closing schools, even occasionally in relatively wealthy areas close to major companies in the new information technology field. A declining birth-rate in the 1970s, causing falling enrolments, exacerbates the difficulties for decision-makers formulating education budgets in many European countries.

Education budgets are constructed in such a way that cuts cannot easily be accommodated, nor funds switched to other purposes. A high proportion of the budget goes to paying the salaries of staff: teachers, administrators and other workers. A further proportion goes towards constructing and maintaining schools and other buildings. Only a very small percentage is available, even in wealthy countries like the United States, for equipping classrooms and providing children with books and materials. Admittedly, in higher education the percentage for equipment and materials is a little higher. Overall, however, education budgets are almost entirely committed to salaries and other fixed costs. As Ahl (1977) noted, for example, telecommunications budgets in American schools are among the first to be cut in times of economic stringency.

In industry and commerce, the second and more optimistic view of investment in new information technology may prevail, and new wealth may be generated in a period of only a few years. In education, it is much more difficult to take this view. Resources available are almost entirely those from government with only minor contributions from parents and students. Western governments are reducing the amount for education each year at present, with substantial, if not majority, support from their constituents. It seems foolish to expect that large sums will be proffered by governments for the purpose of investment in new information technology for education, where returns are essentially long-term, over generations, and virtually unmeasurable. Most governments are obliged, it can be argued, to serve shorter term objectives.

Without massive investment by government of sums that are additional to the budgets needed to keep education systems operating, what are the options? They are limited. Educational institutions may individually decide, within whatever policy guidelines that exist, to divert money from, say, building maintenance or salaries for substitute teachers, in order to purchase small installations of the new technology. Or they may urge their supporters, such as the parents of children in schools or the alumni of colleges, to pay for these extra facilities. These efforts are not be decried, although we must bear in mind that purchasing devices and systems is only the beginning of expenditure: there will be maintenance and repair costs and expenditure on training staff to teach through the new technology. Success in using the technology will only follow a commitment to all these aspects of cost.

Examples of Costs of New Information Technology in Education

Providing examples of costs of new information technology is quite difficult because of variations in different industrialised countries. One common 'currency', however, is a teacher's annual salary, a widely understood basis for comparison. To use this currency is not to suggest that teachers will be replaced by technology.

Microcomputers in secondary school classrooms vary in cost depending on the functions they are to perform and the power and speed required. At the bottom of the market are machines that can be purchased in batches of 12-15, or one for every two or three children, at a total initial cost of less than a teacher's annual salary. Running costs each year might amount to one-tenth of initial costs. These machines would teach computer awareness, BASIC programming and perhaps a little more. They would be linked to a single printer and would have rather limited storage. If we went nearer to the top end of the market to purchase a similar number of machines, feeding two or three better quality printers, we would have to spend the equivalent of five teachers' annual salaries. We would probably obtain high resolution graphics, graphics tablets, more screens, much more storage and a wider range of software and courseware. By paying more each year, in addition to the normal running costs, we could link the microcomputers to computerised databases or possibly to microcomputers in other educational institutions, thus increasing their educational capabilities.

If initial costs are amortised over four years, for a single classroom the cost per year does not look impossibly high. If the equipment is used by several groups of children, the justification for purchasing it may be stronger. The crucial question remains, of course: Is the extra money available and if it is, should it be spent this way? Would it be better spent on extra teachers, for example, or on new pianos?

If we look at another possible acquisition, videotex facilities for a college library, the costs may seem much lower, but so may be the benefits. Let us assume that the college wishes to have two videotex sets in its library, one for students to consult on their own and the other set up where a librarian can teach students how to use it well. Initial costs would be small, particularly if the college already had two television receivers that could be spared for videotex. Two videotex attachments cost less than the equivalent of a teacher's salary for one month. Annual running costs could amount to much more than this sum, however, since videotex use incurs both telephone and computerised databank costs. Even so, the total for a year would be unlikely to exceed half a teacher's annual salary. A cheap printer might save money on running costs because students would be able to make a quick copy of whatever appeared on the screen. How much use was made of the sets would depend partly on how well students were trained in using the videotex search systems and partly on whether the videotex bank contained much information suited to the students' needs. Again, the question for decision-makers would be whether the funds were available and, if so, whether the sets offered the best value.

Hope (1981) gives details of costs of installing the British videotex system, Prestel: £150-200 for an adaptor, plus £13 for a telephone jack, on top of the cost of a television set. Running costs depend on use made of non-free pages and time of day (which affects telephone charges). For information providers, the cost is about £50 per page per annum when everything is taken into account, according to Mills & Allen Communications, a leading provider.

One further example of costs, this time for adults studying at home using interactive videodisc players (and the discs for them). Present technology would require a middle-of-the-market or better microcomputer, plus a videodisc player, at an initial cost equivalent to half a teacher's annual salary, a very large sum for most individuals to provide. There is promise of a player containing its own interactive device, but without a television screen, for about half this cost. Videodiscs for adult education are likely to be quite costly, particularly for subjects in which developers have not been able to achieve economies of scale, but a sum equal to a teacher's monthly salary might purchase enough for part-time study for a year. Public libraries may begin to hold videodiscs for education (just as many now have audiodisc lending collections), in which case the running cost would probably drop greatly.

Schneider and Bennion (1981) attempt a cost analysis for various media used in education, in a hypothetical American school district. Although their analysis omits many factors, such as storage costs, they show that videodisc would be a cheaper medium than film, by far, and probably cheaper than videocassette, for moving pictures. For stills, seldom used in the classroom in conjunction with film or videotape, videodisc has an immense cost advantage: even if the school district were only buying ten copies, videodisc would be about ten times cheaper than colour microfiche or filmstrip, and in larger quantities the difference is much greater. As film prices rise with silver prices, film may become too expensive for educational uses.

Merrill (1980), also writing about videodiscs, provides an example of how difficult it is to get sound costings of new information technology. First, he points out that disc replication costs are low and player costs reasonable (compared with videocassette). But production and mastering costs are high. Development and production costs are very difficult to obtain, partly because organisations making videodiscs do not report all their costs, for good reasons: for example, few discs have been made as yet, therefore there is a fair amount of trial-and-error in their making, more than is likely to be present a few years from now. Should they include costs of motion picture sequences? Are instructional design costs added? And editing costs? What about programming costs if the disc is to be controlled by a microcomputer? In other words, the costing approach will determine the final figure, which could range from £2,000 to £50,000 for making the content for one educational video-disc. To master and replicate a videodisc entails another set of costs: at MCA Discovision, the mastering cost is about one-tenth of the cost to replicate 3,000, assuming both sides of the disc are used.

How do figures like these compare with current provision for books and educational materials? In the United States, public expenditure under these heads for one year in a single classroom averages about $500, in the United Kingdom much less. The annual cost of studying as an adult varies widely but is very seldom as high as the costs shown for interactive videodiscs. Clearly we are considering costs that are additional to those usually incurred, and substantially so. They are not, however, costs that are so high that further discussion is to no purpose. If we consider the investment in equipment for other workers, we see that teachers can claim to be at a severe disadvantage. The average industrial worker is said to have $25,000 worth of equipment for his job; the average agricultural worker, $60,000 worth, and the average office worker has only $2,000 worth (Robertson, 1981). But the average teacher has even less, probably around $1,500 worth. Education is still a labour-intensive, under-capitalised sector of the economies of Western countries.

Costs and Benefits of New Information Technology

The costs of new information technology in education would be more acceptable if benefits could be vividly demonstrated, but the search for clear benefits has not yielded results that inspire confidence among hard-headed politicians and civil servants. In the United States, some trials of the technology in its various forms have included 'before and after' measures of students' achievement by standardised tests. The shortcomings of these tests are well known, although Americans trust the results more than Europeans do. The problems of setting up well-designed trials are also well known. Most of the trials involving television, for example, show that students who use the new technology learn just about as much as those taught by conventional (and presumably cheaper) means. In other words, no significant benefit can be claimed for television. In other countries where standardised tests are seldom or never used, the testimony of teachers weighs more heavily: they attest to the attitudes and achievement of their students. In general, those who have used the new technology in their teaching speak in favour of it. They point out some of the problems, but believe there are benefits. They say that comparisons drawn in American studies are often too facile and that their own students are learning much that cannot be tested by American tests. In fairness, we should note that none of these European teachers (or the Americans) has been asked to give up his or her job so that more technology can be purchased. Rather, these teachers see the technology as enhancing their teaching and their students' learning.

Thus decision-makers at national, regional and local levels are in the position of being unable to advance cost-effectiveness arguments for replacing teachers with machines, or even for replacing textbooks. The evidence does not exist. If the new information technology is to come into education, it must do so despite its costs rather than because of them.

Labour Costs *v.* Technology Costs

Teachers in Western countries are aware of course that the cost of technology is dropping, in real terms. As Melmed (1982) points out, powerful forces in industry and commerce will ensure declining prices for the hardware. Teachers are also aware that the cost of their labour is rising, although it may not be rising as fast as the cost of labour in many other occupations. Are teachers pricing themselves out of the market? Is technology a cheaper substitute? Again, in broad terms, the answer to both these questions must be no. Even in North America, where new information technology is entering very fast indeed one specialised branch of education, industrial training, there is little evidence to support a different answer.

A few large industrial concerns, such as General Motors and Xerox, have set up their own training institutions, catering for the needs of several groups of their workers. They have done so for several reasons. First, they wish to exert greater control over the training of their employees by keeping it in-house. Secondly, they are finding that ordinary colleges and universities cannot afford to install the latest technology, including new information technology, whereas companies like these can and do. Thus at Xerox, employees learn about new information systems and devices through using them, in some cases even before they have been marketed. But these are not clear-cut cases of technology undercutting teachers.

What about correspondence courses for adults, which have a long reputation for being more capital-intensive and less labour-intensive than other courses? Certainly, older forms of information technology are being complemented by newer forms to provide home-based formal education in all Western countries. New information technology is being brought into play in institutions like the Open University of the United Kingdom, the Fernuniversität in the Federal Republic of Germany, Athabasca University in Canada and the University of the Air in Japan. This technology is reducing the cost of paying teachers, although teachers are still important in these systems, both for centralised production of teaching materials and for tutoring. Technology is enabling each teacher, on average, to teach many more students, even at degree level where traditionally one teacher has ten or fewer students. These institutions for teaching at a distance are perhaps the exception that proves the rule, and no government is suggesting general use of distance education as a substitute for face-to-face education. Even the United Kingdom's Open University, Open Tech and National Extension College combined will only account for a small proportion of all students in education in that country by 1990.

Whatever powerful forces are at work to bring down prices of hardware, few such forces will create educational software and courseware, let alone bring down its price, according to Melmed (1982). Yet until there is a large stock of good quality programs and other courseware available, potential educational consumers in schools and homes will not have much to use. Melmed says that some pressure is coming from hardware manufacturers, some of whom are sponsoring courseware development in various ways. He notes a growing private sector investment in training courseware, aimed at improving productivity in offices and factories, but the size of investment needed and the risk of fragmented markets in education are enough to daunt many textbook publishers. If a large and orderly market were created through standardisation of hardware and software, through standardisation of curricula, then risk capital would be found quickly enough. But he points out that such a uniformity would be anathema to many governments, including his own, the American.

Summary

The economic picture we have looked at in this chapter is not a bright one for education. If teachers and learners welcome new information technology, the money will still have to be found, and there are few signs that anyone is ready to pay the cost of installing the technology on a massive scale.

17 TECHNICAL PROBLEMS

New information technology is not free of technical problems. In this chapter we shall look at technical problems particularly relevant to educational applications of the technology. Some may be solved by the time this book appears, because the pace of development is so fast, but others will certainly remain. The capacity of a device or system being used for education is limited by its technical specification. Many technical problems occur simply because people want the technology to do more than it can: they are not aware of its limits. Others are caused by poor design, faulty materials or low standards of manufacture.

Computers, Including Microcomputers

In discussing several major American computer-assisted learning systems, Bunderson, Cole, Gibbons and Kerr (1981) list a number of technical problems associated with them. For example, PLATO (Programmed Logic for Automatic Teaching Operations), developed at the University of Illinois and marketed since 1976 by Control Data Corporation, requires learners to use terminals connected to a mainframe computer, in some cases many miles away. The older terminals suffered from low resolution (a poorly defined picture); newer ones, still black-and-white, have a high resolution screen that is also touch-sensitive. Technical problems remain: in this project, a language, TUTOR, was developed for teachers to use in preparing their own instruction, but it is too complex for many. Attempts to link to the system devices for displaying slides or photographs have not succeeded. Although some 10,000 hours of instruction is said to be available, many of the programs cover only small fragments of conventional school or university syllabuses. Others are designed for business use only.

The same authors comment on TICCIT (Timeshared Interactive Computer Controlled Information Television), marketed by Hazeltine Corporation, a system in which up to 128 terminals can be connected to a nearby minicomputer. They say that few programs are available, compared with PLATO, and TICCIT is still costly at over $50,000 for an installation with only four terminals.

In the IIS (Interactive Instructional System), marketed by IBM, standard IBM equipment is used with courses developed by IBM or IIS-users. Most are data processing courses. Technical problems persist: no graphics are available, the terminals are expensive and the authoring language is difficult to learn, say Bunderson and his colleagues.

In all such time-sharing systems, delays occur if the number of terminals in use at any one time is too great for the central processor. These delays frustrate students: they feel less motivated to use the terminals. In time, an equilibrium is established, but not necessarily one that meets the needs of students.

Technical problems that occur are not restricted to hardware. In the software field, Powell (1981) identifies the problems of acquisition of software by libraries. He says that locating software sources is difficult; the problem is being exacerbated by the spread of microcomputers and by the range of users widening far beyond the original specialists. There are at least eight sources:

(1) computer manufacturers and suppliers;
(2) software houses and software suppliers;
(3) user groups related to a particular machine or make of machine;
(4) special interest groups;
(5) published programs appearing in journals and books;
(6) program exchanges (subject-based or general);
(7) national bodies such as the British Computer Society; and
(8) local groups.

From most of these sources, summary catalogues are available, but other documentation must be obtained before the usefulness of a program can be assessed. Documentation is vital, says Powell, and he notes that often one or more of the following items are missing: purpose of the program, method used in it, method of using it (including details and examples of inputs and outputs), machine requirements (storage, etc.), programming language used, modification and maintenance instructions, a source listing of the program, the form in which the program is issued or distributed, and details of copyright for both the program and documentation itself. Moore and Thomas (1981) support this general approach.

Technical standards for programs and documentation do exist, but are seldom adhered to, as Powell says. There is no standard definition of BASIC. Users face technical problems where no facilities exist for them to try out programs, perhaps in libraries rather than under the eye of a salesman. Since trials require access to appropriate computers, they seldom occur. Such technical problems surround the setting up of any national catalogue of software, as in the case of the new British Library or American Lockheed DIALOG catalogues, but apply particularly to computer courseware (see *CET News*, no. 12, May 1981).

Copyright remains a vexed problem. In the United Kingdom, little or no case law is being built up because copyright lawsuits involving software are being settled out of court and the government is reluctant to act to update legislation. The complexity of copyright issues in new information technology is brought out by Ploman and Hamilton (1980).

Teletext and Videotex

The technical problem of delays crops up again in teletext systems. For example, Chen (1981) reports that on American teletext there is a long wait (up to 25 seconds) before the decoder inside the receiver 'grabs' the frame requested from the cycle of pages being run past it. This problem is caused by the limited memory provided in the decoder, enough for only one page of graphics.

Both teletext and videotex suffer from the technical problem of limits on the amount of alphanumeric information that can be stored in the computer and displayed on the television screen. Bygrave (1979) notes that videotex is really encyclopedic but is highly selective, for technical reasons. He cites *Time Out*, the magazine of events in London, which in 96 pages each week lists all the films, plays, operas, etc. To put the same information on videotex (Prestel) would take up thousands of pages and would require the services of many editing terminals and their staff. Moreover, the searching 'menus' of videotex would be inadequate to the task when a user wanted to find a specific piece of information. Instead, videotex systems must be highly selective in the information they present. A page on the 'Top Ten Plays in London' is much more likely. Similarly, railway timetable information, much in demand in European countries with good passenger services, is too complex to display successfully on videotex, although again selected services could be shown, such as expresses. These limitations have implications for educational applications of videotex, although Hooper (1980) claims that commercial information providers are secretly thinking up ways of using videotex better.

Wright (1980) identifies technical problems in designing the layout of information for use in the new technology. For example, members of the public required to fill in forms need to be able to perceive the 'path' for them through the form, and this may be less evident if the questions are presented singly on a screen. The same could be true of computer-presented tests. On the other hand, explanatory notes that sometimes accompany forms, but on a separate sheet, can now be inserted next to the question or item to which they refer, since each 'page' on the screen will probably contain a single question or item. This practice could be carried over into education, implying a reorganisation of text and illustrations, perhaps. Responding via a keyboard imposes a set of constraints that varies with the equipment in use and the users' skills. Information may be provided in schools in such a form that responses are limited to multiple choice (press button C if you think that is the right answer) rather than requiring a 'written answer' through a full keyboard, which would be more costly.

Videocassette and Videodisc

Here, many of the technical problems are common to both technologies, so far as educational applications are concerned. Both technologies provide audiovisual media capable of moving pictures and both can be linked to microcomputers for interactive learning. In fact, the technical problems relate directly to the level of sophistication of use and the equipment available, as Merrill (1980) points out in a report that specifies six such levels for videodisc. First, all videodisc players operate in linear mode: that is, they play a disc from start to finish without stopping. In this mode, videodiscs offer no overall educational advantage over film or videocassette. Second, all videodisc players permit searching, slow motion and stopping, manually. This is true for some videocassette machines. Being able to provide slow motion or to freeze a frame is valuable in teaching motor skills, such as how to serve in tennis or open heart surgery. But interactive instruction by this means would be very tedious for the learner and nobody has tried to develop it. Third, adding automatic stops increases the potential: chapters can be reached more easily, but the players are still imposing a very limited searching technique on the learner. What is more useful, fourth, is random access, which allows learners (and teachers) to specify which frames or sequences they want to go to next. This is possible with some videodisc players and soon will be with more expensive videocassette players. Fifth, a predetermined series of commands and frame numbers can be entered and stored in the microprocessor built into Discovision videodisc players. This short program may actually be in the videodisc, ready to be transferred to the microprocessor, or the student or teacher may enter it using a keypad, but the latter is rather tedious. Finally, and sixth, the most valuable, but also the most costly, way to use videodiscs (and probably videocassettes soon) is under microcomputer control. Learners interact with the microcomputer keyboard and the display screen. Floppy discs on the microcomputer add to the storage available, and the full logic of the microcomputer provides for very sophisticated branching strategies. Simulations, in particular, can be easily handled with this combination of equipment, but development costs for the courseware are high.

Summary

Overcoming technical problems in using new information technology for education is usually possible, at a cost. Either more powerful technology can be brought into play or new devices and systems developed to take care of particular needs. But technical problems exist. We are not being offered immaculate technology, infinitely reliable, adaptable and flexible. Technical support is and will be necessary.

PART FOUR: INFORMATION TECHNOLOGY IN EDUCATION IN 2000 AD

Part One provides a full introduction to the new information technology, establishing a working vocabulary. Part Two gives many examples of the technology being applied in education at all levels. Part Three stresses the problems and constraints in extending these applications.

Part Four looks ahead to the end of the century. Many readers will think Chapter 18 excessively optimistic, yet it does no more than bring together, without exaggeration, views expressed by politicians and experts in new information technology and, let it be said, more than a few from education. Equally, many readers will find Chapter 19 unduly pessimistic, although it too is a collage of views expressed by political scientists, politicians (of different persuasion than those in Chapter 18) and many more from education. This deliberate polarisation, in Chapters 18 and 19, leads on to Chapter 20, which is my own forecast, based on the broad view of new information technology in education that I provide in the first 19 chapters of this book.

18 LEARNERS' HEAVEN: AN OPTIMIST'S FORECAST

So far in this book we have been considering the present, with an occasional glance at what may lie in the immediate future. In the remaining chapters, we may be able to glimpse what new information technology will bring to education by the year 2000. Why 2000? Why choose the end of the century? Apart from the date being a convenient one to bear in mind, 2000 is about as far ahead as anyone dares to predict. The pace of change in technology is increasing, therefore even more changes are likely to occur in the next 20 years (Evans, 1981, cites examples) than have in the past 20, during which we have seen the developments and inventions of 'new information technology'. Yet to take a date much earlier than 2000 would scarcely allow time for the diffusion and installation of this and even newer technology.

This Utopia is not everybody's Utopia. This chapter asks: What *might* a learner's heaven be like in the year 2000? That is not the same as asking what it *will* be like or even what it *should* be like. It assumes large but not limitless resources being put into new information technology in general, and into this technology for education in particular. Before any description of this Utopia, however, it would be as well to list some desirable goals.

First, there could be no learners' heaven without educational opportunity for all. Barriers of poverty, social class and occupation would have to disappear.

Secondly, and stemming from the first, the limits of time and space, of schedule and geography, would have to be broken down, so that people, including children, could study when and where they needed to.

Thirdly, learners would have access to a very large store of information at many times during their lifetimes, and this store would contain information in a wide variety of forms, subject to some kind of quality control.

Fourthly, learners of all ages would have the means to select information suited to their individual requirements.

Fifthly, every learner would be able to use the technology to process information. This processing might occur in on-the-job training, in a classroom or laboratory, or at home, or indeed in many other circumstances where a learner needed to write, compute, compose, draw or otherwise create something new through processing information.

Sixthly, learners would be able to add to the store of information held locally, regionally or nationally, within liberal constraints of quality control.

We know that to some extent each of these goals is already being achieved, with very little help from new information technology. In Western countries there is greater educational opportunity in the early 1980s than ever before, although we see around us some signs of this opportunity declining as governments cut budgets for education. We can point to heavily subsidised schooling, including many compensatory education projects aimed at removing barriers of poverty, social class and occupation. We can show that some restrictions of schedules and geography have been removed for substantial numbers of students who take correspondence courses, some supplemented by broadcasting and other means. And there is no doubt that very large stores of information do exist in libraries, art galleries, museums and elsewhere. Books, artefacts, films and tapes abound, all under some kind of quality control.

We cannot be sanguine that these goals are being achieved for all sectors of the community, however, particularly the last three. Access to information stores is by no means readily available to all. Learners often lack the means to select what they require, they cannot use the technology to process information and they are rarely able to add to the store. What could be possible by 2000?

Children at Home

Children at home will have access to new information technology of much greater power than is generally the case today. How much they are allowed to use it by themselves will depend on their parents. Undoubtedly they will often acquire the necessary skill to operate the technology if their parents give them the chance. Parents' views will be coloured by the expense, still relatively high, of the more sophisticated devices and systems, and by the technology's vulnerability in the hands of young children. Parents, as always, will also be strongly influenced, however, by how much they perceive their own and other children learning through the technology.

The primary device for young children to learn from at home is likely to be a screen like that of a television set, but one that differs from those we use today by being larger and flatter. This screen will occupy much of one wall in a principal room of the house and will be part of a two-way communication system incorporating television, teletext, videotex, a videodisc or videotape cassette player and a microcomputer. Young children in the family will learn very quickly how to turn on the screen and how to select either a television channel or what is on the disc or tape. Videophones will not yet be widely used, but these children will use a keypad to make ordinary telephone calls, within limits set electronically by the parents. A three-year-old will use the same keypad to call up educational games, singing and dancing, story-telling or old-fashioned educational television broadcasts like Sesame Street. Some of these will enter the home by cable. A five-year-old may use the keypad to check the weather forecast for the day of her birthday party: the screen will display a weather chart with familiar symbols.

Will four-year-olds be using the family microcomputer too in 2000? Perhaps, but before they get that far their parents will have given them several smaller devices, all powered by ordinary artificial light or by daylight. One device will be a pocket calculator, not very different from those widely available today except that it will talk as well as having a window to display the figures. Four-year-olds will soon learn how to add up with it, because one of their daily ten-minute favourites on television will teach just that, with a large, easy-to-press model of the calculator coming up on the screen's touch-sensitive area, low down on the right-hand side where young children can reach it. Some children will learn subtraction, multiplication and division before they go to school, but not the majority. Will any of them know how to compute without the calculator? Will that matter? As Scriven (1981) suggests, poor performance in arithmetic will matter much less with calculators so widely available. Just as engineers moved away from paper-and-pencil to use the slide-rule years ago, so has the general public moved to use the calculator.

Another device, possibly the most revolutionary, will be an electronic reader. Every household will have at least one. It will look like a 'credit card' calculator, that is, it will be about two inches by three and only a quarter of an inch thick. Underneath, it will have an optical character recognition unit. On top, it will have a voice synthesiser, plus the light cell to power it. When a two-year-old runs it over the printed page of his nursery books, it will read aloud to him what is printed. By the time he is four, he will be able to use the device to decode most of the print he wants to read. A child of five may be reading many of the words herself, rather than bothering to run her reader over them, but she will go on using the reader as long as she wants to, long after she has gone to school, because the reader's repertoire of words will include all those she is likely to meet until she is about twelve, when she may be given a more advanced chip to fit into it. As her reading speed climbs, so the incentive to use the reader will drop and she will keep it for words she seldom comes across.

Since three-year-olds soon learn to use a keypad, by four, children will be wanting to try the bigger keyboard of the microcomputer. At first, they may want to do no more than try all the keys, spelling out on the screen all the letters of the alphabet, plus numerals and other strange symbols on the keyboard. Parents will render inoperative certain keys if they wish, because the children's behaviour will be fairly random at this stage, just as it is for most children of that age who try a typewriter keyboard. The difference between playing on a typewriter keyboard and on that of a microcomputer is great, however, and, in 2000, parents will load a disc or tape, or maybe a chip module, which will teach keyboarding, using graphics and sound to the full. A four-year-old girl will find that by pressing the letter A she not only obtains A on the screen but also hears a voice say the letter. She will learn keyboarding via a set of educational games, which will first teach her what the keys can do, within rather simple limits, and then invite her to play games that give her practice in controlling, with the keyboard, what happens on the screen and over the loud-speaker or earphones. The printer attached to the microcomputer will give her a copy to keep and look at afterwards, if she wants it, whether it is a piece of her 'writing' or a drawing or even, perhaps, the letters she needs to press next time to recreate a simple tune. The chances are very good that she will be familiar with keyboarding by the time she gets to school.

A few other facilities will be in the hands of such young children. Some sort of hand-held device will play back recordings, whether of music or voice. This device may also be suitable for making record-ings. At any rate, it will be an amusement, just like a taperecorder today, or, more seriously, it may be a talking encyclopedia. It will take small discs or chip modules, each on a particular topic, and will 'talk' for three to ten minutes. A preschooler will use it for stories and songs, rather than mini-lectures, but may also use it to listen to distant grandparents.

Finally, children of this age will occasionally use the videotex system, probably with some help from parents. They will gain a rough idea of how to search for information in the system, although probably they will explore only a few fields. In America, children may consult the local list of restaurants serving hamburgers on Sunday evenings.

Thus children at home will learn much about how to use new information technology and they will become familiar with it to such an extent that using it will seem far more natural to them than it does to their parents. Beyond that, however, they will learn important skills and will acquire much knowledge that will be valuable to them as they enter primary school at the age of about six.

In Primary School

We should certainly assume that schools will still exist, and teachers in them. We should also assume that parents, the 'consumers' of school-based education, will want their children to come under teachers' influence and control while at school. Most school buildings will be the ones we have today, because they are too costly to replace. Children will still be in groups of about 30 per classroom and in the primary school a teacher will be in charge of each class.

There will be less teaching of the class as a whole. As occurs already in many British primary schools (Galton and Simon, 1980), children will work individually or in small groups, not necessarily on the same tasks simultaneously.

Children will move to 10-15 screens located in various parts of the room, for some, but only some, of their work. Each screen, a smaller version of the television screen at home, will be for use with a variety of interconnected devices and will be essentially interactive (two-way, not merely 'spoon-feeding'). Children will have access, under teachers' guidance, to cable channels carrying many information services, including videotex and teletext. They will use recordings covering a range of selected topics, playing them back either via the screens, or, in the case of audiorecordings, through a small hand-held device (one of a set of 20 provided for the class), fitted with an earphone. Some of the screens will be linked to microcomputers, complete with keyboards, and there will be a printer and copier available in one corner. Again, children will use a selected set of programs on the microcomputers. Each child wishing to use a micro-computer for part of his or her work may well be encouraged to find a partner, since much can be learned through discussing what is happening on the screen and what should be done next on the keyboard.

Textbooks, exercise- and note-books will not disappear, but they will assume less importance. The latter, for example, will still be useful, but not as useful as the disc or discs belonging to each child, for use in the microcomputer. Each child will use his or her disc for written assignments, for artistic work employing the graphics facility and for certain kinds of mathematics. That disc will be a record of learning just as much as today's exercise-books and note-books, but the microcomputer, used with a word-processing program, will do a great deal to help children gain confidence in writing and in creating their own controllable world within it. For the teacher, the disc may be a remedial tool, because he or she can help the child to correct errors until a 'right' version is on the screen. No child will face pages of red ink corrections.

What will a typical day at school be like for a child of, say, ten years of age? Will any day be typical with so much diversity possible? Undoubtedly the teacher will lay stress on a variety of 'socialising activities'. Some of these may involve the whole class, but more likely the teacher will call upon groups of children to work together, perhaps with a few devices to hand, perhaps without. The presence of technology in the classroom will not lead to neglect of humanistic values. The teacher will still want children to learn how to concep-tualise problems and formulate questions, to discover patterns and similarities, to estimate accurately, to seek out and select data according to criteria, to apply strategies to novel situations and so on. And the teacher will still want children to learn how to collabo-rate with each other.

What the teacher is not likely to be doing is spending as much time as today in teaching the three Rs. There will still be remedial teaching of children who have not, for one reason or another, mastered key-boarding, the pocket calculator, simple computing and reading. Spelling exercises for the class will disappear completely, because the microcomputers will be programmed to help bad spellers. Composi-tion and creative writing will, as now, be largely a learning task carried out by children individually, but again with the micro-computers programmed to help. Children will be able to monitor their own thinking, so to speak, as they revise their written work using a word-processing program. Moreover, they will find the task of writing easier, as keyboarding requires less complex motor skills than handwriting, which demands fine control of the pen or pencil. Other subjects, like foreign languages, will be learned only in part through using information technology. In fact, it will be rare indeed for the whole of any subject in the primary school curriculum to be learned this way unless it is outside the teacher's knowledge and expertise. Even in these exceptional cases, a human tutor will still be needed for some aspects of the work.

Individual and small group work will be paramount, with considerable individualisation of each child's programme of work, enabling some children to forge ahead in certain subjects while others do the same in different subjects. To have children working 'out of step' will present the teacher with fewer problems than it does today, because the technology will help children to keep track of their own progress. By the time they reach the end of primary school, at about the same age as they do now (which varies from country to country), these children will have widely differing standards of achievement. Technology is likely to increase the differences among them rather than inducing conformity. Many will have acquired ways of thinking that will stand them in good stead in the secondary school.

In Secondary School

Secondary schools, too, will still exist, largely in their present buildings, in the year 2000. Children will still work with first one subject-teacher then another throughout the school day. Fundamental changes in the system are unlikely to take place by 2000. Each subject-teacher's classroom will be equipped with information technology, as a general rule. Only in a few schools will teachers still be expected to move from room to room rather than the children moving. In these latter schools, every room will have basic facilities, consisting of a number of screens plus associated devices, much as in primary schools.

In Britain and North America, for example, the classroom belonging to the teacher of English will contain 10-20 microcomputers specially adapted as word processors. Children will use them to learn 'composition' or 'creative writing' to a higher level, building on what they began in primary school. Among the facilities they will find valuable will be an automated dictionary, which flashes onto the screen the spelling and, if desired, the meaning and etymology of any word spoken into its microphone. They will also find that the teacher can set the microcomputers to 'grade' their work, that is, to analyse it diagnostically and award a provisional grade. Children may well appeal against the provisional grade, particularly as they will know that the microcomputers grade against a limited set of criteria. By talking over the microcomputers' standards with their teacher, they will internalise sound criteria. They will also benefit from the clear way in which the machine indicates their errors and how these can be corrected. In the same room, children will also use video- and audiorecorders to practise oral composition and speechmaking. In using camera and microphone to record each other, they will learn a little about recording skills, too.

In the classroom of the Mathematics teacher will be a bank of microcomputers, as many as one for each member of the class, together with a full range of programs. This is one subject, perhaps the only one, where a few children will be able to learn entirely through computers if they so wish and the teacher agrees. Those needing help will be able to call up remedial programs, or they will turn to the teacher or to classmates. Those wanting extra time will come after school or take home on disc the work they have begun in class.

Needless to say, the teacher of that relatively new subject in secondary schools, Computing and Information Technology, will have a fully equipped classroom, perhaps along the lines of the one designed for Perth College of Further Education in Scotland, where the microcomputers are arranged in a U on specially-built desks that have good working space yet allow the teacher full access (see *Phase Two*, vol. 2, no. 1, 1982). Children will learn a certain amount of programming, but not very much because most programming in business and industry will be computer-aided. They will gain some experience by working with a computer-aided programming device, and will learn how to organise and search databases of various kinds. They will also learn some of the more sophisticated uses of the special equipment in this classroom: for example, they will learn how to program the music-composer if they have a strong interest in music or, if they have strong artistic leanings, they will work with the dynamic graphics screen (Papert, 1977).

The History teacher will use a class library of video- and audiorecordings of archive material. Children in this classroom will use these recordings either individually or in small groups, although occasionally the teacher will ask the whole class to view or listen to the same recording before a class discussion of it. In the same room, there will be at least one videotex set, which children will use to consult history databases elsewhere, or to discover what publications would be useful to them and where these can be borrowed in the district. Finally, there will be one or two microcomputers on which children will simulate selected historical events, using graphics as well as text. For example, the outbreak of the Second World War, or Japan's turning towards industrialisation, would lend themselves to such simulation.

These examples, from various classrooms, are sufficient to give the flavour of how information technology will be used in 2000 in secondary schools. Each classroom will still have blackboards, books will still be very important, and pen and paper will still be required by every child. Laboratories will still contain large quantities of apparatus, but microcomputers will be particularly valuable in teaching science. Gymnasia and sports fields will remain. Dancing class, school drama and concerts will continue.

How will the children at this level feel about information technology? All who will be in secondary schools in 2000 will be born during the 1980s. They will not take to new information technology as naturally as those born in the next decade, who will grow up with the technology much more in evidence around them. Yet is seems likely that almost all the children in secondary school at the end of this century will learn quickly and easily on the 'user-friendly' machines that will then be installed. Will their teachers too?

In Teacher Training

In teachers' colleges and universities in the 1980s, courses for experienced teachers will receive high priority. Initial training of new young teachers will be needed, but the largest numbers will be found on the in-service courses, which will introduce all the new information technology and its applications in education. A central part of this training will be practical. Teachers will be expected to use the technology to create their own teaching materials, their own programs. They will also gain experience, under master-teachers, of how to organise their classes. They will learn how to group children for different activities related to the technology and how to individualise children's work. Primary school teachers will already know much of this, but some secondary school teachers may be learning it for the first time.

The technology will be provided in teachers' colleges and other training establishments and will include items not yet widely available in schools, such as a speech recognition device linked to a graphics display, invaluable for teaching children with certain handicaps.

In Higher Education

Universities and other institutions of higher education, as in past years, will be well to the fore in the year 2000 in equipping themselves with information technology. While lectures will not be entirely obsolete, they will no longer be considered vital for students (as indeed they are not in some universities today).

Students will spend much of their learning time at screens with full access to library collections in many forms. They will be able to call up video- and audiorecordings from archives, scan books and journals, view films, browse through art collections, consult thesauri and dictionaries, observe master-performers in the arts, obtain updated statistics, trace the origin of certain ideas, compare scholars' views, search bibliographies and cull from encyclopedias. They will have access to collections in their own institution and elsewhere, including those in other countries. They will be able to secure within minutes a translation of, say, a Russian journal article or an editorial in an Indonesian newspaper. They will make hard (printed) copy, perhaps by a process as straightforward as taking a photocopy today, or they will make a recording on disc, for use with hand-held devices in their own rooms. They will use microcomputers to word-process their assignments, which they will deliver to the professor on disc, for him or her to scrutinise and annotate on another screen. The same microcomputers will be used by students for many other tasks: computing, simulation, graphics and so on.

Professors will spend less of their teaching time on preparing and delivering lectures and more on creating and transforming information of many kinds and forms in their own fields. They will have assistance from technicians, but in the majority of cases they will work directly with new information technology. Some will use word processors to write books and papers, not very differently from today, but more fluently. Some will use graphics terminals to prepare computer simulations, mathematical or otherwise, for students to work through. Some will prefer to use a television studio to make videotapes appropriate to their subjects, or they make take a very small crew on location for this purpose. Some will compile reference collections for students' use, stored on videodisc. Others will compile directories of one kind or another, to assist students and academic colleagues in their searches of, say, videodotex computerised databases. One such directory will consist of names and access numbers of distinguished experts willing to answer questions in their field from students and others who may contact them at certain hours by voice, keyboard or even videophone.

There will still be professors who insist on classroom contact. They will have display devices in their classes for playing short segments of video- or audiotape or for calling up data from a computer. Students in their classes will bring hand-held devices for recording more traditional parts of the 'lectures'.

Research laboratories will also contain much new information technology. Indeed, the borderline between teaching and research will be less distinct than it is today. Many students will be trained in research methods at an early stage, probably before leaving secondary school, and will use these methods more and more as they pursue higher education. Much of their learning will take place in research environments, only a few of which will be conventional scientific laboratories. The glass-and-odours image of university chemical laboratories will disappear as fewer students undertake routine procedures, such as titration, by using actual materials. Instead, they will use computers and carry out simulations.

In Continuing Education

Adults wishing to continue their formal education will be able to do so largely in their own homes. They will visit colleges and other institutions from time to time for group discussions, to use specialised equipment or to meet an expert, but most of their needs will be met through the home screen and its associated devices. Some courses will be available via cable television, some will be on videotape or videodisc, and others will be on magnetic disc for use with microcomputers. Printed books will probably accompany each and where appropriate there will be audiotapes, or, occasionally, an old-fashioned radio broadcast, time-shifted from the middle of the night by the microcomputer and a taperecorder.

Adults taking upgrading courses for promotion purposes will receive packaged material from their employers or from colleges and universities, again for use on systems or devices installed in their own homes. Those who wish to retrain for new jobs will be able to commence retraining in the same way, with periods of experience interlocking with theoretical studies.

Teachers in the continuing education field will use telecommunications to keep in touch with their students and will often become highly proficient in devising teaching materials, like their colleagues in higher education. From time to time they will conduct weekend schools for particular groups of students, but most of their teaching will be through media. Like their university colleagues, they will prepare directories to help students make good use of videotex and other information banks.

Informal Learning by Adults

Adults will also have access to a very large store of information for informal learning not associated directly with any course or qualification. Many agencies will offer such information, some of it free, some of it for sale. It will be in books, tapes and records as at present but also in videodiscs for use in videodisc players, with or without microcomputers, in chip module form for plugging into hand-held and larger devices, and as computerised databases accessible by telephone line. In addition, cable television will bring into the home or office or factory a very large number of specialised channels, dealing with gardening, antique furniture restoration and marketing, religion, cultural affairs for ethnic minorities, sport, games such as chess, theatre, music, debate, carpentry and many other interests. One channel will carry nothing but indexes to the other channels, giving full details of all broadcasts.

Koughan (1981) foresees a satellite powerful enough to transmit television signals direct into every home in the United States. For $25 a month, the household will receive 400 hours of television a week on three channels: at a particular time there might be a Broadway play on the first, a children's special on the second, and sports on the third. The satellite will offer a high resolution picture with stereo sound, a second language audio channel, captioning for the deaf, and 100 pages of teletext (only 100 pages). The only missing link will be the talk-back facility, which may be provided by telephone or cable.

Adults will continue to meet in clubs and other groups for certain informal education activities, because they value the social contact these provide. Some of these meetings will include use of new information technology, either to view broadcasts or tapes before discussing them or to link up with other similar groups for exchange of views.

While most of the material provided for informal education will be prepared by professional educators of one kind or another, it seems likely that groups of adult learners, some of them already expert in their fields, will have a strong contribution to make to the store of information held locally, regionally, or even nationally. A cookery club will contribute its best recipes, an electronics group its hints for avoiding mistakes in building kits, a sailing club its frequently updated map of the shifting sands of an estuary popular among yachtsmen, and a religious sect its prayers and texts.

Summary

A learner's heaven based on new information technology will not arrive ready-made. It will spread slowly in each country and among the older people it will be accepted more reluctantly than among the young. By the year 2000, many will not yet be ready to avail themselves of all its benefits, but the rising generation will be eager and will not fear to use what is around them, which will offer them learning opportunities seldom imagined by previous generations.

19 LEARNERS' HELL: A PESSIMIST'S FORECAST

The last chapter focused our attention almost entirely on the benefits that might be brought to education by new information technology. This chapter assumes the worst, with or without the technology. What will happen if there is a general decline of educational systems in Western countries, if current trends continue for the years up to 2000? Alternatively, what are the negative effects that new information technology could bring in these same educational systems? What is the 'worst case' for learners?

Decreasing Budgets and General Decline of Education

If the economic well-being of Western countries declines steadily over the next 20 years, education budgets will be cut year by year. Even Socialist governments will be unable to restore these budgets to former levels because of competing demands for government resources, for example, to pay unemployment benefits. Private enterprise is unlikely to take over public education except at the margins. No more than 10-15 per cent of children will be in private schools, and perhaps even fewer in private universities and colleges. In public education, many aspiring learners will be without educational opportunities, as they were a hundred years before. Even the present low birth-rate, with its effects on enrolments, will not provide sufficient relief. Schools will still be expected to offer compulsory education to the age of 16 and will be sheltering from unemployment large numbers of children who are older.

A grim present-day example: from depressed areas of Michigan in the United States comes the report (*Financial Times*, 5 November 1981) that voters, offered the choice between higher school taxes or no more publicly funded schools, have closed the schools. In two school districts a total of 23,000 children are locked out, with dire consequences for their futures.

The educational system in each country will be in a state of contraction, decline and decay during the years up to 2000. Few new buildings or facilities will be constructed. Old buildings will be maintained poorly, on a minimal budget. Funds for equipment and textbooks will be very limited. Almost all schools and colleges will lack basic teaching materials such as books and laboratory equipment. Prices for these items will be rising faster than inflation as the education market contracts, making their replacement even more difficult. Even in universities, buildings will be closed because they are too costly to heat and maintain for smaller numbers of students. Staff will have to find other jobs and research projects will suffer from shortage of funds, especially for equipment. Libraries will devote all their meagre funds to maintaining existing stock and to continuing subscriptions to a few essential journals. Many journals will cease publication.

Outside the formal education sector, museums, public libraries, art galleries, broadcasting authorities and other agencies of informal education will find themselves unable to carry out their normal educational functions. For example, funds will not be available to transform relatively 'dead' collections of pictures or artefacts into teaching displays, nor to provide enriching series of television programmes for schools.

The most damaging trend will be towards an ageing staff in all agencies concerned with education. Very few young teachers and other staff will be recruited into the schools because the numbers of children will not justify further staff and funds will not in any case be available. Staff numbers will have to fall through retirement and resignations. Even adult education, with increasing numbers of clients, will not be able to afford new staff because it will remain low in government priorities. Informal education agencies will be contracting, like the schools, therefore they too will need very few new staff. Education will be staffed by people in the second half of their lives. These people will feel harrassed and oppressed by the conditions of their occupations, including the even lower status given to them by society. They will be inherently conservative and unwilling to consider changes, particularly those which might increase their productivity and lead to further staff being dismissed. They will turn to supporters such as members of the Back to Basics Movement and will favour 'low' technology, if not the slate and abacus then the blackboard and exercise-book. They will feel alienated from the communities they serve, however, because parents and children alike will be critical of them and the service they provide.

In these circumstances, new information technology will be kept outside the schools, outside the colleges and universities and outside the informal education agencies. If the technology thrives, it will be in the hands of the military, in some sectors of industry and commerce and perhaps in agriculture. Employers will condemn the educational institutions for turning out students who know so little about the technology or how it can be used. They will deplore the ever-widening gap between the needs of the wealth-producing sector of the country, as they call it, and what is provided by the educational system, which they will consider as parasitic. They will make half-hearted attempts to influence schools by offering exchange schemes in which teachers go into industry for a week or a month while an industrial worker goes to a school, but these schemes will be totally inadequate to break down hardened attitudes that will develop by the year 2000. Teachers will see themselves as preserving worthwhile cultural values in the face of blatant utilitarianism on the part of industry, commerce and the military. When accused of creating ghettoes, teachers will be proud of doing so in what they see as the new Dark Ages.

This will be the picture, without adequate funds for education and without the benefits of new information technology in education.

Funds Plus Increased Government Control

Let us now assume that adequate sums are available and that education receives from government, over the years to 2000, sufficient funds to pay staff, recruit a modicum of new young teachers, build a small number of new buildings in place of old and dilapidated ones and provide materials and equipment, including some new information technology. Let us further assume that the price exacted by government from the educational system is increased centralisation and control. This price will be highest in those systems at present decentralised, such as the United States, where States and local communities control education, and the United Kingdom, where local education authorities control it. It will not be as high in countries like France with long traditions of more centralised control, or in Japan, where a nation-wide standard curriculum has been followed for many years.

Governments will justify greater centralisation and increased intervention on their part. The first justification will be economic. In a time of scarce resources, of struggling national economies, it will be argued that there should be rationalisation. Central government will point to wasteful duplication of provision, for example in higher education where similar institutions in neighbouring regions offer roughly the same courses, leading to the same degrees. Central government will exert pressure to bring about greater standardisation of curricula at all levels, on the grounds that transfer of teachers and learners from one part of the system to another will be easier, that the demands of the community, including in particular leaders of industry and commerce, will be more widely satisfied by a standard curriculum and that 'quality control' and economies of scale will only be possible with such a curriculum.

Transfer of teachers will occur more frequently because central government will intervene to reduce staffing in areas with dwindling rolls and to increase staffing in those places with insufficient teachers. Such transfers will be in line with central government's policy for industrialisation, which will focus on 'centres of excellence' and abandon the pretence of trying to save other centres through massive subsidies.

The demands of the industrial and commercial communities will be reflected in a standard curriculum that gives very little time to the liberal arts, emphasises literacy and numeracy in the primary school and introduces direct vocational training at age 15 for all. In higher education, courses not linked to vocations will be eliminated in all except a few selected institutions.

'Quality control' will be the watchword in the educational system. It will be under the supervision of inspectors appointed by central government and reporting to it, and of a central testing, examination and certification agency supported by government funds. Inspectors will ensure that the standard curriculum is being followed at all levels and will also be responsible for monitoring expenditure and efficiency in individual institutions. They will prepare annual 'accounts' of cost-effectiveness, which will reflect not only the main categories of expenditure (and the amounts spent) but also the 'output' of the institution in terms of test scores, examination passes and certificates gained. Cost-effective schools and colleges will be rewarded with extra resources.

Economies of scale will be obtained by bulk purchasing by central government of standard textbooks and other educational materials, by centralised negotiation of all salaries and wages, and by central planning and design of all educational buildings and facilities.

Further economies of scale will be obtained by operating a central testing, examination and certification agency, which will replace scattered smaller and less efficient bureaus.

Such conditions can come about with or without new information technology, but standardisation will favour its introduction. Central governments will be persuaded by powerful private interests seeking to sell the technology that education can benefit from information technology only under these conditions. These interests will argue that the country cannot do without new information technology in its educational system, lest its people fall behind in the international race. They will claim that potential benefits justify changing the system to fit the technology. Schemes such as Bitzer's (1977) proposal for an American million-terminal computer-assisted learning system will command new support.

Education Dominated by Private Interests

Let us assume now that central and local governments by the year 2000 lose interest in education because it is such a depressed sector of society. Government will adopt a *laissez faire* attitude and consider that education should be open to market forces and free enterprise. Those who really want education, government will argue, are ready to pay for it, even if it means a struggle.

Under these circumstances, many learners or their parents will be paying directly for a much larger percentage of the real cost of their education than at present, with a smaller percentage coming from general taxation. Because these 'consumers' of education have to pay more directly, they will demand more direct control over their educational choices. They will want the right to decide which schools are suitable for their children and what they are to learn. For themselves, as adult learners, they will seek freedom to select among courses and institutions, rather than be selected.

Private businesses in the educational sector will thrive. Wealth will apparently buy better education, therefore private companies will set up educational institutions of many kinds to make a profit. Their schools will cream off the more able children from the remaining state-funded schools. The same will happen in higher education, except that many universities will try to save themselves by going into partnership with companies, both for teaching and research, and will be willing to sacrifice much of their autonomy in the process.

Private interests in the field of new information technology will push their products and services at all levels. They will in any case be in a better position to assess markets than publicly funded institutions, which usually do not have the market search skills. Parents and students in the wealthier sectors of society will gain most, because new information technology companies will install cable services only in wealthy suburbs, and will charge prices too high for the rest of the population; microcomputers will be provided in substantial numbers only in private schools and universities; informal education via cable, videodisc and other new media will be the province of those in the upper-income bracket. Videotape companies, apart from those marketing pornography, will move steadily up-market.

Control of new information technology for educational purposes will rest largely in the hands of bodies with little interest in education. Commercial gain over the short term (a few years) will dominate, leading to sales of poor quality programs and hardware, much of it very imperfectly adapted to educational needs. Consumers in education will have few safeguards against the tough sales pitch. Shoddy products with no after-sales service will flood the market.

Costs of new information technology will fall slowly because markets will be relatively small, most people being unable to afford the products. Designers, manufacturers and producers of programs will limit the range of what they make, to serve only the wealthy sector.

Technology Overwhelms Education

Voice recognition will be perfected by the year 2000, in the wake of far greater density of storage in memory devices. If it can be made cheaply enough, the advent of voice recognition may lead to technology overwhelming education. As Scriven (1981) says, the hardware is very likely to be available, even if the software is slower in development on account of the difficult problems of pattern recognition that are involved.

Let us assume that a child is able to speak to a computer for a short while, during which it registers his or her 'voice print'. Thereafter, the child need only utter his or her name to enter into a dialogue with the computer. Such a machine will make it unnecessary for the child to learn to read or write. Even learning to use a keyboard may become superfluous. Foreign languages will pose few difficulties, since translation facilities can be built into the same device. Scriven suggests that these changes will be a natural extension of the realisation that the calculator makes arithmetic virtually unnecessary. In society, the penalty for not being able to read or write will drop as voice recognition is available. But, as Scriven admitted, a person depending on such electronic assistance will be unable to read 'manually' a billboard or any other textual message.

Summary

Why should we consider such developments as a form of hell? The answer to that question is that they will create havoc in our educational systems. They will challenge deeply-held values, derived from pre-industrial society, and long-established practices, and will call in question much of the activity with which teachers and children fill their schooldays. For learners in the year 2000, this will be hell. Technology will dominate education, although the old will not give up without a great struggle. How will written argument, much easier to follow than spoken, be preserved? Can advanced mathematics be studied without writing and reading? Will we have to develop short-hand speech? These are difficult questions, says Scriven, but not as difficult as why we should learn to read and which of us should do so. The teachers' role will need to be clarified too, assuming that enough of them are willing to continue working under what they may well see as technology's rule.

20 NEITHER HEAVEN NOR HELL: A PERSONAL FORECAST

Our view of how the world will be in 2000 AD depends to a large extent on our view of whether world resources are being depleted too quickly or not, and whether we think the population is growing too fast. The Club of Rome said that there are limits to growth. Simon (1981a) argues more or less the opposite: he says the evidence for thinking that overpopulation is leading to widespread starvation or that energy is rapidly running out has been exaggerated, while the evidence for thinking otherwise has been ignored. Energy is dropping in price, in real terms, and the amount of food produced per capita in the world is increasing. He sees these trends continuing indefinitely. The new information technology supports his thesis: for example, it uses much less energy and fewer scarce resources than the old technology. Perhaps, on these and similar assumptions, Martin's (1977) and Evans' (1981) optimistic forecasts are the ones we should have faith in, but most people would rather not take the risk of committing themselves to belief in such an apparently rosy future.

Forecasts regarding new information technology *are* risky, because of rapid evolution of the technology itself and because of powerful forces behind this evolution. Despite the risks, I shall make my forecast, drawing on the inevitable mixture of fact and fiction, of evidence and rumour, of hypotheses and opinions, that surrounds this new technology as it comes into industrialised society (see, for example, Dede's (1981) analysis or Wicklein's (1981) nightmares). I deliberately polarised the views of optimists and pessimists in Chapters 18 and 19, but neither view can be wholly accurate. Neither the best nor the worst will come to pass: instead, something between the two is likely, assuming that we have not brought utter disaster upon ourselves through nuclear warfare before the end of the century. I feel optimism and pessimism, but on balance I am an optimist. I believe that we in education can by our own efforts avoid the worst ills and, for the benefit of our society, take advantage of opportunities offered by new information technology.

We lay bare other assumptions if we ask ourselves the question: How do we want our children's children to benefit from new information technology for their education? Our answer will be idealistic, but at least it sets out the values we hope to maintain. I want these children, in the year 2000, to be able to use new information technology to extend their senses, their understanding and their imagination. Technology of the kinds described in this book will bring to them many visions, visions from the past including that which I now inhabit, from many parts of the world, from the macroscopic and the microscopic, from realms of nature, art and science. I know that these visions will be in every case subjective, somebody's collage, therefore I want my children's children to gain understanding of subjectivity, to welcome it for its richness and to seek their own truth among contrary visions. I want them to be able to use the technology: it will increase their access to these visions and will offer them many choices. At the same time, it will help them to extend their reasoning powers, their capacity to think in symbols. It will help them to use codes and languages, to enhance communication between themselves and others. I want them to understand the society they live in and to contribute to it all they can, from their enhanced awareness and ability to communicate. The problems of their day will be no simpler than those of mine. I know that this is an idealistic statement. It is not particularly original: without the technology, Plato and Aristotle made similar suggestions for educating the young.

Finally, we can base our forecasts on whether or not we have reason to agree with the view of experts about the future. This approach leads us to both optimistic and pessimistic views, and I adopt it in the rest of this chapter.

Optimistic Forecasts

Already we see those who cannot add, adding. I agree with Bowes (1980) that the information-poor may be able to remedy their disadvantage if the technology is made very 'user-friendly' and I forecast that good progress will be made in this direction by 2000. Learners will not always be obliged to depend so heavily on being able to decode the printed page. People who thought of themselves as illiterate or innumerate will be able to use language and numbers in ways at present beyond them. I think Osborne (1977) was wrong in asserting that many people simply will not need computing power because they do no more than add, subtract, multiply and divide —

functions that can be carried out by a pocket calculator. He forgets how the processing power of computers can be brought to bear on many tasks, including transformation of information from one communication mode or one symbol system to another.

Education needs fundamentally new instructional paradigms, ones not based on the belief that computation is a scarce resource, as Brown (1977) points out. I predict that, by 2000, research will be yielding some of these new paradigms. For example, as Brown says, computer-based instructional systems can 'understand' their subject domain and use this knowledge base to help students to experiment with, remove faults from and articulate ideas and reasoning strategies. Progressively more effort will go into research in this field. As O'Shea and Self (1982) say in writing about computers in education, we do not know enough about how students learn, nor about how to teach them. My own field, psychology, has not yet produced the answers, but it must yield them if we are to take full advantage of this new information technology in education.

I agree with Schwartz (1981) that Papert's (1977, 1980) ideas appear likely to be among the most fruitful, and I forecast that they will lead to many new developments by the year 2000. As Papert says, the static technology of paper-and-pencil, as used in schools, obliges us to teach mathematics in a 'denatured' artificial way, whereas the dynamic technology of computers enables us to teach naturally mathematics, and perhaps other subjects. He argues well the case for machines teaching naturally. His turtle geometry uses this dynamic technology, and is, he says, 'more powerful, more accessible and more intuitive than the non-computational geometries of Euclid and Descartes'. His ideas will be used, I predict, in other fields besides mathematics, in fact, wherever computer modelling can assist problem-solving.

I agree with Ahl (1977) that in education we need information technology that is reliable, reasonably priced and adaptable to new needs. It must fit people, rather than vice versa, and preferably should diagnose and repair its own faults. I forecast that by 2000 we shall have information technology in many parts of the industrialised world that will meet these criteria.

Far from predicting the end of textbooks in schools, I forecast that by 2000 there will be a revitalised textbook industry based on new publishing techniques. Gates (1980) argues that the publishing industry will go through certain changes. We may assume that some of these changes will have great significance for education. For example, a move to 'on-demand' publishing will make updating of textbooks easier and more economically feasible. The manuscript will be held on disc or in some other electronic form, and the number of copies ordered, no more, no less, will be printed by new technology on demand. Before a further order is filled, the manuscript may be changed by the author, although clearly there could be problems if too many different editions were in the schools at the same time. Warehouses (and bookshops) full of unsold books may become rarer, and schools may reach the point where they actually print their own books, under licence, on their own equipment, using authors' discs rented from publishers.

I agree with Scriven, who thinks that the handicapped and the poor in American schools may well be the first to get new information technology, with the help of government subsidies. I predict that the wealthy will want their children to have the same advantages and other parents will feel obliged to follow suit. These trends will be backed, as Evans (1981) points out, by 'commercial pressures of unstoppable strength . . . already building up and, like it or not, the pocket teaching computer will soon be upon us. One of the biggest untapped markets in the world is the application of computers to education.' By the end of the century, and not only in the United States, education will be supplied with hardware and courseware.

I extrapolate from Melmed's (1982) estimates of what it would cost to put four million computers into American schools by 1990. He considers this figure would allow a maximum of 30 minutes a day for each student on a computer. If each computer costs $1,000 and lasts five years, the annual cost after 1990 to the government for hardware, including hard disc secondary storage units, would be about $1,120,000,000 at 1980 prices. If there are 40 million students in 1990, he says, the average cost for one student to study for one hour will be about 50 cents, including software and courseware costs. I forecast that, by 2000, this cost will have dropped in real terms by 20-30 per cent. The cost of hardware will have dropped very considerably, but development costs for software and courseware will have risen.

Melmed assumes, on courseware, that in twelve years of schooling a student will, on average, have 864 hours of computer access. He allows for three 'levels' of courseware, for slow, average and fast students, and assumes that altogether about 4,000 hours of courseware will be needed. This figure may not allow sufficiently for variations of curriculum, however, particularly in secondary school.

These variations are both geographical and historical: different districts want different emphases, and individual subjects are changing faster than ever before. He builds in assumptions about courseware life (five years), development and publishing costs, but arrives at a figure that may be low: $40,000,000 a year or $1 per student in 1990. If this figure is tripled, then courseware costs of $3 per student each year are still only a small component of total cost, since the cost of computing facilities he estimates at about $30 per student each year. He makes the further point that, for the United States, this total figure of, say, $33 per student is about 1.3 per cent of the 1990 projected annual per student budget of $2,500. In other words, providing computerised learning in schools should be possible within such a budget. On the other hand, he says, schools now spend only 0.8 per cent of their budget on instructional materials. I am hopeful about United States governments (Federal, State and local) finding these sums of money, and if they do, will other Western governments avoid trying to do the same?

Education (and society) will exploit new information technology selectively, not universally and indiscriminately. Many traditional values, such as personal contact between teacher and learner, will be upheld. I predict that by the year 2000 there will still be many in education in industrialised countries who reject information technology, particularly computers. I do not agree with Evans (1981) that computers' low cost will 'ensure that they, like their predecessors the calculators, will sweep through the educational system of the Western world. Teachers and educators may as well face up to this fact and should decide now how to meet the challenge when it comes, for one thing is certain: any tactic that involves banning or prohibiting their manufacture and sale is doomed to failure.' I think there will be substantial pockets of resistance and I view their existence positively in the sense that they will show independence of thought and action.

Schools will not be deinstitutionalised as Unwin (1981) predicts, because children will still need them and so will their parents. Teachers will still be teaching in classrooms at all levels at the end of this century, despite the attacks of taxpayers.

I predict that by 2000 governments of most of the countries covered in this book will have taken a lead in resolving copyright problems (Ploman and Hamilton, 1980), in setting up courseware libraries and exchanges and in regulating standards, with consequent increased transferability of hardware and courseware. The political pay-off from dealing with these issues will be high enough to ensure that they are not neglected.

Pessimistic Views

As an American academic said to me, 'With technology, it's hard doubting anything.' This is particularly true if one is under some pressure from salespeople from electronic industries in California's Silicon Valley. Nevertheless, I am willing to predict that by 2000 there will be educational institutions where information technology is being used in a dehumanising way. As Hubbard (1981) says 'It is possible, given the wrong intentions, to produce a thoroughly dehumanising educational environment; some of our institutions manage it without using a computer at all.' I am concerned at the possibility that the technology will be used unscrupulously by private interests for personal gain, in institutions that will be outside the few remaining fragments of regulations that government may preserve by 2000 in this field. Some of these institutions will be supporting elitism; for example, in the United Kingdom they will be using new information technology to preserve the belief that the appropriate values in our society should be aristocratic ones, as Gosling (1981) puts it.

I am most concerned, however, that information technology will not be distributed evenly enough through industrialised societies by 2000 for informal education to be available to more or less everyone who wants it. The figures I have add force to this view: for instance, Londoner and Blum (1981), analysts in a firm of New York stock-brokers, in an optimistic report predict that in the United States 40 per cent of households will possess a videodisc player by 1990. Even if that figure rises to 70 per cent by 2000, a great many households, probably in the poorer sectors of town and country, will have none. Similarly, by 1991 only ten per cent of American homes will have videotex (figures reported in *Intermedia*, vol. 10, no. 1), and of these half will be via two-way cable and only 30 per cent via the telephone. By 1991 only 51 per cent of US homes will be on cable, compared with 22 per cent in 1981 (Large, 1982a), and only five per cent of households (7 million) will have teletext, although from 1985 all new colour TV sets made in the US will have a teletext decoder built in. Even the optimistic forecasts of the communications specialists consulted by Pelton (1981) suggest that only a maximum

of 25 per cent of American homes would have a computer-tele-
communications-video centre, suitable for schooling among other
uses, by 2000. Shotwell and Associates (1981) predict that the
number of installed microcomputers in 1984 in the United States will
be three million, of which 750,000 will be in homes and 300,000 in
educational institutions, so there will have to be a sharp increase
even to reach Pelton's figure. If America cannot lead the way to
greater abundance by the end of the century, can any other
industrialised nation? I doubt it, and I fear many people will be
placed at a disadvantage educationally while outside the formal
system. Government-introduced tax incentives, as in the United
Kingdom for television set manufacturers who build in teletext and
videotex adaptors, may not be enough to attract buyers from poorer
sections of the community. Certainly the evidence so far is that
teletext users come from professional or skilled occupational classes,
are prosperous and already make heavy use of information. A
million teletext sets by 1983 in the United Kingdom (Large, 1982) is
only a beginning.

What about other countries? Glowinski and others (1980) provide
four alternative scenarios for French information technology in
2000 AD. Their *téléphonique* scenario envisages 30 million ordinary
telephones, one million businesses on a data network, 50,000 telephones linked for teleconferencing and 500,000 mobile radio telephones. The *audiomatique* scenario provides a mere ten million
ordinary telephones, but 30 million new telephones, 500,000 videophones, 10,000 teleconference telephones and a million mobile radio
telephones. The *videophonique* is even more ambitious, with 35
million new telephones, 10 million videophones, a million telephones linked in a data network and a million mobile radio telephones. Finally, their *videomatique* scenario includes 40 million new
telephones, all with video, and 200,000 mobile telephones. These
scenarios are not so much forecasts of what will happen in France as
speculation, but education simply does not feature in them. In fact,
they include no discussion of the impact of information technology
on education. For Sweden, Svard (1982) says that videorecorders
may be in 25-40 per cent of homes by 1985, but that it is difficult to
predict beyond that date. Chapman (1981), however, gives some
estimates for penetration of videotex in Europe and North America
in 1985 and 1990, and says that North America will grow more
rapidly after a late start. But his highest estimates for Europe in 1990
are for about 17 million sets (12 million in homes) and for North

America 30 million sets (18 million in homes), still a very long way from universal coverage as achieved by television. He predicts that information services will lead, followed by transactional services, but also says that between 1990 and 2000, digital and broadband networks will begin to take over. This changeover will interrupt wider development of ordinary videotex, I predict. I agree with his view that the residential market will probably be dominated by interactive moving picture services: subscribers will be able to call up movies from a long catalogue, among which will be some educational titles. America, with more cable in place, will lead Europe at this stage, although in 1981 cable served more homes (37 per cent in West Germany, and over 50 per cent in Belgium, the Netherlands and Denmark) in some Western European countries than in the United States (Large, 1982a). In the United Kingdom, there will need to be a steep increase in cabling from the present 14 per cent of homes, most of them on obsolete cables with few channels. Probably by 2000 Japan will have developed and installed technology to overcome the problems of its character set and will be forging ahead in videotex. Whether or not education will be well-served is another matter.

I share only some of the concern of technological determinists like Innis (1950, 1951) and McLuhan (1962, 1964) who consider that the form of technology influences the form of society. New information technology will influence society, since it 'has a certain logic, a certain social form through which it must operate' (Ryan, 1981), but I support Gosling's (1981a) view that society influences the technology too.

I am therefore pessimistic about our avoiding a situation, by 2000, in which new information technology is almost completely under the control of large international corporations serving first their own commercial interest. I doubt the will or capacity of Western governments to regulate the affairs of these corporations, for whom educational provision is a very low priority. Woodward (1981) and her colleagues may be right in suggesting that the advent of the information society is merely putting off revolutionary change in Western countries. Dordick (1980) indentifies three 'drives' which are behind new information technology: the technology drive, the market drive and the policy drive. The technology drive and the market drive appear to me to be dominant now and I am pessimistic about the policy drive becoming more dominant by 2000. Even if Polcyn's (1981) forecasts about many more satellites by the end of the century are accurate, education will be the last to benefit.

I agree with Melmed (1982) that three specific conditions could delay provision of computers in schools: lack of money, of courseware and of improved ways of using computers in education. These conditions are mutually reinforcing, as he says. Courseware is expensive because of high development, test and distribution costs. Development requires expensive equipment and specialised authors and designers, if it is to be at a high enough standard for regional or national markets. Testing requires access to children (and their teachers). If courseware is designed for use with different microcomputers, it must be tested on all of them. The costs of ironing out problems that are only noticed later must also be borne. Distribution costs include trouble-shooting of this kind. Once developed, courseware becomes obsolescent quickly in some fields because the state of knowledge is changing rapidly. Thus there are very substantial costs and risks attached to courseware development.

I predict that governments will continue to vote funds for hardware and courseware in schools, but insufficient for universal provision. Companies selling new information technology will take their first profits from the military, industrial and commercial sectors, and will move on to take profits from the agricultural, domestic and government sectors, with education commanding their attention last of all. Melmed is right in pointing out that the non-profit sector in America needs to develop 'examples of increasingly effective approaches to student use of the computer,' otherwise governments (local, regional and national) 'may prefer to delay appropriating a special budget for school acquisition of computer equipment . . . and . . . private-sector developers may continue to delay investment in the production of courseware . . . We may find the schools in 1990 not much further advanced in the student use of computers . . .'

The Last Word

The fact that one company now markets a program called The Last Word, claiming for it considerable powers, is enough, I think, to underline how aggressive selling is becoming in the new information technology field. I am convinced that new information technology in the countries I write about is powered by political, economic and technological forces that will not fade, and that it will influence deeply the lives of many people in these countries by the year 2000. Education, insulated from many technological changes in the last century, will not be able to insulate itself from new information technology. Demands, from parents and employers, for students to learn about new information technology, through it and in preparation for it in their adult lives, will no doubt increase slowly at first but then more quickly. Children and adolescents will themselves seek out new information technology, perhaps by-passing the schools. Even adults will turn more and more towards it for work and leisure.

My view is that here is a new technology with great potential for education. I am sure we do not know enough yet about how to take full advantage of the technology, or about how to avoid some of its dangers, but experience is beginning to accumulate. We are seeing the emergence of synergy, as different devices and systems are brought together, combining powerfully their effects, and synergistic systems may soon become multi-purpose systems, serving learners in many ways. All of us who declare an interest in education should aim at increasing our understanding of this technology, the new information technology. Can education take advantage of it? I hope so, but that depends on us.

REFERENCES

Adams, Charles R. (1981). *Optical Laser Disk Storage for Information Control and Distribution*. London: Altergo Services

Advisory Council for Adult and Continuing Education (1981). *Adults' Mathematical Ability and Performance*. London: The Council

Ahl, David (1977). Does education want what technology can deliver? In Seidel, Robert J. and Rubin, Martin (eds.) (1977). *Computers and Communication: Implications for Education*. New York: Academic Press

Alderman, Donald L. (1980). Evaluations of computer-assisted instruction in mathematics. Paper presented at the Fourth International Congress on Mathematical Education, Berkeley, California (mimeo)

Arnold, E. (1981). Prestel — a lemon in the living room? In Hooper, R. and others (1981). *Viewdata '81*. Northwood, England: Online Conferences

Atherton, Roy (1981). *Structured Programming in COMAL-80*. Chichester: Ellis Horwood

___(1982). Why COMAL is a quiet revolution. *Phase Two*, vol. 2, no. 1

Bakan, Joseph D. and Chandler, David L. (1980). *Access II: the Independent Producer's Handbook of Satellite Communications*. Washington, DC: National Endowment for the Arts

Baker, John, Easen, Patrick, Graham, Alan and Tyler, Ken (1981). Calculators in the primary school. Milton Keynes: Mathematics Education Research Group, The Open University (mimeo)

Banks, Martin (1980). *Living with the Micro*. Wilmslow, Cheshire: Sigma Technical Press

Bates, A.W. (1981). Report on visit to videodisc design/production group, University of Nebraska-Lincoln, 29 October. Milton Keynes: Institute of Educational Technology, The Open University (mimeo)

___(1981a). Report on other developments regarding educational videodisc in the USA. Milton Keynes: Institute of Educational Technology, The Open University (mimeo)

Bejar, Isaac I. (1980). Milliken math sequences. *Creative Computing*, September

Bell, Daniel (1980). The social framework of the information society. In Forester, Tom (ed.) (1980). *The Microelectronics Revolution*. Oxford: Blackwell

Bitzer, Donald (1977). The million terminal system of 1985. In Seidel, Robert J. and Rubin, Martin (eds.) (1977). *Computers and Communication: Implications for Education*. New York: Academic Press

Blizek, John (1981). The First National Kidisc — TV becomes a plaything. *Educational-Instructional TV*, June

Bolt, Richard A. (1979). *Spatial Data-Management*. Cambridge, Massachusetts: Massachusetts Institute of Technology

Borrell, J. (1981). Legislative concerns of the Ninety-Sixth Congress: information technology and policy. *Electronic Publishing Review*, vol. 1, no. 3

Bourne, Richard (1981). Minis and micros. *Guardian*, 14 July

Bowes, John E. (1980). Mind vs. matter — mass utilization of information technology. In Dervin, Brenda and Voigt, Melvin J. (1980). *Progress in Communication Sciences*, Vol. II. Norwood, New Jersey: Ablex Publishing

Brahan, J.W. and Godfrey, W.D. (1981). The big red/green/blue schoolhouse:

videotex and learning in the '80s. In Hooper, R. and others (1981). *Viewdata '81*. Northwood, England: Online Conferences

Bramer, M.A. (1982). COMAL 80 — adding structure to BASIC. *Computers in Education*, vol. 6, no. 2

Bremner, D.H. and Prescott, A. (1981). Primary schools: the first steps in computing. *Phase Two*, vol. 1, no. 3

Brown, John Seely (1977). Uses of artificial intelligence and advanced computer technology in education. In Seidel, Robert J. and Rubin, Martin (eds.) (1977). *Computers and Communication: Implications for Education*. New York: Academic Press

Brown, J. and Stokes, A. (1981). The definitive revelations as to who's using what computer in their schools and how many they've got. *Computing Today*, December

Brown, Mike (1982). Telesoftware standards. *CET News*, no. 14

Bruner, J.S., Olver, R. and Greenfield, P.M. (1966). *Studies in Cognitive Growth*. New York: Wiley

Bugliarello, George and Doner, Dean B. (eds.) (1979). *The History and Philosophy of Technology*. Urbana: University of Illinois Press

Bunderson, C. Victor (1981). Interactive videodisc activities at WICAT. Provo, Utah: WICAT Education Institute (mimeo)

——, Cole, Nancy, Gibbons, Andrew and Kerr, Michael (1981). Educational technology report: video display systems, interactive computers and distributed networks. Orem, Utah: WICAT Systems (mimeo)

——, Olsen, James B. and Baillio, Bruce (1981). Proof-of-concept demonstration and comparative evaluation of a prototype intelligent videodisc system. Orem, Utah: WICAT Systems (mimeo)

Burton, Richard R. and Brown, John Seely (1979). An investigation of computer coaching for informal learning activities. *International Journal of ManMachine Studies*, vol. 11

Butterworth, Judith, Keenan, Stella and Arundale, Justin (1982). Public libraries in the information age. In Tedd, Lucy and others (1982). [Proceedings of the] *Fifth International Online Information Meeting, London 8-10 December 1981*. Oxford: Learned Information

Bygrave, Mike (1979). Writing on an empty screen. *Intermedia*, vol. 7, no. 3

Carpenter, C. (1980). Chem lab simulations from high technology. *Creative Computing*, September

Case, Donald and others (1981). *Evaluation of the Green Thumb Box Experimental Videotext Project for Agricultural Extension Information Delivery in Shelby and Todd Counties, Kentucky*. Stanford: Institute for Communication Research, Stanford University (mimeo)

Caspers, Wesley (1981). Science, Volume 3: earthquakes, minerals, stars and food chains . . . new dimensions in ecology education. *Journal of Courseware Review*, vol. 1, no. 1

Central Computer and Telecommunications Agency (1980). Stand alone word processors: report of trials in UK Government typing pools 1979/80. London: Civil Service Department (mimeo)

Chapman, T. (1981). Videotex applications: an international review of current and potential market penetration'. In Hooper. R. and others (1981). *Viewdata '81*. Northwood, England: Online Conferences

Chen, Milton (1981). Site visits to new communication technologies used by children. Stanford: Institute for Communication Research, Stanford University (mimeo)

Chin, R. and Benne, K.D. (1969). General strategies for effecting change in human systems. In Bennis, W.G., Benne, K.D. and Chin, R. (eds.) (1969). *The Planning of Change*. New York: Holt, Rinehart and Winston

Coates, Jill (1981). Telesoftware goes live! *CALNEWS*, no. 17, September

Coll, John A. (1980). Computer science or computer appreciation? In Stevenson, P. and others (1980). [Proceedings of the Conference on] *Microcomputers in Education*. London, July 1980. Northwood, England: Online Publications

Commission on New Information Technology (1981). *New Media: Broadcast Teletext, Videotex*. Stockholm: Swedish Ministry of Education and Culture

Conlin, Cathy (1981). A computer in an infant school. *CALNEWS*, no. 16, March

Convey, John (1981). The promotion of an online service in the public library. In Holmes, P. and others (1981). [Proceedings of the] *Fourth International Online Information Meeting, London 9-11 December 1980*. Oxford: Learned Information

Crisp, Jason (1982). Why Sinclair thinks small is beautiful. *Financial Times*, 20 March

Czechowicz, Leslie (1981). English basics part II: concepts in language arts. *Journal of Courseware Review*, vol. 1, no. 1

Dede, Christopher (1981). Educational, social and ethical implications of technological innovations. *Programmed Learning and Educational Technology*, vol. 18, no. 4

Deunette, Jacky B. and Dibb, Lesley C. (1981). The Online Information Centre. In Holmes, P.L. and others (1981). [Proceedings of the] *Fourth International Online Information Meeting, London 9-11 December 1980*. Oxford: Learned Information

Dineen, Michael (1981). Mercury on the right track. *Guardian*, 25 October

Donahue, Thomas R. (1980). Technology: using it wisely. *Labour Bulletin*, January

Dordick, H.S. (1980). Information inequality: an emerging policy issue for the United States. In Wedemeyer, D. (ed.) (1980). *Pacific Telecommunications Conference Proceedings*. Honolulu: East-West Center

Drucker, Peter (1969). *The Age of Discontinuity*. London: Heinemann

Dwyer, Thomas A. (1977). An extensible model for using technology in education. In Seidel, Robert J. and Rubin, Martin (eds.) (1977). *Computers and Communication: Implications for Education*. New York: Academic Press

___ and Critchfield, Margot (1978). *BASIC and the Personal Computer*. Reading, Mass.: Addison-Wesley

Eicher, J.C., Hawkridge, D.G., McAnany E., Mariet, F. and Orivel, F. (1982). *The Economics of New Educational Media*, Vol. 3. Paris: Unesco

Ellingham, David (1982). *Managing the Microcomputer in the Classroom*. London: Council for Educational Technology

Evans, Christopher (1981). *The micro millennium*. New York: Washington Square Press/Pocket Books

Finkel, LeRoy (1981). Computer discovery. *Journal of Courseware Review*, vol. 1, no. 1

Finzer, W. (1980) PET programs for the San Francisco State University Center for Mathematical Literacy. San Francisco: San Francisco State University (mimeo)

___ (1981). The gap between the image in the mind and the image on the screen. San Francisco: Math Network Curriculum Project, San Francisco State University (mimeo)

Fisher, James D. (1982). Personal communication

Forman, Denyse (1981). Milliken math sequences. *Journal of Courseware Review*, vol. 1, no. 1

Fort, Ann (1980). Evaluation of the presentation of COIC's information via the Post Office viewdata system (Prestel). London: Employment Services Division, Manpower Services Commission (mimeo)

Fothergill, R. and Anderson, J.S.A. (1981). Strategy for the Microelectronics Programme (MEP). *Programmed Learning and Educational Technology*, vol. 18, no. 3

Futcher, Dave (1981). When deadly maths is nothing like so deadly. *Educational Computing*, vol. 2, no. 7

Galton, M. and Simon, B. (eds.) (1980). *Progress and Performance in Primary Schools*. London: Routledge & Kegan Paul

Gates, M. Yuri (1980). Technological developments in the printing industry from now until 1990. In Maurice, Marcel, Phillips, Edward and Scherff, Hans-Ludwig (eds.) (1980). *The Impact of New Technologies on Publishing*. London: Saur

___ and Maslin, J.M. (1980). Evaluating reactions to the use of Prestel viewdata for information dissemination and programmed learning. In Wanger, Judith and others (1980). [Proceedings of the] *Third International Online Information Meeting, London 4-6 December 1979*. Oxford: Learned Information

Gilmer, Gloria (1981). Compu-Math: arithmetic skills. *Journal of Courseware Review*, vol. 1, no. 1

Girling, Michael (1977). Towards a definition of basic numeracy. *Mathematics Teaching*, vol. 81

Glowinski, Albert and others (1980). *Télécommunications objectif 2000*. Paris: Dunod.

Goodson, Bobby (1981). Elementary, Volume 6. *Journal of Courseware Review*, vol. 1, no. 1

Gosling, William (1981). Remarks following Hubbard's lecture, reported in Hubbard, Geoffrey (1981)

___ (1981a). *The Kingdom of Sand*. London: Council for Educational Technology

Greenagel, F.L. (1981). Arete — a 3000-year-old word for the latest in electronic publishing. *Electronic Publishing Review*, vol. 1, no. 3

Gumpert, Gary and Cathcart, Robert (eds.) (1979). *Intermedia: Interpersonal Communication in a Media World*. New York: Oxford University Press

Hakansson, Joyce (1981). How to evaluate educational courseware. *Journal of Courseware Review*, vol. 1, no. 1

Haney, Michael R. (1981). Scatter: unit on particle scattering. *Journal of Courseware Review*, vol. 1, no. 1

Hartley, Roger (1981). A cool look at computer-aided learning. *Educational Computing*, vol. 2, no 5

Havelock, R.G. (1971). *Planning for Innovation through Dissemination and Utilization of Knowledge*. Ann Arbor: Institute for Social Research, University of Michigan

Hawker, Pat (1981). Electronic cameras: What now? What next? What then? *Combroad,* June

Hawkridge, David and Robinson, John (1982). *Organizing Educational Broadcasting*. London: Croom Helm.

Hechinger, Grace (1981). Tuned-out teachers and turned-off kids. *Channels*, vol. 1, no. 3

Heck, William, Johnson, Jerry and Kansky, Robert (1981). *Guidelines for Evaluating Computerised Instructional Materials*. Reston, Virginia: National Council of Teachers of Mathematics

Hedger, John (1980). Broadcast telesoftware: experience with Oracle. In Haslam, G. and others (1980). *Viewdata '80*. Northwood, England: Online Conferences

Her Majesty's Inspectors (1980). *Mathematics 5-11*. London: Her Majesty's Stationery Office.

Her Majesty's Inspectors of Schools (1978). *Primary Education in England*. London: Her Majesty's Stationery Office

Hessinger, Lynn (1981). Computer and videodisc: a new way to teach CPR. *Biomedical Communications*, September

Hiltz, Starr Roxanne and Turoff, Murray (1978). *The Network Nation: Human Communication via Computer*. Reading, Massachusetts: Addison-Wesley

Hoggart, Richard (1982). The divisive society. *Observer*, 21 February

Hollan, James, Stevens, Albert and Williams, Michael (1980). STEAMER; An advanced computer-assisted instruction system for propulsion engineering. San Diego: Navy Personnel Research and Development Centre (mimeo)

Home Office (1981). *Direct Broadcasting by Satellite*. London: Her Majesty's Stationery Office

Hon, David (1981). What the Space Invaders are trying to tell us. *Video User*, September

Hooper, Richard (1977). *The National Development Programme in Computer Assisted Learning: Final Report of the Director*. London: Council for Educational Technology

___ (1980). Applications of viewdata. In Wanger, Judith and others (1980). [Proceedings of the] *Third International Online Information Meeting, London 4-6 December 1979*. Oxford: Learned Information

___ and Toye, Ingrid (ed.) (1975). *Computer Assisted Learning in the United Kingdom: Some Case Studies*. London: Council for Educational Technology

Hope, Mary (1981). Prestel umbrella noticeboard. *CET News*, no. 13

Houghton, B. and Wisdom, J.C. (1980). Non-bibliographic online databases: an investigation into their uses within the fields of economics and business studies. In Wanger, Judith and others (1980). [Proceedings of the] *Third International Online Information Meeting, London 4-6 December 1979*. Oxford: Learned Information

House, E.R. (1974). *The Politics of Educational Innovation*. San Francisco: McCutchan

Hubbard, Geoffrey (1981). Education and the new technologies. *Proceedings of the Royal Society of Arts*, vol. CXXIX, no. 5297, April

Hutin, François Regis (1981). Télématique et démocratie. *Etudes*, February

Ince, Darrel (1982). How to make a supercomputer get a move on. *Guardian*, 11 February

Innis, Harold (1950). *Empire and Communication*. Oxford: Oxford University Press

___ (1951). *The Bias of Communication*. Toronto: University of Toronto Press

International Commission for the Study of Communication Problems (1981). *Many Voices, One World: Communications and Society, Today and Tomorrow*. London: Kogan Page

Ito, Hiroshi and Harashima, Susumu (1981). The graphic capability of CAPTAIN — a Japanese videotex system. In Holmes, P. and others, (1981). [Proceedings of the] *Fourth International Online Information Meeting, London 9-11 December 1980*. Oxford: Learned Information

Jarrett, Dennis (1980). *The Good Computing Book for Beginners*. London: ECC Publications

Jones, R. (1982). *Microcomputers in Primary Schools: a Before-you-buy Guide*. London: Council for Educational Technology

___ (1982a). *Five of the Best: Computer Programs for Primary School Children*. London: Council for Educational Technology

Kaiser, W., Marko, H. and Witte, E. (eds.) (1977). *Two-way Cable Television: Experiences with Pilot Projects in North America, Japan and Europe*. Berlin: Springer-Verlag

Katz, Martin R. and Shatkin, Laurence (1980). *Computer Assisted Guidance Concepts and Practices*. Princeton, New Jersey: Education Testing Service

Kelly, John C. (1981). Geometry and measurement — drill and practice: math supplement that enhances your instruction! *Journal of Courseware Review*, vol. 1, no. 1

Kendall, Reg (1981). Steady progress in individual skill. *Educational Computing*, vol. 2, no. 7

Kilgour, Frederick G. (1981). OCLC: Aspects of an international network. In Holmes, P. and others (1981). [Proceedings of the] *Fourth International Online*

Information Meeting, London 9-11 December 1980. Oxford: Learned Information

Kincaid, D. Lawrence (1979). *The Convergence Model of Communication.* Honolulu: East-West Communication Institute

Klimbie, Jan Willem (1982). Digital optical recording: principle, and possible applications. In Tedd, Lucy and others (1982). [Proceedings of the] *Fifth International Online Information Meeting, London 8-10 December 1981.* Oxford: Learned Information

Knott, Jack and Wildavsky, Aaron (1981). If dissemination is the solution, what is the problem? In Rich, Robert F. (ed.) (1981). *The Knowledge Cycle.* Beverly Hills: Sage

Koetke, Walter J. (1981). Tribbles: an introduction to the scientific method. *Journal of Courseware Review*, vol. 1, no. 1

Komatsu, S., Hara, O. and Taoka, W. (1981). Overcoming the language barrier in Japan. In Holmes, P. and others (1981). [Proceedings of the] *Fourth International Online Information Meeting, London, 9-11 December 1980.* Oxford: Learned Information

Koughan, Martin (1981). Playing 'The New Television' at table stakes. *Channels*, vol. 1, no. 1

___ (1981-2). The state of the revolution 1982. *Channels*, vol. 1, no. 5

Krugman, Dean M. and Christians, Clifford (1981). Cable television: promise versus performance. *Gazette*, vol. 27, no. 3

Lachenbruch, David (1981). Video disk vs. video disk. *Channels*, vol. 1, no. 4

Large, Peter (1981). The see all, hear all, tell all machine. *Guardian*, 11 February

___ (1982). New technology: investment plan points to government U-turn. *Guardian*, 10 March

___ (1982a). Cable means more to see on TV — and more holes in road. *Guardian*, 23 March

Lefrere, Paul (1982). Beyond word-processing: human and artificial intelligence in document preparation and use. In Hills, P.J. (ed.) (1982). *Trends in Information Transfer.* London: Frances Pinter

Lesgold, Alan M. (1981). Authoring environments for computer-based instruction. Washington, DC: National Institute of Education (mimeo)

Levin, James A. and Kareev, Yaakov (1980). *Personal Computers and Education: the Challenge to Schools.* La Jolla, California: Center for Human Information Processing, University of California, San Diego

Licklider, J.C.R. (1966). A crux in scientific and technical communications. *American Psychologist*, vol. 21

Lindenmayer, Graeme (1981). Information and the technologies for handling it. *Programmed Learning and Educational Technology*, vol. 18, no. 4

Londoner, David J. and Blum, Francine S. (1981). *The Videodisc Goes National.* New York: Wertheim

Lubar, David (1980). Educational software. *Creative Computing*, September

Luehrmann, Arthur W. (ed.) (1971). *Proceedings of the Second Annual Conference on Computers in the Undergraduate Curricula.* Hanover: University Press of New England

McEntee, Patrick and Blum, Vicki (1981). The SCHOOLDISC system. *Videodisc News*, October

McLuhan, Marshall (1962). *The Gutenberg Galaxy.* Toronto: University of Toronto Press

___ (1964). *Understanding Media: the Extensions of Man.* New York: Signet

Machlup, F. (1980). *Knowledge and Knowledge Production.* Princeton, New Jersey: Princeton University Press

Maddison, John (1981). Computer usage must offer advantages. *Educational Computing*, vol. 2, no. 7

Maddox, Brenda (1981). Cable television: the wiring of America. *The Economist*, 20 June

Mahony, Sheila, Demartino, Nick and Stengel, Robert (1980). *Keeping PACE with the New Television: Public Television and Changing Technology*. New York: Carnegie Corporation

Malik, Rex (1982). The Group of Paris and the 'World Challenge'. *Intermedia*, vol. 10, no. 1

Malone, Thomas (1980). *What Makes Things Fun to Learn? A Study of Intrinsically Motivating Computer Games*. Palo Alto: Xerox Palo Alto Research Center

___ and Levin, James (1981). Microcomputers in education: cognitive and social design principles. Report of a conference sponsored by the Carnegie Corporation, San Diego, March 12-14, 1981. San Diego: Laboratory of Comparative Human Cognition, University of California (mimeo)

Mankekar, D.R. (1981). *Whose Freedom? Whose Order? A Plea for a New International Information Order by Third World*. Delhi: Clarion

Martin, James D. (1977). *Future Developments in Telecommunications*. Englewood Cliffs, New Jersey: Prentice-Hall

Marx, Bernard (1980). Production and use of online information systems in universities. In Wanger, Judith and others (1980). [Proceedings of the] *Third International Online Information Meeting, London 4-6 December, 1979*. Oxford: Learned Information

Mason, William F. (1977). Overview of CATV developments in the US. In Kaiser, W., Marko, H. and Witte, E. (eds.) (1977). *Two-way Cable Television: Experiences with Pilot Projects in North America, Japan and Europe*. Berlin: Springer-Verlag

Matthews, J.J. (1981). Computer simulation in university teaching. *CALNEWS*, no. 17, September

Melmed, Arthur S. (1982). Information technology for the schools and nation. *Phi Delta Kappan*, January

Melton, Reginald F. (1982). *Instructional Models for Course Design and Development*. Englewood Cliffs, New Jersey: Educational Technology Publications

Meredith, R. Alan (1981). Practicando Español Con La Manzana. *Journal of Courseware Review*, vol. 1, no. 1

Merrill, Paul F. (1980). Education and training applications of video disc technology. In Sigel, Efrem, Schubin, Mark and Merrill, Paul F. (eds.) (1980). *Video Discs: the Technology, the Applications and the Future*. White Plains, New York: Knowledge Industry Publications

___ (1982). Review of 'School Microware Reviews'. *Educational Technology*, vol. XXII, no. 2, February

Ministère de l'Education (1981). *Le Mariage du Siècle: Education et Informatique*. Paris: Imprimerie Nationale

Moore, J.L. and Thomas, F.H. (1981). The need for more informative descriptions of CAL materials. *Computer Education*, vol. 38, June

Morgan, Eric (1980). *Microprocessors: a Short Introduction*. London: Her Majesty's Stationery Office

Morgan, Gwyn (1980a). Britain's teletext services are a commercial success. In Haslam, G. and others (1980). *Viewdata '80*. Northwood, England: Online Conferences

National Center for Education Statistics (1981). *The Condition of Education*, 1980 edition. Washington, DC: The Center

National Council for Teachers of Mathematics (1979). *Agenda for Action*. Reston, Virginia: The Council

Nayakama, Kazuhiko, Tezuka, Akira and Toyama, Atsuko (1980). Resources sharing network in Japanese universities. In Wanger, Judith and others (1980). [Proceedings of the] *Third International Online Information Meeting, London*

4-6 December 1979. Oxford: Learned Information

Neil, Michael W. (1981). *Education of Adults at a Distance.* London: Kogan Page

Nettles, Patricia (1981). Slow-scan: long-distance pictures by phone. *Development Communication Report,* no. 34

Nora, S. and Minc, A. (1978). *L'Informatisation de la Société.* Paris: Documentation Française

Nuttgens, Patrick (1981). Learning to some purpose. *Higher Education Newsletter,* December

OCLC Research Department (1981). *Channel 2000.* Columbus, Ohio: Online Computer Library Center

Olson, David R. and Bruner, Jerome S. (1974). Learning through experience and learning through media. In Olson, David (ed.) (1974). *Media and Symbols: the Forms of Expression. The 73rd Yearbook of the National Society for the Study of Education.* Chicago: University of Chicago Press

Osborne, Thomas E. (1977). The personal computer in education. In Seidel, Robert J. and Rubin, Martin (eds.) (1977). *Computers and Communication: Implications for Education.* New York: Academic Press

O'Shea, T. (1981). Intelligent systems in education. In Bond, A. (1981). *Machine Intelligence.* Maidenhead: Pergamon Infotech

___ and Self, J. (1982). *Learning and Teaching with Computers.* Brighton, Sussex: Harvester Press

Otten, Klaus W. (1980). Information transfer and the significance of new storage media and technologies. In Maurice, Marcel, Phillips, Edward and Scherff, Hans-Ludwig (eds.) (1980). *The Impact of New Technologies on Publishing.* London: Saur

Paisley, William (1980). Information and work. In Dervin, Brenda and Voigt, Melvin J. *Progress in Communication Sciences,* Vol. II. Norwood, New Jersey: Ablex Publishing

Palmer, Edward L. and Dorr, Aimee (1980). *Children and the Faces of Television: Teaching, Violence and Selling.* New York: Academic Press

Papert, Seymour (1977). A learning environment for children. In Seidel, Robert J. and Rubin, Martin (eds.) (1977). *Computers and Communication: Implications for Education.* New York: Academic Press

___ (1980). *Mindstorms: Children, Computers and Powerful Ideas.* Brighton, Sussex: Harvester Press

Pask, Gordon (1975). *Conversation, Cognition and Learning.* Amsterdam: Elsevier

Payne, Tony (1981). On-line information retrieval in schools. *CALNEWS,* no. 16, March

Pelton, Joseph (1981). *Global Talk: the Marriage of the Computer, World Communications and Man.* Brighton, Sussex: Harvester Press

Phillips, Richard J. (1982). An investigation of the microcomputer as a mathematics teaching aid. *Computers and Education,* vol. 6, no. 1

Pierce, J.R. (1961). *Symbols, Signals and Noise.* New York: Harper and Row

Piestrup, Ann M. (1981). *Preschool Children use an Apple II Microcomputer to Test Reading Skills Programs.* Portola Valley, California: Advanced Learning Technology

Ploman, Edward and Hamilton, L. Clark. (1980). *Copyright: Intellectual Property in the Information Age.* London: Routledge & Kegan Paul

Polcyn, Kenneth (1981). The role of communication satellites in education and training: the 1990s. *Programmed Learning and Educational Technology,* vol. 18, no. 4

Postman, Neil (1979). *Teaching as a Conserving Activity.* New York: Delacorte

Powell, A.J. (1981). Libraries and computer materials: an overview. In Baxter, Paul (ed.) (1981). *Libraries and Computer Materials.* British Library Research and

Development Report No. 5690. London: British Library Research and Development Department

Raitt, David (1982). New information technology — social aspects, usage and trends. In Tedd, Lucy and others (1982). [Proceedings of the] *Fifth International Online Information Meeting, London 8-10 December 1981*. Oxford: Learned Information

Resek, Diane (1981). Personal communication

Rich, Robert F. (1980). Knowledge in society. In Rich, Robert F. (1980). *The Knowledge Cycle*. Beverly Hills: Sage

Robertson, Joseph (1981). Tomorrow's office automation systems will provide greater productivity gains. *Communication News*, November

Rogers, E.M., Eveland, J.D. and Bean, A.S. (1976). *Extending the Agricultural Extension Model*. Stanford: Institute for Communications Research, Stanford University

___ and Kincaid, D. Lawrence (1981). *Communication Networks: Toward a New Paradigm for Research*. New York: Free Press

Ross, B.M., Kellner, A.D., Schmidt, W.H.P. and Schubert, E. (1981). TELETIDE: an experimental military viewdata system. In Hooper, R. and others (1981). *Viewdata '81*. Northwood, England: Online Conferences

Rowntree, Derek (1981). *Developing Courses for Students*. London: McGraw-Hill

Ryan, Michael G. (1981). Telematics, teleconferencing and education. *Telecommunications Policy*, December

Salomon, Gavriel (1979). *Interaction of Media, Cognition and Learning*. San Francisco: Jossey Bass

Schiller, Herbert I. (1981). *Who Knows: Information in the Age of the Fortune 500*. Norwood, New Jersey: Ablex Publishing

Schneider, Edward W. and Bennion, Junius L. (1981). *Videodiscs*. Englewood Cliffs, New Jersey: Educational Technology Publications

Schramm, Wilbur (1977). *Big Media, Little Media: Tools and Technologies for Instruction*. Beverly Hills: Sage

___ (1981). What is a long time? In Wilhoit, G. Cleveland and de Bock, Harold (eds.) (1981). *Mass Communication Yearbook*, Vol. 2. Beverly Hills: Sage

Schubin, Mark (1980). An overview and history of video disc technologies. In Sigel, Efrem, Schubin, Mark and Merrill, Paul F. (eds.) (1980). *Video Discs: the Technology, Applications and Future*. White Plains, New York: Knowledge Industry Publications

Schwartz, Bertrand (1981). *L'Informatique et l'Education*. Paris: La Documentation Française

Scriven, Michael (1981). Breakthroughs in educational technology. In Cirincione-Coles, Kathryn (ed.) (1981). *The Future of Education: Policy Issues and Challenges*. San Francisco: Sage

Sewell, Bridgid (1981). *Use of Mathematics by Adults in Daily Life*. London: Advisory Council for Adult and Continuing Education

Shannon, Claude E. and Weaver, Warren (1949). *The Mathematical Theory of Communication*. Urbana: University of Illinois Press

Sharples, Mike (1981). Microcomputers and creative writing. In Howe, J.A.M. and Ross, P.M. (eds.) (1981). *Microcomputers in Secondary Education: Issues and Techniques*. London: Kogan Page

___ (1982). An evaluation of the Cyclops telewriting system for distance tutoring of Open University students. Paper presented at the Conference on Teleconferencing and Interactive Media, University of Wisconsin, May 1982. Milton Keynes: Institute of Educational Technology, The Open University (mimeo)

Shatkin, Laurence (1980). *Computer Assisted Guidance: Description of Systems*. Princeton, New Jersey: Educational Testing Service

Shaw, K.A. (1980). Computing in chemistry. In Stevenson, P. and others (1980).

[Proceedings of the conference on] *Microcomputers in Education. London July 1980.* Northwood, England: Online Publications

Shinohara, S. (1981). Development of videotex educational programmes. In Hooper, R. and others (1981). *Viewdata '81.* Northwood, England: Online Conferences

Shotwell and Associates (1981). *The 1981 Courseware Market Report.* San Francisco: Shotwell and Associates

Simon, Jean-Claude (1981). *L'Education et l'Informatisation de la Société.* Paris: Documentation Française

Simon, Julian (1981a). *The Ultimate Resource.* Oxford: Martin Robinson

Smith, Ralph Lee (1981). The birth of a wired nation. *Channels,* vol. 1. no. 1

Sternberger, Paul (1981). Using personal home computers to retrieve information from online databases. In Holmes, P. and others (1981). [Proceedings of the] *Fourth International Online Information Meeting, London 9-11 December 1980.* Oxford: Learned Information

Stonier, Tom (1979). Changes in western society: educational implications. In Schuller, Tom and Megarry, Jacquetta (eds.) (1979). *Recurrent Education and Lifelong Learning. World Yearbook of Education 1979.* London: Kogan Page

____ (1981). A little learning is a lucrative thing. *Times Higher Education Supplement,* 1 May

Street, F.P.(1981). To the customer's advantage. *British Telecom Journal,* vol. 2, no. 3, Autumn

Suppes, Patrick (ed.) (1981). *University-level Computer-assisted Instruction at Stanford: 1968-1980.* Stanford: Institute for Mathematical Studies in the Social Sciences, Stanford University

Sustik, Joan M. (1981). Art History interactive videodisc project at the University of Iowa. *Videodisc News,* October

Svard, Stig (1982). Sweden re-regulates its media mix. *Intermedia,* vol. 10, no. 2

Takano, Fumio (1981). The online information service in JICST and the special characteristics of the Japanese language: implementation of automatic processing of Japanese. In Tedd, Lucy and others (1982). [Proceedings of the] *Fifth International Online Information Meeting, London 8-10 December 1981.* Oxford: Learned Information

Teague, S. John (1980). Microform publication. In Hills, Philip (ed.) (1980). *The Future of the Printed Word.* London: Frances Pinter

Technical Authors Group of Scotland (1982). *The Police Use of Computers.* Edinburgh: The Group

Thompson, Vincent (1981). *Prestel and Education: a Report of a One-year Trial.* London: Council for Educational Technology

____ (1981a). Prestel and education I: Educational trial of Prestel. In Holmes, P. and others (1981). [Proceedings of the] *Fourth International Online Information Meeting, London 8-11 December 1980.* Oxford: Learned Information

Tichenor, P.J. and others (1970). Mass media flow and differential growth in knowledge. *Public Opinion Quarterly,* vol. 34

Toffler, Alvin (1970). *Future Shock.* London: Bodley Head

Unwin, Derick (1981). The future direction of educational technology. *Programmed Learning and Educational Technology,* vol. 18, no. 4

VanGrasstek, Jean and Rubens, Donna (1980). My library is a computer terminal! In Wanger, Judith and others (1980). [Proceedings of the] *Third International Online Information Meeting, London 4-6 December 1979.* Oxford: Learned Information

Walker, David D. and Megarry, Jacquetta (1981). The Scottish Microelectronics Development Programme. *Programmed Learning and Educational Technology,* vol. 18, no. 3

Wall, Shavaun M. and Taylor, Nancy E. (1982). Using interactive computer programs in teaching higher conceptual skills: an approach to instruction in writing. *Educational Technology*, vol. XXII, no. 2, February

Watts, A.G. and Ballantine, Malcolm (1981). Computers in careers guidance: an overview. *Careers Journal*, vol. 1, no. 3

Weizenbaum, Joe (1980). Once more, the computer revolution. In Forester, Tom (ed.) (1980). *The Microelectronics Revolution*. Oxford: Blackwell

Wicklein, John (1981). *Electronic Nightmare: the New Communications and Freedom*. New York: Viking. Reviewed in *Channels*, vol. 1, no. 2

Wildenberg, D. (ed.) (1981). *Computer Simulation in University Teaching*. Amsterdam: North Holland

Williams, Frederick (1982). *The Communications Revolution*. Beverly Hills: Sage

Wills, Russell (1982). Personal communication

Wittlich, Gary E. (1981). Interval Mania and Arnold: two musical skills training programs. *Journal of Courseware Review*, vol. 1, no. 1

Woodward, Kathleen (ed.) (1981). *The Myths of Information*. Henley-on-Thames: Routledge & Kegan Paul

Woolfe, Roger (1980). *Videotex: the New Television/Telephone Information Service*. London: Heyden

Wright, Patricia (1980). The design of official information — the new technologies. In Hills, Philip (ed.) (1980). *The Future of the Printed Word*. London: Frances Pinter

Wright, Sue (1981). Encouraging full use of a school's micro. *Educational Computing*, vol. 2, no. 10

INDEX